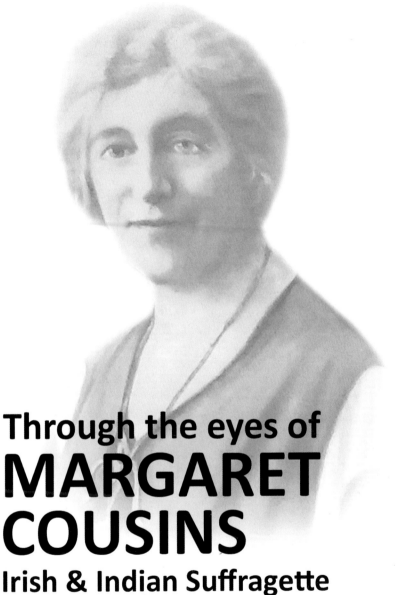

# Through the eyes of
# MARGARET COUSINS

## Irish & Indian Suffragette

## Dr Keith Munro

HIVE STUDIO BOOKS

Published in November 2018.

Copyright © Hive Studios/Dr Keith Munro, 2018.

Every effort has been made to trace the copyright holders and obtain permission to reproduce material used in this publication.

Hive Studio Books
Ráth Mór Centre
Bligh's Lane
Derry BT48 0LZ
www.hivestudio.org
T: (028) 7127 7487

ISBN 978 1 9993479 1 8

A CIP catalogue record for this book is available from the British Library.

The emancipation of women, the achievement of full equality between the sexes, is one of the most important, though less acknowledged prerequisites of peace. The denial of such equality perpetrates an injustice against one half of the world's population and promotes in men harmful attitudes and habits that are carried from the family to the workplace, to political life, and ultimately to international relations. There are no grounds, moral, practical, or biological, upon which such denial can be justified. Only as women are welcomed into full partnership in all fields of human endeavour will the moral and psychological climate be created in which international peace can emerge.

From a document on World Peace released on
United Nations Day 1985
by the Universal House of Justice.

# Contents

# About the Book

To do full justice to the life and works of Margaret Cousins would take many volumes. These I hope will be written in future by historians better equipped. While Gretta did become well known in Ireland and England during the first fifteen years of the twentieth century, this was relatively short-lived when she and her husband James emigrated to India in 1915. Once settled in Madras (Chennai) their fame grew exponentially, especially for Gretta.

This story comes from the mind and the personal experiences of Gretta herself as well as her husband. He became well known in his own right as poet, teacher and playwright, immersed in the Cultural Revival in Ireland during the first decade and a half of the 20th century. Later during the Indian period he became a journalist, teacher of English and Geography as well as lecturer in Theosophy and an expert in the Arts of India. The apex of his career was his appointment as Art Advisor to the Maharaja of Travancore. His creative poetry continued to grow and mature throughout his life. He consistently supported Gretta's efforts in seeking suffrage for women and in seeking full equality with men.

Although the focus during the Irish years is on the Irish Women's Franchise League founded by the Cousins and the Sheehy-Skeffingtons, it should be stated that there were other suffrage movements, both in Ireland and England working for women's franchise during that period in history.

This book draws closely on Gretta's own words and themes. In this way we can, perhaps, catch a glimpse of their lives from her and Jim's point of view. Both were inextricably intertwined from the beginning when they met in Dublin.

In a very real sense this book is not **about** her, rather it is **from** her.

'We Two Together', published in Madras (Chennai) in 1950, is a book of some 780 pages. The hope is that this much shorter book, a distillation if you wish, will be easier to absorb and hopefully will inspire. Jim and Gretta's command of English was such that they use some words with a meaning we are not familiar with some 68 years later. Their style is 'of their time'. The extensive quotes by Gretta and Jim have been kept as accurate as possible to the original. The reader must also appreciate that Jim was a poet and his prose has a poetic ring to it.

Large swathes of their life experience have had to be cut out. What I have attempted to do is to pick out historic, unusual and interesting events – but there is more, much more.

The chapters are purposefully kept short, with many footnotes, that are largely about people or words that are not familiar. Irish culture and Indian culture are both very different.

Both Gretta and Jim seemed to have been airbrushed from Irish history.

Perhaps this is their time. Ireland and beyond should know of this remarkable woman from Boyle, in the county of Roscommon, and her amazing husband – Jim.

# Prologue

As a child, growing up in the 1950s in Belfast, I was aware of a famous great-aunt and uncle who lived in India. That was about it. Great-aunt Gretta Cousins died in India in 1954. Her autobiography, 'We Two Together', written with her husband James sat on my bookshelf for more than two decades until an Indian Bahá'í friend sent me a pamphlet in the early 1990s concerning the **All India Woman's Conference** in which it stated:

> "The All India Women's Conference was founded in 1926 by Margaret Cousins, an Irish lady, who had made India her home. Her main concern was women's education but gradually AIWC took up various social and economic issues concerning women such as purdah, child marriage, divorce, women's property rights etc. It became a leader among organisations fighting for women's rights and equality."

I was jolted into the realisation that my great-aunt was greater than I thought. My wife Anne and I travelled to India on three separate occasions to learn about her achievements and to share Irish connections with the current membership of the AIWC. Our last visit, as invited guests, was to the Platinum Jubilee held in Pune in January 2003.

During this current year - the 100th Anniversary of the hard-fought but persistent campaigns towards women's franchise, both violent and non-violent - it felt appropriate to tell the story of Margaret Elizabeth Cousins (neé Gillespie), known as Gretta.


Keith Munro
Claudy
Northern Ireland

November 2018

# Dedication

One half of humanity which has arisen and
is still rising to recognise their human right
to be considered equal in all things with the
other half of the human race.

And to the other half of the human race, some
of whom already fully support women and
who, in increasing numbers, have become
enlightened to the fact that man and woman
are two wings of a single bird – humanity.

# Acknowledgments

Gretta and Jim for having kept diaries, records and memories of their extraordinary lives together and having decided to gather them into their seminal work: 'We Two Together.'

Janak Palta-McGilligan who had the foresight, in the early 1990's, to send me a pamphlet from India about the All India Women's Conference.

Shobana Ranade, past-President of the AIWC, who invited my wife and me to come to India and see for ourselves the results of Gretta's work, and who subsequently came to Ireland on a pilgrimage in September 1994 to visit Gretta's birth-place. During that visit she had the honour of meeting the then President, Mary Robinson in Áras an Uachtaráin, Dublin.

Maire Egan Paul – past-Mayor of Boyle whose huge enthusiasm for Gretta inspired me to forge ahead.

My long-time friend, Dr Brendan McNamara, who has proofread for me and given advice.

My designer, Joe, who has assisted me through three books.

He always comes up with layouts and designs better than my own ideas.

Last, but not least, to my wife Anne, who has given me a multitude of useful and apposite comments on content and syntax. She is a stickler for accuracy – annoyingly so!

To one and all – my deepest thanks.

# Endorsements

This is the story of a most remarkable Irish girl from Boyle in Roscommon, who, together her husband James and the Sheehy-Skeffingtons, Frank and Hanna, founded the Irish Women's Franchise League in 1908. One of their highlights was a visit to Dublin by Christabel Pankhurst and subsequently by her mother Emmeline who spoke in Cork and Derry amongst other venues during 1910.

Closely working with other suffrage movements Margaret sustained two periods in prison for criminal damage; to the windows of Dublin Castle on the one hand and those of Prime Minister Asquith and Chancellor Lloyd George on the other. These acts were to draw attention to the injustice of lack of a vote for one half of the population.

Both she and her husband disappeared from view in Ireland in 1915, when they accepted an invitation to serve in India from Annie Besant the President of the International Theosophical Society.

She continued her suffrage work founding the All India Women's Conference in the 1920's helping to achieve votes for women in all Indian States by 1929. She later established the All Asian Women's Conference in the 1930's.

Margaret was invited to become the first non-Indian woman magistrate, an honour she cherished.

Driven by her passion for women's equality she devoted the rest of her life to the education of women in India and the raising of their status. It is significant that this book is being released during this historic year of **Vótáil 100.**

'Through the Eyes of Margaret Cousins – Irish & Indian Suffragette' is a book all women can enjoy and, for that matter, men as well. It demonstrates in no small measure how one women with a passion can make a huge change in the world for the betterment of human kind.

Mary Robinson, 7th President of Ireland
Founder of the Mary Robinson Foundation – Climate Justice
United Nations High Commissioner for Human Rights (1997-2002)
Amnesty International's Ambassador of Conscience Award (2004)

* * *

As Cathaoirleach of Roscommon County Council, I initiated the **Vótáil 100** Roscommon Commemorative Lecture Programme which was held in King House, Boyle in April 2018. It celebrated the centenary of women's suffrage and reflected on Margaret Cousin's legacy and the pioneering work of the Irish Women's Franchise League. It is important to recognise, honour and show our gratitude to the suffrage movement that secured women's right to vote and to continue to challenge the barriers to female representation in politics and decision making. I welcome Dr Keith Munro's publication 'Through the Eyes of Margaret Cousins' which tells the story of a pioneering women in Ireland and India drawing on her autobiography, 'We Two Together' written along with her husband James.

Cllr. Orla Leyden, Cathaoirleach<br>
Roscommon County Council (2017-2018)

* * *

This decade of commemorations has brought some very rich new information and source material on women of the revolutionary era to light. In particular, family members and relatives of extraordinary activist women like Margaret Cousins recognise how important their lives and contributions were, and have, as in this welcome volume, taken ownership of those histories and given us all new and welcome insights to the private and public woman.

Dr Mary McAuliffe<br>
Assistant Professor in Gender Studies<br>
University College Dublin

* * *

Dr Munro's great-aunt, Margaret Cousins, jointly founded the Irish Women's Franchise League in 1908 and collaborated with my great grandmother, Emmeline Pankhurst and her daughters on the quest for suffrage, suffering a period in Holloway Prison as a result. Mrs Cousins emigrated to India in 1915 and played an important role in Indian women's fight for the vote, subsequently devoting her life to the education of Indian women and striving for their equality with men in all things. She was also a vegetarian and a Theosophist who lived a long and purposeful life, dying in India in 1954.

My thanks to Dr Munro for bringing Margaret Cousins' life and work out of the shadows, sharing her story primarily through her diary records and those of her husband James. So many women fought to make a difference to the lives of others and yet their contributions are being, or have been, forgotten. Hopefully this book will ensure a better fate for Margaret 'Gretta' Cousins.

Dr Helen Pankhurst
Great granddaughter of Emmeline Pankhurst

\* \* \*

Keith Munro has skilfully produced a welcome, timely and fascinating story of Margaret Cousins. Relatively unknown in her homeland, Margaret Cousins became a leading Theosophist, and a powerful advocate for the rights of women. She was connected to many of the most important figures in Ireland on the eve of the birth of the nation. In midlife she, and her husband James, set out for India in search of spiritual and cultural inspiration, eager to share the lessons of the Irish cultural revival on the subcontinent in opposition to Empire. She was among the courageous instigators of the suffrage movement. Margaret was jailed in England, Ireland and India as a consequence for her support for women's issues. A truly transnational figure of substance, she has left a rich legacy which deserves attention.

Dr Brendan McNamara
Study of Religions Department University College Cork

\* \* \*

In this centenary year of Irish women's participation in parliamentary elections, it is fitting that we remember the work and sacrifices of the women who helped us reach this point. Margaret Cousins was one of those. This book provides insight into Margaret's life, her dedication to freedom and fairness and her efforts as a "natural equalitarian" who exploited her own privilege to highlight and overturn injustice and inequality.

We owe much to Margaret Cousins; and to Keith, for bringing her story alive and reminding us of Margaret's due.

Marcella Smyth
Deputy Director
Department of Foreign Affairs and Trade

\* \* \*

Margaret Cousins, also known as Gretta Cousins (née Gillespie), was part of a new generation of Irish women in the 19$^{th}$ and 20$^{th}$ centuries who fought for women's emancipation and equal rights. In James Cousins she found both a life and a political partner and their life together was a truly remarkable one – as author Keith Munro so beautifully portrays here, through the eyes of his great-aunt Margaret. With their friends Hanna and Francis Sheehy-Skeffington, Margaret and James established the militant, non-partisan Irish Women's Franchise League in 1908. The woman from Boyle paid a price for suffragette activities, serving time in Mountjoy and Tullamore Gaols and went on hunger strike. The second half of the Cousins' life spent in India was just as extraordinary, where Margaret again fought for women's equality and children's rights and spent time in jail for her endeavours. Munro notes that 'Gretta and Jim' seem to have been airbrushed from Irish history; no longer is this the case.

Claire McGing,
Athena SWAN Project Officer
Social Sciences Institute,
Maynooth University,

# CHAPTER ONE

## THE DONKEY INCIDENT
### Early education and introduction to politics

As the clock in Boyle Town Square, in the county of Roscommon, struck midnight on 7 November 1878 granny was summoned from the other end of the town to help usher in the first-born of fifteen children created by two handsome and musical parents. Her daughter, committed at that moment to 'hard labour', was Margaret Annie Gillespie (neé Shera). Her husband was Joseph Gillespie, a petty-sessions clerk. The family was strongly Protestant and Methodist by denomination.

The birth was proceeding apace inside the middle house of the Crescent at the top of the town square, when granny arrived. Unfortunately she had had to plod through two feet of snow by the light of a paraffin lamp but made it none-the-less. All went well and Margaret Elizabeth Gillespie was welcomed into this world by all. Young Margaret, known as Gretta by the family, grew rapidly in health and abundant in energy and was topped with fine red hair.[1]

She acquired a reputation as a 'good and wise child' who could be trusted and who made original remarks. It was decided she had 'brains' and could actually think for herself. Early on Gretta decided that not only should children be seen but they should be heard as well. This, however, would frequently get her into trouble.

The start to a rebellion against inequality

---

1 Most so-called redheads are in fact ginger. The small percentage are either admired or known for their fiery-temper. We will leave the reader to decide into which category Gretta falls.

19

"When I was about eight years old I innocently threw my leg across the saddle of my donkey when the stirrup of the lady's side-saddle broke. A friend of my father met me in this heterodox manner, and reported his amusement to my very proper papa. When I returned home I got well spanked for behaving in such an unladylike way. That was my introduction to the inequality of opportunity which then belonged to being a girl. I was born a natural equalitarian, and rebelled exceedingly from that early age against any differential treatment of the sexes."

In similar vein she later wrote:

"I saw that it was counted a kind of curse in those days to be born a girl. One of my missions in life, equal rights for men and woman, was finding me."

That brief event with the donkey, and thus being saddled with inequality, proved of life-long significance to Gretta. It seared into her very heart and soul. It drove her forwards in all her subsequent striving for equal treatment for both sexes, right to the very end when she passed away in India in 1954. Equality was like a mantra for her, which, coming from a very unequal society, made her prone to bouts of righteous anger.

A strong Methodist background seemed a practical pattern for life at that time with its regular reminder of hell and fear of punishment on the one hand and a loving Father who gave security on the other. As a young teenager, Gretta attended a series of mission meetings and was determined to dedicate her life to the service of God and humanity. She noted well the way her granny took part in the Sunday services, praying, singing and preaching as well as any man. There seemed, in that small western Irish country town of Boyle, more freedom for opportunities for women than later she found in great cities. The love of her granny continued to be a major influence, infusing culture, love of flowers and nature, appreciation of painting and encouragement to fall in love and appreciate the best of music and literature. It was the embroidering of silk costumes that particularly stirred her young heart, generating a longing to see the East, particularly India. Little did she realise that India was indeed firmly on the path of her destiny.

The seeds were sown. Now they needed watering. Fortunately the water was pure and progress good. If Gretta learned beauty and the love of nature and music from her granny she learned politics from her father. In front of their house was the Town Square shaped as a triangular common area and used for regular community events. Monthly fairs were a regular occurrence with its merry-go-rounds and the occasional inevitable political gatherings.

"Politics has been called 'the national game of Ireland.' It was the subject in which the Irish masses were most vividly interested; the struggle for freedom from alien domination. Balfour and Gladstone, were the powerful figures of the Conservative and Liberal side of English politics. Charles Stuart Parnell, Dillon, O'Brien, Davitt, and lastly John Redmond, were the Irish names that dominated the swirls of patriotic emotion by which I was surrounded and influenced from my tenth to my sixteenth year. My father used to get me to read to him the political news of those stormy times. Through this good custom I was brought up to understand coercion laws, agrarian troubles, Home Rule Bills, Fenianism, the clash of Catholic and Protestant; and all my life through I have felt quite at home in politics. I remember watching Parnell speaking from a platform erected on the Crescent space. He was tall, bearded, frock-coated, pale and tense yet masterful. Our parents forbade us children to go to such meetings or to look out of the windows; but from behind the curtains I missed nothing that could be seen, and later read what was unheard to my father from the newspaper."

Gretta was quite clear on her path forwards:

"I belonged in my heart, from the beginning, to the fighters for freedom…"

# CHAPTER TWO

## EDUCATION – BOYLE TO LONDONDERRY

Gretta was given a sound elementary education in a co-educational National School in Boyle. Apart from the usual three R's she was taught French and given piano lessons by two cultured gentlewomen who made a deep impression on her with their cleverness and sense of public service. One of her best skills, one might say a gift, was her inherent voraciousness for reading. Once she got into a book she was dead to the world. Gretta was not a bit interested in dolls but was fascinated with biographies. Women saints particularly attracted her such as St Catherine, St Teresa but chiefly St Joan of Arc.

From her elementary education she moved to the Intermediate School, also co-educational and ruled by a headmaster who was extremely bright and one of the pioneers in the production and use of electricity. This lit up her love for science. She won a three-year scholarship to The Victoria High School for Girls in Londonderry. With her noted talent for music she was encouraged to specialise in that direction. Gretta's three years stretched to four in the end. The school, situated at the top of Crawford Square just off the Northland Road, was run successfully by Miss Margaret Mackillop a forward thinking Head Mistress.[2]  Having settled in with a group of some eighty other girls she commented that:

> "Living with girls, between fourteen and twenty knocked the corners off my priggish provincialism, and developed my power of working in organised groupings of women."

One of Gretta's sisters was also a pupil at the school and indeed became captain of hockey. Gretta enjoyed all the school excursions, not just as left-wing on the hockey team but as pianist for the school orchestra. These activities fed her love of music, adventure and group activity.

---

2 The original school – the **Ladies Collegiate School** - was founded by the Misses Mackillop in 1877. This became the **Victoria High School**, then **Londonderry High School for Girls**. Eventually it merged with the **Foyle College**. As **Foyle & Londonderry College** it became the first co-educational Grammar School in Londonderry. The school has now recently moved to a state-of-the-art campus on the Waterside adequate for the 21st Century. The name has reverted to **Foyle College**. A note in Gretta's own handwriting from 1892 was discovered in the archives of the College during research on her life. The Headmaster's surname at the time was Gillespie (Gretta's maiden name). The writer's mother, **Marion Cousins,** attended Londonderry High School for Girls back in the 1920's and much later three of his four children attended Foyle and Londonderry College.

The four years spent at school in Derry strengthened her independence of character, moulded her a framework for community life through interaction with large numbers of assorted fellow students and teachers. All of this gave her almost a sixth sense in judging character, which helped throughout her life. She was very proud, during her last year at school as a prefect, to be invited for tea in the city tuck-shop by the two exhibition winners[3] from Foyle College for Boys. She felt honoured to meet the most intelligent as well as entertaining of the male students of that year.

Gretta's intense love and thirst for 'getting lost in books' was fulfilled by a fine school library. She would climb to the highest shelves. Once she found a character sketch of a most remarkable woman, Madame H.P. Blavatsky, who was the Founder of the Theosophical Movement. Gretta knew nothing about Theosophy[4] at this time and therefore was oblivious to the fact that it would play a large part in her future as well as that of her husband-to-be.

Her musical talents effloresced and between the ages of 13-16 she was considered a semi-prodigy. She would roam through Beethoven's first twelve sonatas as well as Chopin's mazurkas and waltzes. It was her unusual musical talent which, in the end, persuaded her to study for her Batchelor of Music in Dublin.

The last piece of advice, prior to moving to Dublin in 1898, was from her wise headmistress, Miss Mackillop.

"She advised me that I should not be so independent. Life would be easier for me if I was more like other girls. I listened to her politely, and often recalled her words. But my nature was free and original in its bent. I could be happy only in doing what I felt was right in principle, not because other people did it."

Life has many twists and turns. As she left her formal schooling full of joy, free at last to pursue her love of all things musical, historical events were to bring her back to Derry a decade later. Aged nineteen, however, she was largely ignorant and unaware of the rapidly rising women's movement seeking not just suffrage, but eventual equality with men in all things.

---

3 Top students who have one prizes in a particular subject or subjects.
4 **Theosophy** was not a religion but a society. Their motto is 'There is no religion higher than truth.'

# CHAPTER THREE

## TRANSFER TO DUBLIN'S FAIR-CITY
## AND FREEDOM
### Music, music, music

In the autumn of 1898 Gretta started a four year specialised course of study at the Royal Irish Academy of Music. This consisted of composition, orchestration, piano and organ playing, musical history and biography as well as analysis of musical scores. Her time was also well-filled with widening cultural experiences which expanded her mind greatly. She felt privileged, realising that this opportunity came to very few girls. Free of the sheltered life of a community she felt liberated.

"I found myself racing on my bicycle about 'dear dirty Dublin' thinking myself the luckiest, freest and happiest girl in Ireland because I had a clear course before me of musical study which I had always longed for. For the first time I was my own mistress. I had found lodgings which I was to share with the newly arrived first-trained kindergarten teacher, who had been engaged as a historic experiment by my uncle by marriage in Sandymount Castle."

Apart from her studies in music Gretta was alive to the Irish Cultural Renaissance and this aspect of her exciting Dublin life was now becoming much more intense. For the moment musical experiences, however, thronged her mind. Perhaps the high point was the visit of Paderewski in 1901 whose masterly performances sent her to seventh heaven.[5]  While her music was never far from the surface she became more rapidly absorbed in the renewal of culture which was all around her, like a warm bath.

"I soaked up new experiences like a sponge. Dublin had always been a city of intellectual and artistic preoccupation. Its interests lay in ideas rather than industries. It valued wit and gifts of entertainment more than blue blood or money bags in a newcomer. In those days the art of conversation ranked high. It would have been considered a social failure if three hours could not have been filled up with sparkling talk. Those were pre-bridge and pre-radio years. And what a range of subjects: literature, poetry, the latest plays, players and playwrights, politics,

---

5 Gretta was to meet **Paderewski** in Europe some decades later.

Rule Bills, Queen Victoria's visit to Ireland, the Parnell scandal, music Irish and European, the renaissance of Irish culture, the Gaelic League, Irish myth, folk-dance, song and costume."

Diving into this pool of kaleidoscopic thoughts and new experiences, Gretta began to feel drawn towards international life. These were years of expansion on her artistic side as well as years of work on an academic and professional level. She was preparing herself for both physical and economic independence. Gretta was a product of that same process of growth that was pushing Ireland itself through cultural self-consciousness towards a hunger for self-government and through patriotic aspiration into courage and strength to fight for freedom.

While all these new experiences were being processed, her heart and childhood memories of injustice for girls kept surfacing. The outcome of the 'donkey incident' came flooding back. She had been the eldest of a dozen sisters and brothers, which had started with four girls in a row.[6] Families of ten or eleven were not uncommon in the late 19th century although it was rare not to lose at least one child, if not two, during early life.

She had sensed an air of disappointment after the fourth girl was born as boys were wanted and expected. There was an observable preference for boys. Once they did come they always seemed to get more attention as well as more money.

She well-remembered the suffering of her mother who was never given money of her own, while there was no scarcity in the family home on the Crescent.[7] What money there was 'belonged' to her father. He never gave her mother a regular allowance in order to run the house. Accounts were 'on tick'[8] in the various shops in the town and her mother had to present the passbooks to her husband, who would regularly grumble at the amounts being spent. He would speak as if it was all her mother's fault. It had seemed a curse to Gretta that she had been born a girl and indeed often wished she'd been born a boy.

Now settled in Dublin she was able to look back with a fresh perspective on her upbringing. She realised that she had been steeped in the all-too-common home atmosphere of that period:

"The continuous production of babies, growing parental friction, a queer mixture of autocracy, kindliness, love of music and beauty, an irrational kind of religious faith and an overall sense of congestion."

---

6 Eventually three more siblings were born.
7 Later they moved to a larger house in the town called – **'Belmont'.**
8 A slang word for payment later, like a 'bar tab'.

The overwhelming nature of Gretta's home life peaked when an old friend of her mother's asked her a question which profoundly affected her: "With all these youngsters around you, Gretta, are you not afraid to get married?" This, together with her deep sense of inequality between male and female, created a surge within. She now knew that she had to do something about it. The injustice of the 'donkey episode' surfaced again and she was more than ever determined to act upon it.

"One of my missions in life, equal rights for men and women, was finding me."

# CHAPTER FOUR

## MEETING 'HIM' & 'HIM' MEETING 'ME'
### Big Changes

Romance came naturally to Gretta after release from four years in a girl's boarding school. She met plenty of young men during her first year in Dublin, feeling that it would be a tragic fate if she were to end up an old-maid. Like many girls her age she had formulated an image of her ideal man. 'He must be tall and dark, a professor with a beautiful voice.' Her dreams, however, were crushed when 'he' materialised. He was small and fair, an accountant in business and, worst of all, spoke with a strong North-of-Ireland accent which she detested.  He had one saving grace. He was a poet!

'He', James Henry Cousins,[9] had come down to Dublin after braking-off his engagement to a Belfast girl. Writing his biography some fifty years later he could not recollect precisely when he met Gretta. His diary of the time only indicated when he had begun a relationship by recording: 'Roses for Miss Gillespie 2s 6d.' He had attended a public meeting during the Annual Conference of the Wesleyan Methodist Church, he on the ground-floor and she in the balcony. Bumping into her afterwards, and as they were going the same way, he invited her to join him on the top deck of the tram from Nelson's Pillar in O'Connell Street.

There followed a pattern of 'going out with each other'. They shared many a cultural evening from Shakespeare to Wagner. Gretta, her image of the perfect man shattered, decided to 'give it a go'.

On 1 July 1900 Gretta was on her way to see her parents in Boyle. Jim was saying his usual good night after seeing her back to her lodgings. 'Good-night' up to then had consisted of a 'hearty handshake'. On this particular evening she asked him, what should she tell her parents? His answer was short and pithy. "Tell them we are getting engaged." She responded: "You may kiss me if you like."

During their period of engagement they got to know each other in depth. Their 'wooing' was, to say the least, unconventional by modern standards. In the early 1900s sex before marriage was **not** the social norm, made stronger by the fact they had both come from a somewhat rigid Methodist Christian upbringing. Gretta's thoughts at the time can be summed up:

---

9 **James** was born at 29 Cavour Street, Belfast on 22 July 1873. He was son of James Cousins and Susan Davis. He had three brothers, George, Thomas John and William Cousins, grandfather of the author.

"Often I asked myself why it was that in that first year of knowing him I had such a dislike for him. I cried with disappointment the night after he proposed. But I knew he was good and clever and full of the highest ideals…. I thought this was probably my only chance of marriage. I must not rashly throw it away. I knew he was a poet; and I loved poetry. Perhaps a poet might work out as well as a professor. I decided to give him a trial. My interest was aroused in him by his poetry and later by his dramas, also by his love of all beautiful things. For six months I forced myself to suffer his company so that I might, as I told him, "learn what he was really like." Scandal began to wag its tongue. So I agreed to an engagement but made the provision that I reserved the right to break it at any moment. So there was no temptation or forcing into marriage. In the three years following 1900 I was completely won over."

It might be a convenient moment to pause and see where Gretta was placed on her journey through life. She had had the joy and freedom of her upbringing and fine educational opportunities both in Boyle and Derry. Her gifts for music were being honed, satisfied and developed. Above all she had this deep yearning to seek equality of opportunity in all things for both men and women. At this point, however, she had not an inkling where or how this might be satisfied. While showing interest in the politics of the time, she had not become immersed. She had shown no interest in Theosophy, in which Jim was becoming increasingly involved, nor was she a vegetarian which he was. Finally she had met a man who seemed to disappoint her at first. The worry that she might not have another chance overcame her. As yet any urge to seek votes for women was only at an embryonic stage and even that embryo was very, very small. Things were about to change.

While there was still the absence of cinema, radio, electric light as well as cars, electric trams and aeroplanes in 1900, they visited botanical gardens, parks, museums and the National Gallery; or went to plays, concerts or lectures. Every Friday evening, firmly engaged, her 'poet' took her home after presenting her with a bunch of flowers. She recalls 'they were not many, but choice: a tree carnation, Parma violets, lilies of the valley, which even now after 50 years I could still smell the 'wafture[10]' of their respective fragrances.' She was stimulated by listening to Æ, a close poetic friend of Jim's, expounding Indian philosophy, or Harvey Pelissier[11], or indeed Leslie Pielou, who later married Gretta's sister, Annie. In fact the stimulating talk of these cultural giants seemed to make Jim pale in comparison, whom she thought of only as 'her wee man from the north'.

10 The act of **wafting** a sound or perfume – in this case the smell of flowers.
11 **Harvey Pelissier** became Jim's bestman.

Sometime during 1902 she was jolted to change. Her strict Methodist beliefs had crumbled and she had now, for the last two and a half years, been a 'humble agnostic'. She read many books on higher criticism, rationalism and socialism. Then:

> "My fiancé brought me to a lecture by Mrs Besant, one of the Founders of Theosophy, sometime during 1902; but I was neither attracted nor impressed by either her subject-matter or her personality. Little children can feel superior to their elders; and I was still but a little child in wisdom."

In fact Jim wanted Gretta to experience something more about Theosophy and so exposed her to a lecture arranged by the Dublin Theosophical Society, which had been formed back in the 1880s. The subject was 'Theosophy & Ireland.' It was Mrs Besant's birthday – 1 October. As you can see Gretta was none too impressed. Jim had been warned off Theosophy by his parents in Belfast some years previously. They had heard that Besant was an 'agent of the Devil,' and doubly dangerous by her immoral association with the atheist Bradlaugh.[12] At this time Annie Besant was one of the leading proponents of the Theosophical Movement. Jim's experience of the meeting was very different. He gathered from the lecture that information by means of clairvoyance[13] had been 'revealed' that Ireland was ultimately to emerge as 'the spiritual mentor of Europe', even as India had been for Asia. He noted that Mrs Besant then 55 years old, short, grey-haired, pleasant yet serious, had an intelligent face, spoke with ease in plain language and without notes. She had an attractive full-tone voice. His conclusion was that Theosophy was a much bigger matter than he had derived from small manuals – and so was Ireland.

He records that it was all a lot to learn in one afternoon. Despite Gretta's initial negativity she was destined to grow into it.

The second half of their three-year engagement helped her build knowledge, respect, admiration and affection for this truly worthy man. It made them enjoy each other's company. While growing closer to the big day she began feeling some indifference and not a little uncertainty about the future. She was feeling unworthy of him and didn't feel the fictional sort of emotionalism that a bride was expected to feel. Jim had already broached the subject of children and made it clear that anything about having children was

12 **Charles Bradlaugh** was an English political activist and atheist. He founded the National Secular Society in 1866. In 1880, he was elected as the Liberal MP for Northampton.

13 **Clairvoyance**: The psychic faculty of perceiving things or events in the future or beyond normal sensory contact. Literally means 'clear vision'.

entirely her choice. In fact they later, agreed to live a companionate marriage. It seems they pledged to develop themselves towards the higher mental and spiritual aims of their life. This, by any modern standards, was an unusual decision. How this panned out in reality we do not know. One thing we do know, however, they did not have children.

Another hurdle presented itself which, though difficult, was in the end jumped fairly easily.

> "One of the first things that I disliked about this Mr Cousins was his vegetarianism. Yet he did not draw attention to it or preach it. He simply did not eat fish, flesh or fowl. Somehow he managed to get enough vegetables, fruit, nuts, cereals, to keep him healthy. Although I argued against this food-faddism at first, and had no natural inclination towards it, I found certain points connected with it appealing. The Dublin Vegetarian Restaurant was a rendezvous for the literary set, of whom Æ was the leader. We frequently joined these idealists at lunch, and later met a number of Hindu vegetarians, who had come to Dublin for medical or legal studies.
>
> After about six months I suddenly realised as in a blinding light of unarguable Truth: "If it is not necessary for health that I should demand living creatures, small and large, to be slaughtered, and their flesh to be cooked for food for me, then it is murder, and a crime for me to be a party to such cruelty and wickedness, and as soon as I am free to order my own food I will be a vegetarian."

Gretta kept her pledge not to violate the Law of the Sanctity of Life. Jim was naturally delighted. They were married on 9 April 1903 in Sandymount Methodist Church by the Rev J.W Ballard, who had baptised Jim some 25 years earlier. Harvey Pelissier was best man and Jim announced at the wedding breakfast to one and all, that Gretta had become a vegetarian. It is interesting to note what Gretta recorded, decades later, in 1943.

> "The mutual happiness that Jim and I had in one another's company we brought to our wedding day in Dublin, and we have not lost it in forty years. The cynicism behind the phrase, "How to be happy though married", was displaced, in our case, by the affirmation, based on experience that, begun in happiness, based on love, knowledge and spiritual aspiration, marriage is secondary, not primary. We learned "how the be married though happy!"

With the surprise announcement at the wedding breakfast that Gretta was ceasing to eat fish, flesh or fowl, they managed to survive on wedding cake to keep them alive until they reached Killarney on their honeymoon.

# CHAPTER FIVE

## THEOSOPHY & PSYCHIC EXPERIENCES
### Blavatsky & Besant – Founder and Protagonist of Theosophy
### The Krishnamurti episode. Was he the new Messiah?

Settling into married life in Dublin, Gretta found she had more time to get involved in other things. She had been awarded her Batchelor of Music from the Royal University of Ireland in October of 1902. Jim was now fully occupied rehearsing his play '*The Sword of Dermot*' and Gretta with practising the *entr'acte* music for the play.[14] Both were now immersed in the green-ocean of the Celtic Revival. Both, but mostly Jim, were associated with the Irish Literary Theatre, the National Dramatic Society, the Abbey Theatre and the Theatre of Ireland. The visits of actors to their home some late evenings introduced Gretta full-on to the world of drama in Dublin. Various famous people popped in from time-to-time such as George Augustus Moore: Irish novelist, short-story writer, poet, art critic, memoirist and dramatist. James Joyce: Irish novelist, short story writer, and poet. Padraic Colum: Irish poet, novelist, dramatist, biographer, playwright, children's author and a collector of folklore.

As we say in Northern Ireland, the 'craic was ninety'.[15]

By 1905 Jim's intimate involvement with theatre in Dublin came to an abrupt end. While his heart lay in these artistic fields and he was contented to be wrapped in the warm blanket of the Cultural Revival, it was financial pressures, as well as disagreements with some of the protagonists in the field, that brought it all crashing down. In Jim's own words:

"Thus ended my theatrical phase; here beginneth my second phase.
The gulf between the making of a living and living a life had widened."

Pressured by the necessity of making a living he sent out eighteen letters of inquiry, receiving just two replies. One was a flat refusal and the other an invitation to call on the Headmaster of the High School (Dublin). Within ten minutes into an interview he was appointed Assistant Master, teaching English, English literature and Geography. (21 October 1905). Jim had noticed on the very first day, presumably by looking at engraved boards of prize-winners festooning the walls, that the name Charles Johnston appeared

---

14 James sometimes acted or wrote using the stage name **James Sproule.**
15 **Craic:** Refers to the laughter and banter that goes with having a good night out with friends. It is pronounced 'crack'.

four years running, as winner of the first exhibition cup in the Intermediate exam. He commented to William Wilkins, the Headmaster, that Johnston must have been exceedingly clever, to which he got a terse reply.

"Oh! That fellow, Charlie Johnston. *He* was an Olympian. He might have gone to the very top, but he made a fool of himself by marrying the niece of the charlatan, Madame Blavatsky."

He also learned that WB Yeats had attended the same High School, which was the 'feeder' for Trinity College. Jim's Irish career in teaching lasted some eight years when further pressures brought about his resignation.

Returning to 1903, we see Gretta, with time on her hands and teaching music only part-time. Her mind was 'ready for flowing to the ocean'. She managed to get hold of the first two volumes of 'The Secret Doctrine' written by the controversial and mysterious figure Madame Helena Blavatsky. This enigmatic Russian lady was the Founder of Theosophy (1875).[16] This philosophy, with its motto: "There is no religion higher than truth" was circulating with increasing general interest at this time in the western world as well as the east. In November 1889, Mme. Blavatsky had welcomed a young Indian lawyer, Mohandas Gandhi, who was studying the Bhagavad Gita. He became an associate member of her Theosophical Lodge in March 1891 and continued to emphasize the close connection between Theosophy and Hinduism throughout his life.

The two-volume book, The Secret Doctrine was reviewed for the Pall Mall Gazette by the social reformer Annie Besant. Impressed by it, Mrs Besant met Madame Blavatsky and joined the Theosophical Society. In August 1890, Mme. Blavatsky moved into Annie Besant's large house at 19 Avenue Road in St. John's Wood.

As a teenager, Gretta had already read about Madame Blavatsky in 'papers' she had found in the library at the Victoria High School in Derry. Now she was intrigued by the volumes and read avidly day by day. Although she didn't understand a tenth of what she was reading the whole experience brought her an expansion of consciousness about time, space, ethnology, cosmography, symbolism, magic and religions in general.

Gretta's agnostic state, which had lasted for several years, now gave way to esoteric[17] Christianity, by way of a book by Dr Anna Kingsford called "Clothed with the Sun". Added to this mix, every Sunday night during 1906, Dr Khedkjar, from Kolhapur in the Indian State of Maharashtra, came to

16 **Theo Sophia** means God Wisdom.
17 **Esoteric:** Intended for or likely to be understood by only a small number of people with a specialized knowledge or interest.

their home and read passages from the Bhagavad Gita, the Hindu Scriptures. Thus Jim and Gretta were being drawn evermore towards Theosophy and Hindu thinking along with their practice of vegetarianism.

## What is Theosophy?

The term Theosophy comes from the Greek theosophia, which is composed of two words: *theos* ('god,') and *sophia* ("wisdom"). Theosophia, therefore, may be translated as the "wisdom of the gods," or "divine wisdom". The word was first used in writing during the 3rd to the 6th century by the Alexandrian Neo-Platonic philosophers. They used this term to denote an experiential knowledge that came through spiritual, not intellectual, means. In the course of time, several mystics and spiritual movements in the West (mainly Christian-based) adopted the word 'theosophy' in their teachings. Among them we find Meister Eckhart in the 14th century, and Emanuel Swedenborg in the 18th century. In 1875 Madame Blavatsky, Col. Olcott, and a group of like-minded people, founded the Theosophical Society, thus bringing the term back into the light again. They claimed the work of the TS was a continuation of previous Theosophists.

In the modern Theosophical movement the word has been used with several different meanings: It is frequently used to describe the body of teachings that allegedly 'came through clairvoyantly' via Mme. Blavatsky and other Theosophical writers. It is also used to refer to the universal Ancient Wisdom underlying all religions when they are stripped of accretions, deletions, and superstitions. The process of becoming more and more receptive to these theosophical insights is termed the 'spiritual path'.

Modern Theosophy postulates that this world of existence embraces more than the material world that we perceive through our senses. In fact, the lack of knowledge about the higher aspects of reality makes us see things from a distorted perspective. Theosophy states that we can gain knowledge of Reality, both in the universe and in human beings by means of a holistic spiritual practice that includes study, meditation, and service.

\* \* \*

Returning to the story, Mme Blavatsky appointed Annie Besant to be the new head of the Blavatsky Lodge, and in July 1890 inaugurated the European headquarters of the Theosophical Society in Mrs Besant's house. While living there, Mme. Blavatsky authored a book containing questions and corresponding answers, calling it 'The Key to Theosophy'. This was followed shortly by 'The Voice of the Silence'. As with 'The Secret Doctrine', most scholars of Buddhism have doubted that this latter text comes from authentic Tibetan Buddhist documents. She continued to face accusations of fraud. During the winter of 1890 Britain had been afflicted with an influenza epidemic. Mme. Blavatsky contracted the virus. Subsequently this led to her death on the afternoon of 8 May 1891 at the home of Annie Besant in London.

Gretta and Jim never actually met Mme Blavatsky and were yet to become intimately associated with Annie Besant, now emerging as the leader of the modern Theosophical movement. She, in due course, would invite them to come to India in 1915 to work together on her campaign: HOME RULE FOR INDIA. Theosophy may have fired the spiritual side of her but the other side was definitely political and nationalist in character.

* * *

At this juncture, it might be helpful to mention something about Annie Besant herself as her life-motivation has some parallels with Gretta and Jim's evolving thinking in Ireland.

Annie Besant (1847-1933)
President of the International
Theosophical Society 1907-1933
Political reformer, women's rights
activist, women's educationalist
and Indian nationalist.

Mrs Besant stated in her autobiography:

"Please or displease, whether it bring praise or blame. That one loyalty to Truth I must keep stainless, whatever friendships fail me or human ties be broken"

Embedded in this statement is the age old conundrum: What is truth?

This is a subject that has concerned philosophers and theologians for centuries.

Born in Clapham on 1 October 1847 Annie Besant came from Irish roots. With the early death of her father in 1852, the family was brought up in relative poverty. In 1867, aged 19, she married a clergyman Frank Besant, seven years her senior. The marriage soon experienced difficulties. Annie became increasingly radicalised in her political views, whereas Frank was generally conservative. Annie instinctively supported the rights of workers and poor farmers. She began writing, but her husband forbade her to keep her earnings. Other issues emerged and finally Annie left him taking her daughter Mabel to London. Looking back on her marriage, she realised that her temperament was not suited to the Victorian expectations of the 'passive wife'. She wrote at the time:

"…for under the soft, loving, pliable girl there lay hidden, as much unknown to herself as to her surroundings, a woman of strong dominant will, strength that panted for expression and rebelled against restraint, fiery and passionate emotions that were seething under compression—a most undesirable partner to sit in the lady's arm-chair on the domestic rug before the fire."

In London, she became noted for her radical political views. She espoused freedom of thought, women's rights, secularism, birth control and the rights of the working class.

Bernard Shaw in 1911

She became a popular public speaker associating herself with the ideas of Charles Bradlaugh especially on contraception. A turning point in the movement for the dissemination of information on contraceptives was the Bradlaugh-Besant trial in 1877.[18] The publicity surrounding the trial radically increased the demand for information about contraception.

---

18 The case was dismissed in the end on a technicality, after a tortuous path.

After this Annie became more influenced by the new Socialist organisations such as the Fabian society. In particular, she was impressed by the views and personality of George Bernard Shaw (then a struggling Irish writer living in London).[19] They shared many natural sympathies such as Irish home rule, and a concern for social justice.

In 1885, when Gretta Gillespie was only seven years old and still being educated in Boyle, Annie Besant stood for election to the London School Board. Campaigning on a policy of 'No more hungry children' she came top in a poll in Tower Hamlets with over 15,000 votes. She was now becoming an early role model for women politicians. Though women didn't have the vote in general elections she encouraged the increase of women's participation in local government.

After meeting Mme Blavatsky, and reviewing 'The Secret Doctrine,' her interest in Theosophy grew rapidly as her commitment to left wing politics declined and her membership of Socialist societies lapsed. Annie Besant moved to India in 1893, further to Mme Blavatsky's death in May 1891. Once settled she became extremely active in the Theosophical Movement which was established at a Centre at Adyar in Madras (Chennai). By 1909, Besant had become President of the International Theosophical Society.

One key aim of the Theosophical Society, at that time, was to find, educate and prepare a New World Teacher for his important mission. She and C.W Leadbeater, a self-styled psychic, came into contact with two remarkable Indian boys, and declared that the elder of the two, Jiddu Krishnamurti (14) was destined to become the 'vehicle' of the expected 'World Teacher', the Bodhisattva Maitreya, the Universal Buddha promised to bring peace to the world. Leadbeater noticed Krishnamurti walking on the Society's beach on the Adyar River, and was amazed by the 'most wonderful aura he had ever seen, without a particle of selfishness in it.'

Jiddu Krishnamurti

In 1910 Annie Besant assumed guardianship of J. Krishnamurti and his brother, and, despite great difficulties, launched him on his remarkable career. The two boys were educated in the west, then, in

19 **George Bernard Shaw** (1856 – 1950), known, at his insistence, simply as **Bernard Shaw**, was an Irish playwright, critic, polemicist, and political activist. His influence on Western theatre, culture and politics extended from the 1880s to his death and beyond. He wrote more than sixty plays, including major works such as *Man and Superman* (1902), *Pygmalion* (1912) and *Saint Joan* (1923). With a range incorporating both contemporary satire and historical allegory, Shaw became the leading dramatist of his generation, and in 1925 was awarded the Nobel Prize for Literature. He was also a vegetarian.

the 1930's in Holland, Jiddu was enthroned and the assembled multitude informed that he was the 'New World Teacher'. Krishnamurti subsequently renounced this manufactured role as a World Teacher and broke away from the Theosophical Movement, but remained close to Mrs Besant whom he held in high regard as his surrogate mother.

Krishnamurti continued to share his profound thoughts for spiritual development but insisted he did not want 'followers', nor did he wish to create a new religion. Despite Krishnamurti's plea he remained surrounded by 'followers' for the rest of his life. He was admired by many for the courage of his convictions in turning his back on Prophethood and all the advantages and disadvantages it brings in its wake. He died of pancreatic cancer at Ojai in California, in Feb 1986, aged ninety years.

In 1916, Mrs Besant became an early member of the Indian National Congress and launched the Indian Home Rule League which agitated for Indian independence. She stated:

> "India demands Home Rule for two reasons, one essential and vital, the other less important but necessary: Firstly, because freedom is the birth-right of every nation; secondly, because her most important interests are now made subservient to the interests of the British Empire without her consent, and her resources are not utilised for her greatest needs."

Her campaign helped strengthen the Indian belief that self-rule was a possibility. For a year she was made President of the Indian Congress – preceding such leaders as Mohandas Gandhi and later Jawaharlal Nehru.

Mrs Annie Besant died in India in September 1933. She left instructions, "I ask no other epitaph on my tomb but: **'SHE TRIED TO FOLLOW TRUTH.'**

Mohandas Ghandi

Jawaharlal Nehru

In due course Gretta's life and that of Annie Besant would become intertwined. Both these feisty freedom-fighters sought to raise to a higher status the equality of men and women in India. Annie Besant, on the political road, was more concerned with 'Home Rule for India' **and education** while Gretta focused on 'Votes for Women' **and education.**

# CHAPTER SIX

## THE AWAKENING OF HER CHILDHOOD PASSION FOR JUSTICE
### Meeting her destiny in Manchester

Towards the end of 1906 Gretta was invited to speak at a vegetarian conference in Manchester. As fate would have it the National Council of Women was also holding a conference in that same city. She had been encouraged to attend by Ernest Bell, head of the publishing house George Bell & Sons. Gretta contacted the NCW and as a result walked into a whole new world with fresh horizons for half the human race. The immediate goal, however, was to campaign for Women's Suffrage.

> "It impressed me deeply with the possibilities that were latent in womanhood. It made me aware of the injustices and grievance which were taken for granted as the natural fate of my sex. Here I found a large organization already challenging the continuance of inequality of opportunity between man and woman. I was spiritually excited and stimulated by the meetings of the conference. I had never, in my insular life in Ireland, heard of the movement till I went to Manchester. But even as a child I had felt that girls and women did not get fair play in life. I was a born rebel against conventions which gave women less freedom than men, fewer opportunities, smaller pay, less education, lower status. The writings of Anna Kingsford, had already affirmed women to me as spiritually co-equal with man.[20]
>
> This, I felt, was bound to demonstrate itself out to its uttermost. Advanced men and women had, between 1800 and 1905, used every method of constitutional agitation to bring women within the expanding circle of democracy. But their efforts had proved unsuccessful. Then Youth took the matter in hand in 1905. In that

---

20 **Anna Kingsford**, (1846 – 1888), was an English anti-vivisectionist, vegetarian and women's rights campaigner. She was one of the first English women to obtain a degree in medicine and the only medical student to graduate without having experimented on a single animal. She pursued her degree in Paris, graduating in 1880. Her final thesis, *L'Alimentation Végétale de l'Homme*, was on the benefits of vegetarianism, published as *The Perfect Way in Diet* (1881). She founded the Food Reform Society that year. Kingsford was interested in Buddhism and Gnosticism, and became active in the theosophical movement in England, becoming president of the London Lodge of the Theosophical Society in 1883.

year Christabel Pankhurst, a young law student of the Manchester University, and Annie Kenney, a typical young mill-hand of Lancashire, became the voice of awakened women-hood in the opening years of the twentieth century."

Gretta's sponge-like mind quickly soaked up the various aspects and workings of the National Council of Women and so, on return to Ireland, she immediately got in touch with its local leaders. These were Thomas and Anna Haslam an elderly but energetic couple who were nearly seventy years old.[21] They were both devoted to the advancement and enfranchisement of women. She was a dynamo of energy, small and sturdy. He was intellectual, tall, rather like a university don, a good speaker and refined. Anna Haslam was born in Youghal in 1829, the 16th of 17 children. She was educated in Newtown School, Waterford. She met Thomas when teaching at Ackworth School, Yorkshire. They married in 1854 in Cork Registry Office and lived together happily until his death in 1917. When Thomas became unable to work due to illness she established a stationery and toy business at their Rathmines home to support them both.

Thomas had been a feminist theorist and from 1868 he wrote about many topics concerning female rights and issues such as prostitution, birth control and women's suffrage. Both he and Anna were expelled from the Society of Friends due to their interests in social reform but both still maintained links with that community. Thomas was said to have been disowned for harbouring ideas contrary to Quaker teachings. In 1868 he published a pamphlet called 'The Marriage Problem', in which he raised and supported the idea of family limitation and outlined a number of contraceptive methods including the safe period.

Gretta joined the local branch of the National Council of Women and immediately attended drawing-room meetings at homes of leading Dublin women. She and Jim had moved, in July 1906, to a house on the Strand Road, Sandymount, which had larger rooms ideally suited for such meetings. A month later they were both more than happy to host suffrage meetings in their home.

In January 1907, Lady Dockrell presided at one such meeting while Anna & Thomas

Anna Haslam (1829-1922)

---

21 **Anna Haslam** had joined the Dublin Women's Suffrage Association, set up in Dublin back in 1874. She was one of their first secretaries.

Haslam both spoke. Gretta's publisher friend, Ernest Bell, who had been the catalyst for her attendance at the NCW in Manchester sent her back-copies of VOTES FOR WOMEN, the organ of the militant suffragettes. The newspaper had been launched in October the previous year and was owned and edited by Mr & Mrs Pethick-Lawrence.

> "I eagerly followed the doings of the militants, with full understanding of their aims, methods and spirit. I felt so much one of them that I longed for some way in which the women of Ireland might be colleagues in such a soul-stirring movement for the freeing of world-womanhood from the shackles, injustice, inequalities and denial of citizen rights and responsibilities under which women suffer."

Gretta and Jim were spending some days in London with two of Gretta's sisters towards the end of June 1907. Jim had won a prize for an essay on Vegetarianism and this gave them a little surplus money for the trip. Up till then Gretta had not met any members of the Women's Social and Political Union (WSPU). She had only known them through newspaper publicity. They found themselves on a crowded footpath near Parliament Square when they saw a small band of women, seemingly under arrest, being marched to the local police station. They were told that they were leaders of the suffrage movement.

> "In their simplicity, respectability, and quiet dignified demeanour they were deeply impressive. I was so hurt by the indignity of the struggle that women would have to make to secure any freedom from the subjection which they had had to endure through the ages, I suffered the insult in my own soul in sympathy with those self-sacrificing women whom later I met and knew and worked with, Mrs. Pankhurst and Christabel, Mrs Pethick-Lawrence[22], noble elderly Mrs Despard, and others."

The Women's Suffrage strand of Gretta's destiny was enhanced by this experience. The other main strand, involvement in the Theosophical Movement, also received a significant boost.

---

22 **Emmeline Pethick-Lawrence** had started the publication *Votes for Women* with her husband in 1907. The couple were arrested and imprisoned in 1912 following demonstrations involving breaking windows, though they had disagreed with that form of action. After being released from prison, the Pethick-Lawrences were unceremoniously ousted from the Women's Social and Political Union (WSPU) by Emmeline Pankhurst and her daughter Christabel because of their ongoing disagreement over the more radical forms of activism which the Pethick-Lawrences opposed. They then joined the United Suffragists.

Jim and she had an invitation to attend a Convention of the Theosophical Society at the British Headquarters in Albemarle Street in London on 6 July 1907, even though they were not yet members. The function was a reception by the President, Annie Besant. When their sponsor announced "Mr and Mrs Cousins from Ireland", Mrs Besant smiled warmly and shook hands, repeating, "From Ireland!" Later on Mrs. Besant approached them again. Jim records:

"Being lamentably honest we told her that we were not members of the Society; that we are regrettably young; that we knew very little, though we wanted to know nothing less than everything. None of these considerations weighed on her. She loved Ireland, and was thrilled by its future as the spiritual leader of Europe. She put a hand on Gretta's shoulder, saying, "Go back to Ireland, my dear, and form a Lodge of the Theosophical Society and when it is formed I'll come and lecture for you.""

Once back in Ireland they took part, initially from the side lines through the pages of 'VOTES FOR WOMEN', in the increasing support for woman suffrage being played out on the streets and in the courts of London.

"We read of the first deputation of about 60 women, headed by Mrs Pankhurst, to Parliament, and their arrest and imprisonment in Holloway as common criminals. There was later the exciting and inspiring account of the first meeting organized by the 'Women's Social and Political Union' which packed the Albert Hall on 19 March 1908. 'Never before had there taken place so large a gathering of women under one roof.' In June 1908 there was a demonstration in Hyde Park of over a quarter of a million people, a triumph of organization. Following it, came the 'Rush the House of Commons' attempt to protest, after a mass meeting in Trafalgar Square - 1 Oct 1908 - and the sensational trial in Bow Street Court in which Christabel Pankhurst conducted her own defence and cross-examined Herbert Gladstone and Lloyd George."

# CHAPTER SEVEN

## AROUSING IRISH WOMEN TO ACTION
### Formation of the Irish Women's Franchise League

These exciting and enthusiastic events in London roused the mettle of similar-minded women, as well as some men, in Dublin. On 4 November 1908, at the home of Frank and Hanna Sheehy-Skeffington,[23] Gretta and Jim suggested that such a movement or organization was needed as much in Ireland as in England.

However it was not a simple matter. The quadrumvirate[24] sat down to discuss the possibilities in greater depth. They reached the conclusion that

Hanna & Frank Sheehy-Skeffington

---

23 When marrying in 1903, recognising equality, they agreed to both take each other's names. Thus **Hanna Sheehy & Francis Skeffington** became **Hanna and Frank Sheehy-Skeffington.**

24 Quadrumvirate: A group of four powerful or notable people.

they would now invite other friends and together work out a scheme for a similar militant suffrage society, but more suited for the differing political situation in Ireland, as between a 'subject' country seeking freedom from England which was a free country.

They felt that votes for women *must* be incorporated into the Home Rule Bill for which Ireland was fighting. They also felt that the women of Ireland should do this themselves and not under women leaders in England who, they felt, would not understand the complexities of Irish politics! A small group went to see the 'dear old leader' of the constitutional suffragists, Anna Haslam, to explain that the younger women were ready to form a more militant movement. She expressed her regret on two issues, one that it would duplicate efforts and, secondly and more to the point, she was against any form of violence. She was 'law-abiding to the finger-tips'. They parted friends, agreeing to differ on means, though united in aim and ideals.

On 11 November 1908 the new society, named **The Irish Women's Franchise League**, was born. Gretta was its Treasurer, Hanna Shechy-Skeffington was its Secretary and Alice Oldham its President – all honorary. Finally, on 17 November at the home of the Oldhams, the League was made public for the first time. That night Gretta felt that both she and Jim were now on a mutual path in striving for women's equality and rights. He supported her to the hilt in all her endeavours throughout the next forty-six years.

This is a summary of the aims and purposes of the IWFL, as outlined by Gretta:

The Irish Women's Franchise League was to obtain the parliamentary vote for the women of Ireland on the same terms as men.

Its policy was to educate by all forms of propaganda the men, women and children of Ireland to understand and support the members of the League in their demand for votes for women, and to obtain pledges from every Irish Member of Parliament to vote for Women Suffrage Bills in any Irish Home Rule Bill.

The forms of propaganda of the IWFL were to be both constitutional and non-constitutional, as dictated by political circumstances.

Its own structure would consist of a Headquarters in Dublin, manned by a Committee, President, Secretary and Treasurer, and voluntary organizers who should tour the country and form Branches of the League with an annual Branch subscription to the central funds.

Only women could be members.

The League would cooperate, where possible, with the suffrage societies of Great Britain and other countries, especially with the militant suffrage organizations.

Mary Gawthorpe

Within a fortnight of its foundation the IWFL had a welcome boost. Mary Gawthorpe,[25] one of the recently imprisoned London suffragettes had been invited to speak on Women Suffrage by the 'Solicitor's Apprentices Debating Society' at the Four Courts in Dublin. Tom Kettle,[26] the vibrant politician and poet was to have been the second speaker but had to cancel. His slot was then offered to Gretta - who was scared to death. She had little preparation and there would be about a thousand people present. She was to follow on from Mary, a brilliant speaker, who had sustained severe physical beatings as a result of her arrests and imprisonments. This predicament was torture for Gretta. But she survived!

**The First open-air Meeting of the Irish Women's Franchise League**
Gretta was the main speaker at the first open-air meeting held on a Saturday afternoon in Phoenix Park near the base of the Wellington obelisk. Both Frank and Jim were there fully supporting their wives, though, as stated, men could not be paid up members.

The Wellington Memorial obelisk in Phoenix Park, Dublin, c1994 (Mrs Shobana Ranade, President of the All India Women's Conference, and Anne Munro are standing at the base)

25 **Mary Eleanor Gawthorpe** (1881-1973) was a British suffragette, socialist, trade unionist and editor, described by Rebecca West as «a merry militant saint». Gawthorpe also spoke at national events, including a rally in Hyde Park in 1908 attended by over 200,000 people.
26 **Thomas Michael Kettle** was an Irish economist, journalist, barrister, writer, poet, soldier and Home Rule politician. As a member of the Irish Parliamentary Party, he was Member of Parliament for East Tyrone from 1906 to 1910 at Westminster.

Jim has recorded his observations including banter from the audience which gives, perhaps, some flavour of the occasion, not all positive. The following is a lightly edited version:

"Frank Sheehy-Skeffington carried a banner wrapped around two poles. Someone carried a chair borrowed from the gate-lodge. At the meeting-place the group of well-dressed ladies, obviously with a purpose, drew the familiar crowd of the unemployed and the curious. The banner was unrolled flat on the grass. The raising of it, as the signal of a new era, was given to an English women and myself, one at each side. When the words IRISH WOMEN'S FRANCHISE LEAGUE were seen against the background of elms, Skeffy led the applause. This drew the scattered watchers closer and encouraged others.

By the time the first speaker, standing on the chair in front of the banner, had got into the ways and wherefores of the occasion, a large crowd was eagerly listening. I moved unobtrusively from the platform to the back of the crowds to catch its sentiment. Mainly it was friendly; but there was a spot where some kind of kafuffle suggested possible opposition. I edged my way, as though I was one of the audience, to the middle of the commotion and found it to be made by a typical back-street woman, with bright eyes and a Dublin brogue. She was happily engaged in interjecting comments such as Irish crowds always enjoyed. Gretta was on the chair at the front. I edged to the side of the woman in question.

**Woman:** (*towards Gretta who could not hear the comments*) "What you want is a husband." (*laughter*)

**Jim:** "I believe ma'am, the lady is very happily married – which I hope you are." (*loud laughter and a gleam in the eye of the woman*)

**Woman:** (*unable to resist*) "You ought to be at home cooking for your husband, if you have one" (*laughter*)

**Jim:** "If I'm not wrongly informed, ma'am, the lady, though she has her own servant, is a very good cook. I hope you have arranged as good a meal for your husband as she has for hers." (*loud laughter*)

**Woman:** "What you should be do'in is sewin' or darnin' instead of standin' there talkin'"

**Jim:** "She has as much right to be standing there talking as you have to be standing here talking, and in any case she's talking sense. And I think I'm not far wrong in saying that the very nice dress she has on she made with her own hands for this very occasion – maybe this is more than you can say about your dress."

**Woman:** *(exasperated and with innuendo).* "You seem to know a divil of a lot about this woman!"

**Jim:** *(casually with a trace of triumph):* "I do know quite a lot about her, ma'am. She happens to be my wife." *(applause and guffaws)*

I then worked my way back to the platform. None of them knew, until afterwards, what had gone on in the back of the crowd."

The arousing and educating of the population spread throughout country towns but experiences were varied. The IWFL felt strongly that they had to get pledges for inclusion of women's suffrage in the Home Rule Bill. As with the Women's Social and Political Union in England, the IWFL was convinced early on that they must get an interview with Ireland's political leader of the day, John Redmond. He agreed to a meeting and a deputation was headed by Miss Deborah Webb, an elderly Quaker lady of high standing who had a quiet disposition. Before their memorandum could be read, Redmond made it quite clear that none of the proceedings could be reported in the press. After a quick consultation with Hanna Sheehy-Skeffington, who knew this was contrary to usual practice, Miss Webb rose from her seat and stated with dignity that under such conditions the deputation would be a farce and serve no purpose. She then left the room followed by the others of the League.

They were never able to make women's suffrage a Nationalist Party question, however, the majority of its members became strong supporters in their private capacity.

In the summer of 1909 Gretta offered her services for three weeks to the Women's Social & Political Union in London. This voluntary work consisted of chalking pavements with announcements of meetings and selling the newspaper: VOTES FOR WOMEN.

On return to Ireland events moved quickly. Charlotte Despard[27] came

---

27 **Charlotte Despard** (1844 – 1939) was an Anglo-Irish suffragist, socialist, pacifist, Sinn Féin activist, novelist and vegetarian. She was a founding member of the Women's Freedom League, Women's Peace Crusade, and the Irish Women's Franchise League, and active in a wide range of political organizations over the course of her life, including the Women's Social and Political Union, Labour Party, Cumann na mBan, and the Communist Party of Great Britain.

from England and spoke for and to the League. Gretta observed that she was a leader of highest quality, an aristocrat and one of the most democratic political thinkers among them. She was also one of those rare Catholics who had become a Theosophist, and was both warrior and pacifist. She was a sister of the future and final British Lord Lieutenant of Ireland from 1918, which made for interesting conversations between brother and sister.

Charlotte Despard
(1844-1939)

Shortly afterwards, Gretta paid a visit to Portrush where she gathered a crowd to spread the message and sell copies of VOTES FOR WOMEN. During this visit, as luck would have it, she was approached by an attractive and well-dressed young mother 'wheeling a perambulator,' who turned out to be Lady Sybil Smith. Her father was the Earl of Antrim, owning most of Portrush. Her aunt was Countess Minto, who had been a Lady-in-waiting to Queen Victoria.

"Lady Sybil invited me to stay with her and have a series of open-air meetings. Together we made many converts to the cause. Lady Sybil was a fine musician, and a well-trained soprano. We made much music together. She was interested in socialism and other kindred subjects, and a lover of good poetry. One day, when admitted to her bedroom, I came across a book on Raja Yoga by Swami Vivekananda, the famous Indian exponent of the Vedantic philosophy. "Now, Lady Sybil," I exclaimed," I understand the secret of your life! You work from the centre of a realization of the One Life, as Vivekananda expounded to the west." She told me that Lady Minto had personally known Sister Nivedita, an Irishwoman, Margaret Noble by birth-name, who had been a devotee of the Swami and who wrote beautifully about the philosophy, life and people of India. Our mutual interest in oriental thought made a strong and lasting link between us. A couple of years later Lady Sybil was arrested in London for speaking in protest against the Governments treatment of the suffragettes."

By 1909 there was no political issue within living memory that aroused so much support or generated so much enthusiasm as woman's suffrage. Many were the open-air meetings that boosted an upsurge in support. Even some well-known men stood by them. One in particular was the famous actor

James Forbes Robertson, who addressed a packed audience in the Molesworth Hall in Dublin, supporting the suffragettes and their movement. Amongst his advice he said.

"You cannot trust even the best of men to guide your movement. Keep its leadership entirely within your own control. I would not trust my own advice to you though I am heart and soul with you in this, which I regard as the greatest reform of modern times; but our view of things, man's view, is ever unconsciously warped by self-interest."

He, and men like him, fanned the spirit amongst the women of the IWFL as well as other suffrage groups.

\* \* \*

Mrs Besant's offer to speak in Dublin did not wait for the formation of the Dublin Theosophical Lodge as requested by her. A letter to Gretta announced that she would break a return-journey from the United States at Queenstown and asked for an afternoon reception and an evening lecture to be organised. The afternoon reception, held in the Contemporary Club on 10 October 1909 was by invitation only. The lecture in the evening, in the Molesworth Hall, was filled to capacity. The title was **"The New Era"**. Jim had sent a hand-written invitation to Sir William Barrett, the eminent physicist and parapsychologist. Jim asked if he would sit on the platform. His terse reply was that he would have nothing to do with the eminent speaker nor her works. Later, as the meeting started, Jim noticed a man who was hiding his identity. Later he confirmed that it was indeed Sir William. Jim again:

"Mrs Besant spoke for about an hour in a rich tone and clear enunciation, in perfect plain diction, with an occasional gesture, working out a logical theme to a fine peroration." [28]

Applause was cordial and long. Then, as she turned to leave, the voice of Sir William called out from the back of the hall, "Ladies and Gentlemen." Jim felt cold shivers down his spine dreading a possible confrontation. However, Sir William went on to say:

"I was invited to take a seat on the platform tonight. I declined the invitation as I did not wish to be identified with the ideas held by the

---

28 **Peroration:** The concluding part of a speech, typically intended to inspire enthusiasm in the audience.

lecturer. But I wish to say that in my long life, in which I have heard the greatest speakers of English in the world, I have never listened to anything finer in substance and delivery than what has been given to us tonight, and I wish to express my personal thanks to Mrs Besant and to the organiser of the meeting."

That night Mrs Besant stayed with Jim and Gretta in Sandymount, before leaving next day from Kingstown[29] to return to England.

---

29 **Kingstown:** Now called the port of **Dún Laoghaire**, previously called Dunleary until 1821. It was renamed Kingstown in honour of King George IV's visit during that year. In 1920 it reverted to its former name but with the original Irish form of spelling.

# CHAPTER EIGHT

## THE PANKHURSTS VISIT IRELAND

The biggest venture of the IWFL so far was a visit, in March of 1910, of Christabel Pankhurst, illustrious daughter of Emmeline. Dublin's largest Hall, the Rotunda, was booked. It seated some 3000 people. After intensive publicity, the hall ended up packed to the gunnels and as Gretta put it:

"She came: we heard and saw: she conquered."

**IRISH WOMEN'S FRANCHISE LEAGUE,**

Miss Christabel Pankhurst,

FRIDAY, MARCH 11th, 1910,

8 p.m.

ROUND ROOM, ROTUNDA.

Admission    -    -    2/-

Jim Cousins and Frank Sheehy-Skeffington were on the door trying to control the crowd when a voice shouted, "Let me in Cousins. Let me in!" It was Æ[30]. Needless to say he got in. Gretta describes the event:

"Christabel's personality was very charming. She disarmed criticism. Young, slight, fair, pretty, well-dressed, with a clear and telling voice, one imagined her as a kind of Joan of Arc. She was very clever with a natural flair for politics and promotional strategy. She was in her twenty-sixth year when she took Dublin by storm. In that suffrage decade, which changed world history for women, she was the brain of the campaign, the Political Secretary of the Women's Social & Political Union. I had occasion to travel with her in Ireland, and saw for myself how, when she

Christabel Pankhurst

---

30 **George William Russell** who wrote with the pseudonym Æ, was an Irish writer, editor, critic, poet, painter and Irish nationalist as well as a vegetarian.

had finished a speaking engagement, she curled herself up like a kitten and conserved every atom of her energy for her public work. Sincerity, concentration, intrepid courage, determination, a belief that they were 'women of destiny', were characteristics of the Pankhurst family, which included daughter Sylvia as well."

In October 1910 Gretta was responsible for organizing public meetings for Mrs Emmeline Pankhurst in Cork and in Londonderry. She describes what happened:

Emmeline Pankhurst

"We had invited her to come over and help us. I went a week in advance to Cork to arrange a Reception Committee of women and to enlist new sympathizers and organize the meeting. The Town hall had a capacity audience, all seats paid for, and I felt very happy at the ovation she received from my country-people on her first appearance in Ireland. I travelled with her from Cork to Dublin."

A frantic hiccup occurred at the railway station in Mallow. Emmeline had asked Gretta to send an urgent telegram to her headquarters in London. Gretta got off the train to look for a telegraph office. On returning to the platform, to her horror, she watched the train slowly moving out of the station. She dashed across the lines and shouted at passengers staring out of the windows of one of the carriages. She managed with difficulty to climb

Mallow railway station to Dublin

onto the footboard. Somehow passengers held her there while the door was opened and she was pulled into a carriage some way from Mrs Pankhurst. As there was no corridor on the train she had to wait until the next station before being able to return to her guest. She was fairly shaken. Her arms were stiff for a week from the muscle-strain of being pulled off the rails. That night Emmeline Pankhurst spoke at the Dublin ice rink.

Gretta travelled on to Derry in order to organize a large meeting in the Guildhall. However, fire had destroyed all but the clock-tower during Easter 1908. Most functions had been transferred to St. Columb's Hall within a stone's throw of the Guildhall, so on Friday 7th October 1910 the Irish Women's Franchise League public meeting was held.

St Colomb's Hall, Londonderry

Mrs Pankhurst called for the women of Ireland to have the same vote, on the same terms, as their sisters across the water, and votes on the same terms as their male counterparts. 'The Londonderry Sentinel' of 8 October commented that Mrs Pankhurst had said:

'They were fully determined that this question must be settled at once, and then they would have a nation well governed, contented and happy.'

'The Derry Standard,' printed a long article. It was published on the following Monday morning, 10 October 1910.

# VISIT OF MRS. PANKHURST
## LARGE GATHERING IN ST. COLUMB'S HALL
## WHAT WOMEN WANT AND HOW THEY ARE TO GET IT

"A LARGE AUDIENCE, REPRESENTATIVE OF ALL CLASSES IN Derry, welcomed Mrs. Pankhurst to the city on Friday 7th October night at a meeting in St. Columb's Hall under the auspices of Irish Women's Franchise League. The spacious platform was very tastefully arranged for the occasion, the floral decorations being on a lavish scale. The air was laden with the aroma of sweet smelling flowers, and through tall variegated pot-plants and autumn-tinted leaves, half-concealed lights shed a soft radiance around the speakers and others on the platform. Cordial congratulations are due to those to whom the excellent work was entrusted.

The Mayor of Derry, Counsellor John McFarland presided.[31] At the outset he expressed his delight at appearing on the platform for the first time in that magnificent hall, which was a credit to the old city. He was also extremely pleased to see such a large audience. As to his own views on the subject which was to engage their attention that night, he need hardly say that they were well-known in Derry. He had been enlightened on the matter a few days ago by a lady who called to ask him to preside at the meeting.[32] He had always understood that the ladies were claiming a franchise-right similar to that possessed by men, and that every woman would claim a vote on equal terms with her husband. He could not agree with such a principle as that. (*laughter and applause*). However, in regard to this Conciliation Bill, which would give votes only to women who paid rates and taxes, he demanded that such a concession should be granted. (*applause*). To give votes to women in an indiscriminate way would be to give what the men themselves had not got, but in so far as the women paid taxes and were rated occupiers he was with them in their claim to the Parliamentary franchise. (*applause*).

Mrs. Cousins, the secretary of the Irish League, explained what the League stood for, and what it had been doing in the country. She said the League had been established for about two years, chiefly for having their views as Irishwomen clearly expressed on this subject and showing sympathy with the women's leagues across the channel. Ireland had

---

31 **Sir John McFarland** was founder of McCrea & McFarland, engineering contractors. He was also Chairman of Brewster's Bakers, owner of Lough Swilly Steamship Co and Chairman of Lough Swilly Railway Company. He was Mayor 1910-1912.

32 Gretta

been left out of beneficent legislation in many directions, and the Irish Women's Franchise League hoped that when this matter came to be dealt with it could not be said that Ireland was not interested in the matter and had not expressed any opinion. The women of Ireland asked for this vote on the same terms as their sisters across the channel, and that was on the same terms as men had it - property qualifications. They had held meetings all over Ireland during the past two years and had everywhere been received with favour and enthusiasm (*applause*). The Dublin Corporation had unanimously passed a resolution to favour the Conciliation Bill, and demanding facilities for its passage. Belfast Corporation had promised favourable consideration of the matter, and she hoped Londonderry would follow suit. (*applause*).

She then moved:

'That this meeting approves of the enfranchisement of women and calls on the Government to grant facilities before the end of the session for the third reading of the Conciliation Bill, which had already passed its second reading by a majority larger than that gained by the Budget or the Veto proposals'.

Mrs. Pankhurst, in seconding, said she would like to express her gratitude to the people of Ireland, both in Londonderry and elsewhere, for the particularly keen interest taken in the women's suffrage movements, and for showing that they were ready and willing to hear all that was to be said about it, and give the movement a courteous reception. It was necessary to explain how this movement for votes for women had come about. Unless they could realise the urgency of the need for women's enfranchisement it was impossible to understand the real force behind the movement.

She asked them to consider whether women could have done all that was reported of them across the channel, going out into the streets, faced thousands of police, and gone into crowded meetings unless there were many real grievances which had made matters intolerable for them. The movement was not a new one, as women had been putting forward a demand for the vote for the past fifty years. Up to 1832 there was nothing against men having a vote, but the Reform Act then passed, which opened the door for so many male voters, shut the door in the face of the women, as only men were expressly named. Further Acts had conferred still greater extension of the franchise, and all this time women had been trying in vain to secure some rights.  Men had been able to find means of bringing pressure to bear on the Government of the time to force them to grant extension of the franchise, and the women of to-day sought to convince the Government that it was politically dangerous to neglect women's claims any longer, and politically expedient to grant them. (*hear, hear, and applause*).  The great majority of men held the opinion that the women's claim was not urgent, as they were well protected and shielded by men from the hardships of life and provided with homes. Let them examine that contention.

In the United Kingdom there were five and a half million women entirely dependent on their own exertions for a livelihood.  Men had not been able to provide homes for these women, and, indeed many of these women had not only to protect and shield themselves, but had others, sometimes husbands, depending upon them. (*hear, hear and laughter*). Now, if men found it most desirable that they should have votes for the purpose of protecting their interests and securing legislation for the purpose of assisting them to earn a better livelihood, surely women were entitled to the same facilities to protect *their* interests. (*hear, hear, and applause*).

Another reason put forward against women's claims to a vote was that the interests of the women could be left quite safely in the hands of the men who made laws not only for themselves, but also for the best interests of women. But if the case were reversed she wondered if men would be quite willing to allow a body of women to legislate for them - women who would be in no way responsible to the men.

Why, as a matter of fact, they found that the varying classes of men found it necessary to have each of these classes represented in Parliament, so as to put forward the point of view of each particular class on the matters dealt with by Parliament.  So far from men being able to look after the interest of women, every man at one time or another felt forced to admit that if there was one thing a man could not understand it was a woman. (*hear, hear and laughter*).

She stated deliberately that even with the very best intentions in the world men could not help dealing with legislation from their own points of view. (*hear, hear*).  But still they found men claiming that they could do all the legislation for women, and indeed, one Member of Parliament had recently stated that man knew much better WHAT WAS GOOD FOR WOMEN than women themselves (*laughter*).

Many men quite honestly agree with that Member of Parliament, but she ventured to say they were mistaken, and she pointed to the Acts of Parliament affecting women as proof of her statement. There was for instance, the Property Act, under which, if there were ten children, heirs to an estate, and the first nine happened to be daughters, they were all passed over in favour of the youngest if he happened to be a son.

Next, there were the laws relating to the guardianship of infants. These laws recognized only one parent, the father. The mother of the youngest infant, even girls, had in law no legal existence, and the father could decide anything relating to the future of the child. In the case of the child born out of marriage, the law again, while recognizing only one parent, made that parent this time, the mother. The father of such a child escaped all responsibility, but the unfortunate mother was held responsible and could be severely punished if the child were neglected. If members of Parliament when making such laws had been responsible to women voters she was convinced those laws would have been different, and the father and mother would have in each instance been held equally responsible for the care of the child. (*hear, hear*).

She also pointed to the English divorce laws as another instance of the injustice under which women were placed by man-made laws. These matters had all been brought before the attention of members of Parliament, and most of them agreed that these grievances were real and should be removed. But it all stopped there. Even to-day laws were being passed which did women an injustice. There was, for instance, the 'Deceased Wife's Sister Act,' which had roused women to a sense of indignation and impatience which they had not felt before, and whether the new law was good or not women had not been consulted….Again, there was the 'Registration of Nurses Bill,' which Parliament legislated not on what the nurses thought should be done, but on what Parliament felt was good for the nurses.

They also saw how the Government, as employers of labour, placed women on a different footing to men. Whether as factory inspectors, post office clerks, or in the telephone service, the Government insisted on women being PAID LESS THAN MAN and for doing exactly the same work. The matter did not end there, so when the Government gave out contracts, fair wage clauses were enforced in the case of the male workers, who had votes, but not in the name of women workers, who had none, and that led to intolerable sweating. (*hear, hear*)………

Women were tired of being classed with lunatics, paupers, aliens and others deemed incapable of exercising a vote. They were only asking that a million and a-half women should have the vote and that if they paid taxes, they should *not* be robbed of the vote. And for simply putting forward that claim, over 600 women, including herself had suffered imprisonment. What else were women to do?

If the man did not like a law, they used their political power to have it changed; but women could do nothing except submit or protest. They demanded time in November for the committee stage and the third reading of the Conciliation Bill. After waiting fifty years to get this question settled women thought they were certainly entitled to twelve hours for the passage of this Bill through its final stages. If Mr. Asquith refused to grant the necessary time, then they would send a deputation of women to the House of Commons and they would refuse to go away until they got satisfaction.(*hear, hear*). That was what they hoped to do in November, although that question might be relatively new in Londonderry, she hoped there might be some women from here, as there would be from Dublin, Belfast, Cork, and elsewhere, to go with them. On this question of the elementary rights of citizenship English and Irish women would be at one. (*hear, hear and applause*). They were fully determined that this question must be settled at once, and then they would have a nation well governed, contented, and happy. (*applause*)."

On show of hands the resolution was carried unanimously. Miss Mackillop moved a vote of thanks to Mrs. Pankhurst for her eloquent and earnest address.

Alderman Anderson, seconding, said Mrs. Pankhurst has proved her case up to the hilt. The vote was passed with acclamation, and with a similar compliment to the Mayor the meeting ended."

Gretta, as we know, had a very personal connection with Londonderry. It was here she received her higher education for four years before moving to study music in Dublin. She was delighted when she had been invited to stay with her old headmistress, Miss MacKillop during her visit.

"In that familiar city of my schooldays I was the guest of my old boarding-school and its respected Head Mistress, Miss Margaret MacKillop. She had always been a public-spirited citizen of the historic old city, and kept abreast of the times. When I left the school ten years before, her last kindly-meant advice was not to be too independent. And there I was, one of the foundation members of the now notorious Irish Women's Franchise League, and one of the best-known and independent of its organizers. She welcomed me kindly, and gave me all assistance in arranging the large public meeting in St. Colomb's

Hall and was herself proud to know Mrs. Pankhurst, and to declare herself a supporter of votes for women. It interested me particularly to find that the old High School was now specializing in Domestic Science training. The more women came into public life, the more they paradoxically became trained students of home-making!"

After the historic public meeting in Derry Mrs Pankhurst travelled to Belfast for various engagements while Gretta returned to Dublin. Prior to her departure from Ireland Emmeline outlined the future work in London and throughout England. She said that for fifty years successive British governments had been using every form of tactic to prevent the securing of a Woman Suffrage Bill. She expected a further deputation would be sent in November to the Prime Minister, Herbert Asquith, to protest against the omission of suffrage from the Party programme on which the Liberals would go to the country in a new General Election.

Gretta immediately volunteered when Mrs Pankhurst asked for members to make up the deputation.

"There and then I rose from my seat and volunteered for militant action knowing it would result in my imprisonment. I knew that if I discussed my decision with relatives or friends they would feel bound to try to save me from suffering. It was my own responsibility, and, I felt, my own privilege. My dear husband upheld and helped me, he being as enthusiastic and revolutionary as I was myself. Six women from Dublin travelled to London on November 17. And took part in the Parliament of Women which met in Caxton Hall, Westminster, and from which four hundred women, in groups of twelve, made their way towards the House of Commons."

# CHAPTER NINE

## PEACEFUL DEPUTATIONS
### Militant resurgence and then Holloway prison

The educational campaign for women suffrage in Britain from 1906 had been so successful in turning an academic and intellectual question into a vital political issue demanding immediate action, that the many supporters in different parties joined together and had drafted what was then called a **Conciliation Bill,** the object of which was to acquire enfranchisement for women householders and occupiers of business premises with an annual rateable value of ten pounds. The militants had not been happy with this as they were hell-bent on demanding 'Votes for Women' on an equal basis. However it seemed there was a good chance that the Bill might be passed. The WSPU[33] as well as the IWFL both agreed to call a truce on militancy which lasted some ten months during 1910. However, when it came to the crunch, the country went into a General election without any indication in the Liberal mandate of votes for women.

Gretta recollects:

> "This roused the women of the British Isles again to take up the weapon of militancy; and they were now ready for mass protest and its consequences: prosecution, imprisonment, suffering, and in a later phase, the hunger-strike, force-feeding, and readiness to face death."

The rejection of any progress towards votes for women raised the ire of the Irish Nationalist Politicians in Parliament as well as members of the Irish Women's Franchise League.

Gretta had been one of the first up when, in Dublin, Mrs Pankhurst had invited ladies to join the deputation: Gretta relates now what happened when six volunteers sailed from Dublin to London to take part:

> "A contingent of the IWFL, of which I was one, was to represent Ireland in the Deputation planned to wait on the Prime Minister in protest for the omission of suffrage from the Liberal election programme. Having been sick crossing the Irish Channel I was now fit for any fray on the morning of 18 Nov 1910. I was brought by my hostess,

---

33 **The Woman's Social and Political Union** – The leading militant suffrage organisation 1908-1917 in the UK.

Mrs Merryweather, to the Women's Parliament in Caxton Hall, not far from the House of Commons.

A purple-white-and-green scarf, bearing the words VOTES FOR WOMEN was worn by all 400 volunteers for the Deputation to Downing Street. We also wore a card with our name on it. Mrs Pankhurst and Mrs Pethick-Lawrence made inspiring speeches. It was my first opportunity of hearing the latter at her best. She was highly magnetic, appealed to the heart, was intensely spiritual and did not hide it.

After the Resolution had been enthusiastically passed we each took a copy and formed ourselves into the constitutionally permitted groups of twelves having the right to seek interviews with the Prime Minister or his deputy. I felt deeply the high privilege of a place in history as I moved forwards from Caxton Hall in the spaced processions second group towards Westminster. The first two groups were allowed to stand on the steps of the entrance to the House of Commons. We waited five hours to get an opportunity in person to place the Resolution in the Prime Ministers hands. From our point of vantage we watched the police, whom the then Home Secretary, Winston Churchill, had specially drafted from the docks and slums of East London, obeying their orders not to arrest the women but to "put them out of action." Nevertheless 119 were arrested. Fifty had to receive medical attention for the injuries they received in fulfilment of Churchill's order."

They were so incensed at the treatment meted out that day that a call went out for volunteers for an immediate second Deputation, this time to the Prime Minister's residence in Downing Street. When they arrived they were met with solid phalanxes of police who forced them out of Downing Street. Gretta comments that a young woman fainted beside her and that she 'thumped her into consciousness.' As she came too she called out "Which way to Asquith?"

She learned later that this young woman was a medical doctor, whom she met again in India some twenty-five years later. By then she had become the wife of a high-up Government official.

The experience of the previous two days turned the suffragettes to a new form of militancy. They decided to first break the windows of the houses of Cabinet Ministers. The Irish suffragettes, with a few of their London colleagues, set out on 20 November for the home of The Hon. Augustine Birrell, the Chief Secretary for Ireland. Gretta describes the events:

"Our missiles were potatoes which we bought on the way and carried in our pockets and muffs. There was not a policeman in sight as we broke all the windows within our reach. Later at our prearranged rendezvous we heard that over 200 women, who had broken Government glass, had been arrested, but the windows of Asquith and Lloyd George were intact as Downing Street had been too well-guarded for our volunteers to get into it. As we Irish women were free, it fell to our lot to carry on the fight. We waited till midnight when we, along with some male supporters, were escorted to the corner of Downing Street. The November fog was so thick that we could not see across the street or make out the group preceding us.

My escort was Captain Gonne of the Royal Artillery, a cousin of Maud Gonne.[34] He left us after pointing out that "This is Downing Street. Go straight up there." Anna Garvey-Kelly and I had to call all our courage to our aid. The only missiles we had been able to secure at our friend's house were pieces of flower-pot that had been broken for the purpose. In the heavy silent fog we reached the official residence without meeting anyone. Then we heard the crash of glass from the preceding group. Immediately there was the shrilling of a police whistle. I flung my pieces of pottery and heard the result of the impact. I dashed across the street to be lost in the fog to avoid being caught but then came to my senses realising I was deserting my comrades. I dashed back to Lloyd George's residence and, as I threw my last pieces, a policeman actually asked me excitedly, "Will you stop here while I catch her?" referring to Anna. I laughed heartily and gave

Anna Garvey-Kelly

34 **Maud Gonne** was an Irish revolutionary, a romantic muse for William Butler Yeats, and mother to Nobel Peace Prize-winner, Sean MacBride. She founded the Irish Nationalist group, 'The Daughters of Ireland.' She married Major John MacBride in 1903 and their son, Sean was awarded the Nobel Peace Prize in 1974. He previously had been Chief of Staff of the IRA.

the required assurance to the poor man. But I was relieved when we were safely in his care. The police of the Westminster district were gentlemen compared to the bullies that Winston Churchill had turned on us at Westminster."

At one in the morning they were bundled into Cannon Row Police Station where they found the other members of their group. Shortly after, Fred Pethick-Lawrence[35] arrived and bailed them out. Gretta finally found her way back to Mrs Merryweather's flat. Next morning she was escorted to Bow Street Police Court. Crowds of suffragettes were there and stories were rife with excitement. Even the officers were asking for autographs and some for souvenirs such as their badges. About 100 women, who had not broken windows, were released by order of Churchill.  Eventually seventy-five of them were sentenced for criminal damage. Gretta was one of them. She was remanded to court on the following day. Till then she was taken in by a comrade and was so exhausted that she quickly fell into a deep sleep.  Next morning she felt fully revived and later, in Court, she was sentenced to a month's imprisonment in Holloway. Most of the trial she couldn't recollect other than the cost of the glass – which was ten shillings. She was conveyed to prison in a Black Maria. The others sang as they were driven through the streets of London.

Holloway
Prison for
women –
1914

---

35 **Frank Lawrence** met Emmeline Pethick, an active socialist and campaigner for women's votes. They married in 1901 after Lawrence converted to socialism. They kept separate bank accounts and they both took the surname ‹Pethick-Lawrence›. He published various left-wing newspapers, including **Votes for Women** and became involved in the Labour Party. His involvement with the WSPU, on behalf of women's rights, led to a nine-month prison sentence in 1912  following Christabel Pankhurst's window-smashing campaign, even though he had disagreed with that form of action; because of his disagreement he was expelled from the WSPU by Emmeline Pankhurst and Christabel. On account of his prison sentence he was expelled from the Reform Club. Early in the First World War Pethick-Lawrence joined with others in founding the Union of Democratic Control (UDC), a leading anti-war organisation of which he became Treasurer. After acceptance by a Tribunal in Dorking in 1918, he worked on a farm in Sussex as a conscientious objector.

"My memories of that month sum themselves up as a species of living death because of the solitariness of the confinement. My watch had been taken as well as all trinkets. The arrival of the three meals a day, pushed in through a locked aperture was the only way we knew of the time. The heat of the cell from hot water pipes was suffocating. Ironically, the only relief we got was to break the window panes with the heels of my shoes. As a vegetarian I was given an extra quantity of milk at each meal, no tea or coffee for the month. A piece of brown bread was given at each meal. Vegetables were limited and the only cutlery was a blunt tin knife and a spoon – no fork. We were allowed any number of 'improving books' sent by friends. No writing materials were allowed. There was a short church service daily which each prisoner was expected to attend. I deeply rebelled against the spy-hole in the locked cell door and felt degraded by being known and spoken to only as a number. The daily hour of exercise was spent in walking behind one another in complete silence, round and round a narrow path in a high-walled enclosure. I was fully convinced that such imprisonment as the supposed civilized Government was giving to women (women who were thinking, self-sacrificing, politically minded, educated, seeking only reforms and justice) was a stupid, cruel and useless way of suppressing their agitation, and was only wasting time."

Gretta was released on 23 December 1910. No one met her outside the gates, while others were picked up by relatives and friends. Eventually Mrs Merryweather arrived in a taxi apologizing that she had been held up in traffic. Gretta's loneliness was quickly dispersed at seeing her welcoming face.

## IRISH SUFFRAGETTES

### SENT TO PRISON IN LONDON

In all, seven members of the Irish contingent, sent by the Irish Women's Franchise League to take part in the militant deputation to Westminster, have been arrested, and six of these have been imprisoned. On Tuesday, Mrs. Earl, Miss Webb (member of Committee, I.W.F.L.), Miss Stephenson, and Miss Houston were arrested in connection with the demonstrations in Downing street, but were subsequently discharged without any evidence being tendered against them. On Thursday, Mrs. Cousins, Mus.Bac. (treasurer, I.W.F.L.), Miss Allen, and Mrs. Garvey Kelly were brought before the police magistrate in Bow street, charged with breaking Cabinet Ministers' windows, and sentenced to one month's imprisonment each. On Friday, Miss Webb, Miss Stephenson, and Miss Houston, who had been arrested a second time, were again brought up, charged with breaking windows of Cabinet Ministers, and were sentenced to two months' imprisonment each.

Dublin Daily Express – Monday 28 November 1910
Note: 'On Thursday, Mrs Cousins, Mus.Bac. (treasurer, I.W.F.L.), Miss Allen, and Mrs Garvey Kelly were brought before the police magistrate in Bow street, charged with breaking Cabinet Ministers' windows, and sentenced to one month's imprisonment each.'

# CHAPTER TEN

## BACK TO IRELAND – MORE SMASHING OF WINDOWS
### A month in Tullamore jail

Anna Garvey-Kelly and Gretta arrived back in Ireland at Kingstown on the next day, Christmas Eve 1910. Jim met her on the quay with a bunch of lilies-of-the-valley. They boarded the train into Dublin and found Westland Row station crammed with suffrage supporters. A torchlight procession was waiting and they were escorted, together with a band, in an open two-horse carriage. This unexpected reception made up for the recent arduous times in London. They stopped outside the Antient Concert Rooms in Pearse Street where a meeting of the IWFL took place. Once finished she and Jim were driven home by the same carriage-and-pair to be received by relatives and friends at their own home which had been specially decorated for Christmas.

In the general election of 1910 the Liberals just scraped in. The Conciliation Bill presented to the new Parliament in February 1911 was passed by a majority of 176 votes. However, the tempo of the suffrage movement in England increased when it became evident that Liberal Government under Asquith had no intention of passing the Woman Suffrage Bill. The WSPU again resorted to a campaign of window-smashing, followed by the inevitable imprisonment where they starved themselves out of jail. They had clearly shown that the majority of the population of England were in favour of votes for women.

In Ireland the work was mostly educational, holding open-air meetings in summer and indoor meetings in the winter. It looked, at the time, as if the Home Rule Bill would pass, gaining freedom for Ireland. It was not to be, however. When it was passed no mention of Irish women being made full citizens in their own country appeared – not a single word. Irish Nationalist Members of Parliament were heckled wherever they spoke in public. They didn't like this.

Gretta went to London:

"My task was to try to persuade them to add a women suffrage amendment to the Irish Home Rule Bill. I lobbied Tim Healy, Hugh Law, John Redmond and five or six others, all of whom were cross with Irish women for trying to gate-crash their sacrosanct politics. They felt that it would be time enough to think of women's status when Ireland was free. I had an hour's interview with Joe Devlin of

Belfast, then very powerful in the Irish party. He stormed at me that he had always been in favour of giving votes to women, but the way suffragettes were interrupting Cabinet Ministers, and in Ireland the very Members who were fighting for Home Rule was turning him against the whole movement. He would not move a hand to improve the draft Home Rule Bill, but would promise us that he himself would introduce an Irish Women Suffrage Bill in the first Irish Parliament (Dáil Éireann). Those Irish politicians had no use for women citizens; they were sufficient for themselves and for the country. We measured them by principle and democracy and found them wanting. We knew other Irish members, some younger like Tom Kettle, who were more understanding of women in the world of labour; other men of vision like Sir George Plunkett, James Connelly, Jim Larkin, Æ; poets of the Irish revival like Pádraig Pearse, MacDonagh and my husband; some women political leaders like Countess Markievicz, and Mrs Despard, Mrs Tom Clarke (afterwards first woman Lord Mayor of Dublin),[36] and particularly Frank and Hanna Sheehy-Skeffington, who were heart and soul for getting the rights of citizenship into any and every Home Rule Bill, and working for women's rights through the Conciliation Bill or any other Bill the English Parties might introduce either before or during all contemporaneous phases of the seven hundred year struggle for the freedom of Ireland."

In 1912 Prime Minister Asquith came to Dublin to speak in favour of the Irish Home Rule Bill. He was to speak in the Theatre Royal. The IWFL publicized the fact that they would find some means of protesting against the Bill which did not include Irish Women as full citizens of the country along with men. The organizers were, to say the least, anxious and decreed that no women should be admitted to the meeting. Members of the IWFL chalked the pavements advertising that they would hold an open-air meeting beside the Custom House, the nearest suitable ground to the Theatre Royal. The Prime Minister was secreted via a side entrance.

What they didn't know was that Frank Sheehy-Skeffington had managed to get a pass into the meeting. He high-jacked friends in a dramatic company to disguise him as a Protestant Clergyman so he would be given a prominent place in the stalls. Once Asquith was well into his speech, Frank's voice rang out as he shouted:

---

36 **Caitlín Bean Uí Chléirigh** was elected Lord Mayor of Dublin in 1939. She was the widow of Tom Clarke who had been a signatory of the Proclamation of the Irish Republic and was executed for his part in the 1916.

Theatre Royal – Dublin 1912

"Give votes to women. Stop force-feeding of women prisoners. Put votes for women in the Home Rule Bill."

Pandemonium broke out. Voices shouted, "Its Skeffy!" So the 'respectable clergyman' was handed over to infuriated stewards and then ejected from the building. A group of friends spirited him away to a local café where he related his story to Jim and others. Meanwhile Gretta, together with other members of the IWFL, were on a lorry from which they had announced the meeting. An angry crowd, however, had been sent to break them up. Police got in between and managed to abort a nasty fracas. They managed to escape safely, but it took Gretta two hours to get back home to Sandymount. When the second reading of the Liberal Home Rule Bill was due – without mention of women's suffrage – the League decided it was necessary that more extreme militant action was now justified to ensure world-wide publicity.

Three members of the Irish Women's Franchise League, Mrs. Connery, Mrs. Hoskins and Gretta volunteered to break the windows of Dublin Castle, the official 'seat of English domination.'

"The sound of breaking glass on 28 January 1913 reverberated round the world and did what we wanted. It told the world that Irish women protested against an imperfect and undemocratic Home Rule Bill. We were marched from the Castle to College Street police station, next door to the Vegetarian Restaurant, each between two policemen, who, at our request, did not hold our arms or handcuff us, but allowed us to walk freely as they accepted our word that we would not try to escape.

We were the first women prisoners on behalf of women's demands for their sex in a Home Rule setting. The court was crammed for the trial. Though the damage to the windows did not amount to five shillings each, we were sentenced to a month's imprisonment as common criminals. We stood up and protested against the status to which we were condemned, and demanded to be treated as political prisoners, a classification which had been won by men in the Land League and Home Rule clashes with the English Government. As I was escorted from the court someone handed me a bunch of beautiful pink-and-white double tulips that were my companions to the last day of the hunger strike we were forced to undertake."

The sentence given down was one month with hard labour. The first night Gretta was held in Mountjoy Gaol in Dublin. The authorities were not prepared for them. They refused neither to be searched nor to remove their clothing. They were separated to single cells which were bitterly cold, unlike Holloway in London where the cells were too hot.

"Much tension and nervous strain had made me so tired that a final tussle with the jail authorities, because I wouldn't give my thumb impression, exhausted me, and I had to lie down on the plank bed. It was terribly hard and hurt me. What was worse was the sickening, disgusting smell from a grey blanket that had evidently been used by former unwashed prisoners. I eventually slept through the raw winter night conquered my nausea and gave me oblivion till morning. Next morning we three were packed, with a couple of police men, into a car, driven to a railway station, and taken by train under escort some thirty miles to the prison in the town of Tullamore."

After arriving at the station in Tullamore, visitors, station porters, car-drivers, newsboys all formed a procession of sympathy behind them with their police guard. They cheered as the prisoners finally entered the gate of the Prison. The IWFL had increasing evidence that the groundswell of the Irish population were sympathetic to their cause. Prison conditions were much better in Tullamore than Mountjoy. Each had a separate room in the prison hospital. A fourth suffragette joined them, who had also been sentenced for violent protest. This was Mrs Mabel Purser, wife of an eminent physician.

Meg Connery, Mabel Purser, Barbara Hoskins & Margaret Cousins

They were all allowed a fire, an iron bedstead, clean and warm bed-clothes, a chair, a table, a writing slate and pencil, their own clothes, some 'moral' books and edible food of a poor kind, as well as the right of association in work and exercise. The Superintendent of the jail and the female warders were all humane. The sentence had included 'hard labour' which was not implemented. In fact, unknown to the higher authorities, they were treated as political prisoners. They were addressed by their names, not as numbers as they were in Holloway. Only a 'spiritual advisor' was allowed to visit. As each of them had differing religious persuasions they were allowed one each. They had decided, from the start, to go on hunger strike.

"My spiritual advisor was not permitted to give us any outside information or to take any from us. All the same he managed to do both. On his first visit he was tight as an oyster. I knew he was full of news and I was frantic to get at it. But he was loyal to his duty. Before leaving me, after a short empty conversation, he exercised his right to pray with me. What he could not tell me he was, without restriction, able to tell to 'God!' His prayer went something like:

"O God! Bless the efforts that are being made by the friends of those noble women to secure them honourable status or release; and influence the Lord Lieutenant to grant the request that has been made in the widely signed memorial to His Excellency."

I could have hugged him. As it happened, God didn't or couldn't influence the 'principalities and powers' of Dublin Castle. By the third day hunger had entirely left us. On the sixth day Mrs Hoskins collapsed and was said to be in danger of death from heart failure. This frightened the Governor and he sent for the chief Medical Officer of Prisons. He ordered the immediate unconditional release of Barbara

Hoskins. He then interviewed the rest of us, with only the Tullamore prison doctor present. I was ready to face death from starvation, but shrank from the horror of forced feeding, which we knew had been inflicted on suffragette hunger-strikers in England. He put difficult questions to me, three of which I remember. "I hear you are a musician. Are you ready to give up all your music for a political object?" He then asked me about my duty to my husband. I replied that he understood the women's cause so thoroughly that he gave me his moral support in all I was doing. "And are you so fixed in this course as to part from him forever?" he continued. "We shall meet again." I replied, "We are not afraid that death will separate us eternally."

The local doctor, using horsy vernacular, summed up the situation: "You can do nothing with her. She's a thoroughbred." With my own horsy tradition from childhood, I deeply appreciated his evaluation of my spirit. I reversed the questions and answers. "Are you going to order forcible feeding for us?" "No!" he replied we are not going to use that in Ireland." I jumped up, snatched my slate, and wrote on it: 'WE ARE PROMISED THERE WILL BE NO FORCEABLE FEEDING.' Then I turned it over and wrote, on the other side. 'NO SURRENDER'"

The interest that the protest and sentence had evoked throughout Ireland was remarkable. Gretta's younger brother, Alfred, an electrical engineer in County Cork, who had been vehemently opposed to the Movement, now wrote to her on 3 February 1913:

"Your imprisonment has created more interest and discussion than anything done for women suffrage so far in Ireland. The whole thing has been a great success and you and your comrades are indeed to be congratulated on doing your part so nobly."

Rumours had filtered out from the gaol that the hunger strike had started and was by that time in its third day. Jim had received a telegram – from which name and address had been redacted. It was discovered that it had, in fact, been sent by one of the spiritual advisers who had visited the prisoners. It read: MATTHEW SIX SIXTEEN & GENESIS ONE THIRTEEN PASS ON. This he realized must be code. Hurriedly a Bible was dug out and he read the following:

MOREOVER, WHEN YE FAST, BE NOT AS THE HYPOCRITS, OF SAD COUNTENANCE. + AND THE EVENING AND THE MORNING WERE THE THIRD DAY.

He immediately got in touch with 'Skeffy', and the press of the world knew the next day that the suffragettes in Tullamore Jail had gone on hunger strike on 3 February because no response had been received to their petition to the Lord Lieutenant.

Jim had written to Gretta in Prison in Tullamore on 1 February to ask if she would like him to visit. The Governor wrote back that if he could get permission, she would be glad to see him. So, on 4 February, he spoke to the Chairman of the Prisons Board, Max Green, son-in-law to John Redmond. He was quite happy to give permission but he would have to keep quiet about it. He explained that the prisoners were being provided with all the facilities of political prisoners although this had not been officially sanctioned. He added, "We have to cod the public!" Jim told him that 'codding' was not one of the techniques of the suffragettes. He therefore withdrew his application to visit. The Chairman was very sorry as he was a firm supporter of the movement. However in the middle of the one month sentence Jim *would be* entitled to visit.

"All arrangements were made for my mid-month visit to Gretta on 15 February 1913. Whispers came that she had been in good form during the strike and helped to keep the others up. The Governor met me with an affable smile and a warm handshake, and assured me of the honour they felt in having such fine ladies in their care. This was a good start. He took me personally to the visiting room and assured me we were given 15 minutes. Then when Gretta entered the passage escorted by a wardress, the Governor left me in the care of the clerk and women warder.

Now, strike finished, she was looking much better. I was about to share a list of points of information but she was more interested in me and sprawled along the edge of the circular table until, before the 15 minutes were up, she was touching my hand. The Governor returned a minute before time saying, "Would you not be more comfortable on your seat, Mrs Cousins?" "Thank you, Governor, this *is* my seat." she said and, like a shot, was on my knees and holding onto me with an arm round my neck. The Governor had turned away. He said to the clerk, "They may have another ten minutes." And left the room. After her release, like a well-mannered guest, Gretta wrote a letter to the Governor thanking him for his courtesy to her during the month under his care. He replied:

"My duty here with you and your fellow prisoners was made very light indeed by the kindly consideration and good sense you have always shown towards myself and the other officials in the discharge of our duties…I am not writing words of empty flattery when I say the Cause you have so much at heart will lose, by your departure, a lady and a leader of more than the ordinary ability and tact, whose place it will not be easy to fill with a person of equal qualifications."

And if anyone has a nicer testimonial from their jailer with which to start on a new era, they are welcome to it".

As a result of this publicity and general support from the population the inclusion of women suffrage was 'assured' in the Home Rule Bill. Margaret Connery, Mabel Purser and Gretta all completed their month's sentence in 'peace and honour.' They were pleased that Ireland, at least, had come through humanely and not 'stained its history as England had stained hers, by forcibly feeding suffrage prisoners.'

Gretta ruminated many years later:

"No one in 1913 thought that Home Rule for Ireland would come in any other way than through the peaceful passage of the Bill promoted by the Liberal party then in power. We knew a number of the leaders in politics and labour; but names that in a few years were to become starred in the record of Ireland's fighters for freedom Collins, McSweeney, Cosgrave, De Valera were unknown to us or to anyone else. We had no idea that the Ireland of our first twelve years together would, by the time we promised to return in five years, not be in existence. During those five years Ireland was to go through undreamt of agonies and tragedies. When we did return in 1925 it was an Ireland of transition, rent and bitter, in which we did not feel at home, where there was now no room for such as we were; though, to our deep satisfaction, Ireland was functioning through its own Parliament, and Irish women were voting citizens of the Irish Free State and of the enforced province of Northern Ireland."

Gretta and Jim 1915 before emigrating to India

# CHAPTER ELEVEN

## WHY THE 'SUDDEN' MOVE TO INDIA?

The decision to leave Ireland at what could be termed the zenith of the work of the IWFL and Jim's immersion in the Cultural Renaissance with his poetry and his plays seemed daft to friends and relatives. It was no ordinary attractions or repulsions that forced them towards making this life-changing decision. They had been very happy in Ireland and indeed felt they had been useful.

It was, in the end, a mixture of push and pull.

The main 'push' was monetary. The Episcopalian Committee of The Dublin High School, where Jim taught, could not be expected to increase his salary, especially as his notoriety as a poet and playwright with a tint of 'green' in his work and his meetings in halls with 'red' ties had become very public indeed. James Connolly had said to him once, "Better a socialist *in* a job than *out* of one." Jim was considered very unorthodox. He was noted widely for dabbling in Theosophy and psychic affairs and of being a vegetarian. He had been given two labels, Nationalist & Socialist, but unorthodox within each. In a very real sense Jim could be considered a maverick.

"This was doubled by the notoriety of my wife as a militant suffragette whom I did not 'keep in her proper place' but actually aided and abetted her in "The Irish Citizen" of which, in the last year of our Irish career, I was shamelessly the editor.

Economically I was in a cleft stick. My school salary was fixed while the expenses of life were growing. While I was an undischarged bankrupt I was on thin ice in a respectable school and ineligible for a responsible post in commerce ever again. I almost became one of Æ's agricultural demonstrators![37] These were the expulsive forces in our life in 1912."

---

37 **George William Russell** (1867 – 1935) who wrote with the pseudonym Æ, was an Irish writer, editor, critic, poet, painter and Irish Nationalist. He was also a writer on mysticism, and a central figure in the group of devotees of Theosophy. Russell started working as a draper's clerk, then for many years worked for the **Irish Agricultural Organisation Society** (IAOS), a society initiated by Horace Plunkett in 1894. In 1897 Plunkett needed an able organiser and WB Yeats suggested Russell, who subsequently became Assistant Secretary of the IAOS.

The 'attracting force' came from India itself. Visitors from the subcontinent, intent on studying medicine and law, saw the possibility of service to education and womanhood for the Cousins. Five years abroad would be their longest intention, then to return to Ireland equipped for teaching or journalism. Then the 'pull' from India suddenly became stronger in an unsuspected and roundabout way.

Their vegetarian activities brought to Dublin a pioneer in the manufacture of meatless food products. This Food Reform movement resulted in the establishment of Health Food Stores. Hugh Mapleton was founder and CEO of a factory for such foods based in Garston, near Liverpool.

George Russell (Æ)
Poet, Theosophist & vegetarian

He gave a public cookery demonstration for the Irish Vegetarian Society and stayed with the Cousins. He, guess what, was also involved in Theosophy and invited Jim to lecture to the Theosophical Lodge in Liverpool. He accepted and, during Jim's brief visit to Garston, Hugh asked him to look over his factory (Autumn 1912). After lunch on that particular day Mapleton enthused that Jim was just the man he was looking for to manage a new branch of his business to be opened in Bombay (Mumbai). He had received a capital sum from an Indian philanthropist and was going ahead with the project. Then came the icing on the cake. He offered Jim a salary *four times* what he was earning as a teacher in Ireland and promised, once settled in Bombay, this would then be *doubled.* He was to talk it over with Gretta. After cool considerations of all aspects they decided to accept once the official invitation came from Mapleton, which it did on Christmas Day 1912. Both of them began the painful process of 'pulling up the stakes' in order to move lock, stock, and barrel to Garston in June 1913.

Family-wise, back in Ireland, Leslie Pielou and Gretta's sister 'Florrie' (Florence) were married. A final good-bye function was held in Hardwicke Hall on 29 May 1913, when dramatic, vegetarian and suffragist friends all came together. Two of Jim's plays were re-enacted, "The Sleep of the King", and "The Racing Lug." with Mary Walker playing the characters she had made her own some eleven years previous. Gretta was then presented with a bag of sovereigns, as Jim was still not released from bankruptcy. W.J Lawrence, art critic and theatrical historian, in a last minute handshake, said with pathos, "It's the end of an era".

Once settled in Garston, some seven miles from the heart of Liverpool, in Mrs Entwistle's in Island Road, where they rented a spare bedroom and use of a parlour, they began their nine month stint prior to sailing for India. Jim, during this period, needed training for his planned managerial job in India.

On 10 June 1913 Jim received a letter from Dublin from one of the leading lights of the Irish Literary Revival, Padraic Colum.[38] In it he expressed regrets at having left the farewell function so early, which he wouldn't have done if he'd known they were leaving Ireland so soon.

He then wrote:

"I thought it was a great privilege to be asked to speak. I am sorry I had not considered the splendid poem you sent 'The Irish Review' before my speech. I said I had difficulty in placing you in relation with the Gaelic poets. Now, when I read your poem I am surprised that I said this. I have seen nothing so Gaelic in feeling and form. I think it is a grand poem and I am publishing it this month with one of the best of Æ's."

Padraic Colum

Jim's poem was "The Fire of Love, the Wine of Love and the Wings".

---

38 **Padraic Colum** (1881 – 1972) was an Irish poet, novelist, dramatist, biographer, playwright, children›s author and collector of folklore. He was one of the leading figures of the Irish Literary Revival.

# CHAPTER TWELVE

## TRANSITION BEFORE INDIA
### Attending Emily Davison's funeral
### The Women's Church
### Charlotte Despard's visit to Liverpool

Just because they had moved across the Irish Sea, did not prevent Gretta from engaging in suffrage work both in England and Ireland. Hopelessness in Ireland and exasperation in England were driving the two sister movements (IWFL & WSPU) towards a crisis. The 'violence' in Ireland had got no further than window-breaking and painting VOTES FOR WOMEN on Government letter-boxes.

Only four days after their arrival in Garston Jim was sent off to Hamburg to investigate the affairs of a food manufacturer, similar to Mapleton's, which was in danger of bankruptcy due to misappropriation of funds. If he confirmed these matters, then Mapleton's would take over the concern, discharge its liabilities, and thus make a large boost for the business of 'food-reform' of which Hugh Mapleton felt he was a real pioneer. Upon return Jim confirmed that the Hamburg firm was a going concern, but, as had been thought, was financially tottering on the edge because of fraud.

It was a shock to both he and Gretta when Mapleton announced that funds earmarked for opening the branch in Bombay (Mumbai) were now diverted to buy the Hamburg business of Rothfritz. It was still hoped that finances would be sorted by the time Jim was trained and ready for Bombay. India seemed to be receding in their minds. Then, as fate would have it, war broke out, some fourteen months later on 2 August 1914 and Mapleton's foreign money invested in the Hamburg business was 'confiscated' by the regime.

**Attending Emily Davison's funeral**
Meantime the exasperation of the suffrage movement in England was short-lived. Gretta received a sad and urgent message:

"I had to make an unexpected trip to London, to attend the funeral of Emily Davison,[39] who, as a protest against the treatment of the women's

---

39 **Emily Wilding Davison** (1872 – 8 June 1913) was a suffragette who fought for votes for women in the United Kingdom. A member of the Women's Social and Political Union (WSPU) and a militant fighter for her cause, she was arrested on nine occasions, went on hunger strike seven times and was force fed on forty-nine occasions. She died after being hit by King George V's horse **Anmer** at the 1913 Epsom Derby when she walked onto the track during the race.

demand, and for the securing of publicity that was restricted by those in power, stopped the King's horse in a race by rushing in front of it, and was killed. (8 June 1913).

Emily Davison

Six years previously I had spoken with her at the Cobden Statue in St Anne's Square in Manchester. She was a college woman and as steady as a rock. She spoke well but unemotionally and had a store of historical knowledge. I thought she had no imagination; yet she had thought out a wholly unexpected and individual act of militancy that she knew was almost certain to cost her life, or permanent disablement, in the service of the cause.

I left Garston on June 14 1910 at 7.30am and was back by 10pm. There was a long procession of women through famous London thoroughfares lined by thick crowds whose men showed their recognition of the occasion by solemnly raising their hats and caps. The simplicity, the quietness, the purity of that interminable line of women-mourners, in whose sorrow there was a glory of sacrifice, carried the impersonality and meaning of the act deep into the consciousness of the people. Triviality over the movement had left the male mind for some time. Here was an example, a final dissipation of the misrepresentation by politicians and press that the suffragettes were only out for cheap notoriety. One did not get killed just to enjoy the sensation. There had been a general attitude of giving the 'suffs' enough rope and they will hang themselves; but the epic sacrifice of Emily Davison began to make the public realise that the rope was on another neck, and that the incomplete and hypocritical 'old order' was itself on the way to a scaffold of its own raising.'"

The work continued with Gretta attending meetings under the auspices of the Women's Social & Political Union with occasional free-lance speeches to local societies.

## The Women's Church

The suffrage struggle, as it developed, brought a number of other questions to the fore. One of these was the place of women in the church. Gretta by now was not an enthusiastic church-goer, although psalms and hymns stirred something deep within her musical spirit. With her open mind and her endless search after truth Gretta moved among Englishwomen of various classes, creeds and interests. This made her aware of a growing dissatisfaction among them regarding their relationship to 'organised churches'. This was particularly marked among women of the Church of England. The stock phrase: "Dearly beloved brethren" first amused them as an obsolete antiquity, but afterwards began to irritate them as an ancient assertion of their inferiority.

Gretta had by now no regular connection with any church, but her thoughts on such matters drew a number of questioning women around her. She had no ambition towards leadership, but was, however, fully in sympathy with this desire for a religious body that gave woman their rightful place. Gretta assisted the movement, and after many meetings, talks and plans, an organisation grew from these consultations that had considerable influence on the religious life of Liverpool and its vicinity. The new organisation was to be called The 'Church of the New Ideal'. Its departments were entrusted to various women. Gretta was given the task of compiling an order of service. As news of the soon-to-be-opened church spread, interest grew widely and quickly reached even London.

The Church was opened in Liscard Concert Hall in Cheshire on Sunday, March 29, 1914, by the Rev Hattie Baker, who had been consecrated to the ministry by her father, a well-known non-conformist clergyman. She had acted for him in his pulpit in the past.

Gretta writes about the formation of the Women's Church.

"The afternoon service drew a large congregation of women only. The open evening service filled the large hall with men and women who, whatever natural curiosity or other reason brought them, paid reverent attention to the new and solemn occasion.

The Order of Service was as follows:

1. Short invocation by the officiant. 2. General prayer. 3. Hymn. 4. Lesson. 5. Hymn and Offertory. 6. Extempore prayer and Lord's Prayer. 7. Sermon. 8. Hymn. 9. Benediction.

The Rev. Hattie Baker, mature, ascetic, intellectual, preached a sermon of great impressiveness. Yet for all her care to explain that the church was not an anti-male institution, some of the newspapers played up the false premise that what is *for* something is therefore *against* something else. How far the influence of the new church had grown in a couple of months can be seen in a report which appeared in the London paper, 'The Daily News and Leader,' of 20 May. The report was head-lined:

# Women in the Pulpit
### Far-reaching claims at Liverpool conference.
### "It is not good for man to be alone—even in the pulpit."

In this epigrammatical adaptation of the Biblical dictum, Mrs Cousins, the well-known Liverpool suffragist, summed up a far reaching claim for a larger place for women in Church life in the course of an address at the spring conference of the Liberal Christian League at Liverpool yesterday. The Church, she declared, had lent itself to the subjection of women, and it was not supporting women in their efforts to emancipate themselves as it ought, not-withstanding that women were the mainstay of the Church. 'If it were not for the women in the Churches you might shut them all up.' Yet women are treated in the churches as if they were children. We are simply to be seen and not heard. Preaching has been a masculine monopoly, but the women's time to preach is coming. Women would no doubt preach the same things as men, but they would view them from a different angle. It was the habit of men to think and talk of property and 'things'. Women from the time they were born always looked at human affairs. Women had asked to be made wardens, vestry women, and sides-women, but the Bishop of Leeds had said it was not seemly for women to collect money in the church.

Did his Lordship think it seemly for women to be there at all? The religious half of the race, she claimed, was the feminine half, and if it were not for women we would be a set of atheists. Even in the Free Churches the door was shut to women. "If the churches," declared Mrs. Cousins, pointing to the fact that a church with a woman preacher and officers had been founded at Liverpool, "do not voluntarily and willingly ask us to come into their administration on absolute equality with men, that will happen which has already taken place as a first step in one part of Liverpool. Women will organise their own churches. (*applause*)."

The Church of the New Ideal went on steadily with its services. I preached at times. The first phase, that of having its services conducted only by women, ended in a year. The new phase was opened by admitting a man-preacher on 9 May 1915. The choice fell on my husband both because he had reached a position of literary eminence and had been a frequent and appreciative and understanding attendant at the services. Characteristically he chose as his subject "The Eternal Feminine," and took as his double text one from Haggai: 11 1-9, "The glory of the latter house shall be greater than the former", and from Revelation X I I: "There appeared a great wonder in heaven; a woman clothed with the sun, and having the moon under her feet, and upon her head a crown of twelve stars.""

The Church of the New Ideal continued its work for some time after she and Jim had moved to India.

## The visit of Charlotte Despard to Liverpool

On 10 November 1915 the Liverpool Vegetarian Society welcomed Charlotte Despard, described by Gretta as 'that perpetual centre of ideal inspiration'. She and the Pethick-Lawrence's had broken away from the Pankhursts on matters of militant action. She now headed up the new 'Women's Freedom League', but all suffragettes loved her. The aims were the same but the manner in which they were to be gained was different. Some quotes from The 'Liverpool Express' of the time fills out some facts about the visit:

> In recognition of her twenty years' labours for food reform, a luncheon was given today for Mrs Despard by the Liverpool Vegetarian Society, at the Vegetarian Restaurant, Eberle Street. Their guest, said Mrs Cousins (the President), was an arch-reformer and pioneer of the cause of freedom. Many of them looked to her as being the real Queen Mother of Freedom, from the soles of her feet, where she wore sandals, to the top of her head, where she did not wear a hat (*laughter & applause*).
>
> …Mrs. Despard expressed the opinion that vegetarianism was really at the base of a great many things. Food seemed only a humble thing, but if they realised what did, and might, go into them and through their bodies, then perhaps they would think the question of food was one of the greatest importance.

During the huge crisis that had suddenly overwhelmed Europe, militancy by the various suffrage groups was suspended. Asquith's 'musty' slogan that "a women's place is the home" was drowned out by his call for women to take their place in the munitions factories. In due course the inconsistency of this sudden *volte-face* became abundantly clear. Women were soon to win the vote,[40] first with an age limit, and then finally with full suffrage. In time, women were to become members of Parliament. However only a very few made it in the first decade. It was still felt that women were basically homemakers.

It has taken 70-80 years for the numbers of women elected to Parliament to rise significantly. Men still dominate. In the 2017 election 208 women were elected out of a total of 650 MPs in the Westminster Parliament.

The first woman to be elected to Parliament was Countess Markievicz (1868-1927). Of Anglo-Irish origin, she was married to a Polish Count. As a member of Sinn Fein, she had played a part in the Easter Rising of 1916 and stood for election for a seat in Dublin and won, even while still in Holloway prison in London in December of 1918. Once elected she did not take up her seat on a principle that Sinn Fein has adhered to ever since. Viscountess Nancy Astor (1879-1964) was the first woman to actually take up a seat in the Westminster Parliament. Born in Virginia, she moved to England following her divorce from her first husband and subsequently married William Waldorf Astor[41] in 1906. In 1919 her husband, who was MP for Plymouth Sutton, succeeded to the peerage and she was elected in his stead for the Conservative party. She held that seat until she retired in June 1945.

---

40 **Women's suffrage UK** finally succeeded through two laws in 1918 and 1928. In 1872 the fight for women's suffrage became a national movement with the formation of the **National Society for Women's Suffrage** and later the more influential **National Union of Women's Suffrage Societies** (NUWS). The movements shifted sentiments in favour of woman suffrage by 1906. It was at this point that the militant campaign began with the formation of the **Women's Social and Political Union** (WSPU). The outbreak of the First World War led to a suspension of all politics, including the militant suffragette campaigns. Lobbying did take place quietly. In 1918, a coalition government passed the **Representation of the People Act 1918,** enfranchising all men, as well as all women over the age of 30 who met minimum property qualifications. This act was the first to include practically all men in the political system and began the inclusion of women, extending the franchise by 5.6 million men and 8.4 million women. In 1928, the government passed the **Representation of the People (Equal Franchise) Act** giving the vote to **all** women over the age of 21 on equal terms with men.

41 In 1916, **William Waldorf Astor**, American by birth, was elevated to the peerage as Viscount Astor. When his father died in October 1919, Waldorf became the 2nd Viscount Astor despite Waldorf's attempts to disclaim the title. As a member of the House of Lords, Astor was forced to forfeit his seat in the House of Commons, though he remained active in the government. The seat was won subsequently in a by-election by Astor's wife **Nancy**, who became the second woman elected to the House of Commons but the first to take her seat. Nancy retained the seat until she stepped down in the 1945 general election.

Countess Markievicz

Viscountess Nancy Astor

# CHAPTER THIRTEEN

## THE TIDE OF EVENTS RISES
### India calls and the picture shifts

With the outbreak of war against Germany on 2 August 1914, as already stated, the Mapleton's money in Germany was misappropriated by the Kaiser's regime.

It appeared that the duo was condemned to remain in Garston indefinitely. Their immediate reason for moving to India had been destroyed. The pressures that had pushed them from Ireland had not changed. India was still calling but they did not know how this would or could come about. Events, however, fell into place opening up their future destiny on the Indian sub-continent.

Jim described the outbreak of the First Great War with a short and pithy comment:

> "Someone shot someone; and in revenge, with that marvellous intelligence to which Europe then laid unique claim, everybody got to shooting at everyone else as quickly as possible."

Gretta returned one night from one of her regular meetings with a group of Theosophical students who met in Birkenhead. She was excited. During the meeting, apropos of nothing, she had found herself enveloped in a sudden joyous state of consciousness and, with it, came the strong insistence that Jim should write to Mrs Besant at the Theosophical Headquarters in Adyar, Madras (Chennai), offering his services as a journalist in connection with an important enterprise she had undertaken – 'Home Rule for India'. Both concluded that no harm could come by contacting Mrs Besant as a result of this 'psychic' event.

Jim sent her a short telegram, mentioning her visit to Dublin when she had stayed at their home, stating that he was, amongst his other skills, a trained journalist. Both their services were at her disposal. On 6 March 1915 an equally short note came in reply, asking them to come to Adyar for a period of three years. This was followed by another note on 21 June of that year enclosing a cheque for £80 to pay second-class fares from Liverpool to Madras. They started immediately to pack in preparation for the 'great shift'.

As it was likely they would not be back for many years, in spite of the initial invitation covering only three years, they decided to pay farewell visits to both sets of parents back in Ireland. This happened between 27 July and 10 Aug. They went first via Belfast to bring Jim's parents up-to-date and to take them for their first-ever 'motor-drive' over the hills. Then on to Dublin where Jim visited the Pielou family to catch-up on old friendships, while Gretta then detoured to Boyle to say goodbye to her own family. During Jim's stay with Leslie and Florence Pielou they became joyous parents when twins were born – a happy event indeed.

Before leaving Dublin Jim met with Æ, who had manoeuvred himself into a very negative position with regard to some Theosophical writings. His parting shot was: "Cousins, beware of that charlatan Annie Besant!" Next day he accidently bumped into Tomás MacDonagh while down town in Dublin. He had joined the Southern Volunteers, whose purpose was to help the British Government to establish Home Rule once it became law. These volunteers were being arrested under various pretences. He said with a glow of pride, "For one volunteer arrested we enrol ten more." Jim asked, "And to what end?" to which MacDonagh replied "We don't know – but whatever it is we are going on to it." History records that Tomás was subsequently executed by firing squad on the 3 May 1916 at Kilmainham Gaol in Dublin, as one of the leaders of the Easter Rising.

A few months later after they had returned to Garston, Gretta and Jim embarked from Birkenhead on the good ship **The City of London** (10,000 tons) holding some forty passengers. It was by now 4 October 1915. Thirty friends saw them off at the gangway. They were a superb mixture of unorthodox folk, dietetic, political, social, intellectual, aesthetical and religious. Gretta was presented with a bunch of crimson carnations which lasted as far as Suez. A packet of sealed letters was also handed over numbered 1-18. One was to be opened each morning thus conveying a touch of individual and group friendship. The last letter was for Mrs Besant sending greetings from the Theosophists to their President. As the ship was making ready a woman beside them on the deck, who apparently knew India quite well, shouted, "Goodbye chilblains!" Rumours were rife that a German submarine was awaiting them in the Mersey. This delayed the sailing till the morning of 6 October. They passed through the Bay of Biscay with only half a day in their bunks due to sea-sickness and entered the Mediterranean. It was like entering summer and silk-calm waters.

Jim records:

"Halfway through the Mediterranean, after a few hours' pause in Marseilles, the daily round of seven meals, games, music, exhibitions of diving by swordfish, after-dinner views of phosphorescent fragments passing alongside the steamer, our morning read of a letter-a-day, and snipping a tiny piece off the ends of our carnations began in earnest. It now seemed as if the picture was shifting smoothly. When we got to Port Said it was explained that we had escaped one or more German U-boats that had made their debut in the Mediterranean the day after we left Marseilles and had sunk a fat innocent looking cargo steamer that had been birthed alongside us."

Blackout at night was in indicator that the ship was not quite beyond the reach of war. They then entered the Suez Canal, then sailed steadily crossing the Indian Ocean finally birthing at Colombo in Ceylon (Shri Lanka). A Buddhist, Dr Vijetunge, who had visited Gretta and Jim in Dublin, had made them promise that if ever they passed through Colombo they must make contact. They did and Dr Vijetunge met them off the boat. They were immediately immersed in a total change of environment in colour, form, odour and personality, which plunged them both into a new and wonderful experience. It was like being wrapped in Joseph's coat of many colours.

The boat embarked again after three days, arriving in Madras on 1 November 1915. They were met at the harbour and conveyed by car to Adyar, a district of Madras (Chennai) before arriving at the International Headquarters of The Theosophical Society. By way of further immersion in this new and fascinating milieu they were driven along the beautiful Beach Road, with its margin of yellow sand, white breakers and rhythmical green sea to the left.

Jim mused:

"There was deep consolation around both mosquito-curtained beds in the realisation, as we passed into our first sleep on solid and unmoving ground in 28 days, that India…India…India was north, south and west of us, and that, after ten years of dreaming and aspiring and planning, the picture had shifted."

# CHAPTER FOURTEEN

## Settling IN & unsettling OUT

The International Headquarters of the Theosophical Society
at Adyar, Madras (Chennai)

### Settling IN

The first Indian week was, as a result of the kindly attentions of Mrs Annie Besant, filled with rest and absorption of the pleasures and beauty of nature, the sea, the flowers and the trees. The birds especially presented to them new and intriguing species as well as the most heavenly of sounds. Jim began his job as literary sub-editor of 'New India', Mrs Besant's newspaper and platform for her Indian Home Rule project. At first he rode a bicycle to the office, some nine miles away near the harbour in Madras. He soon became so exhausted with his daily commute, not to say 'sweaty' in the intense heat, that he soon abandoned the two wheels. The Editor–in-Chief, Annie Besant, ordered him to be 'taken somewhere and wrung out!' From then on her car called for him at 8.30am each morning at Leadbeater Chambers, their new living quarters.

The Chief, after reading the morning papers looking for suitable subjects she could use as 'leaders' for New India, held short conferences with a rising young lawyer, Mr C.P. Ramaswami Aiyar. What puzzled Jim was the fact that he was the advocate *against* Mrs Besant in the trial with regard to her two wards, J Krishnamurti and his brother K Nityananda. Mrs Besant was, at the time, preparing Krishnamurti to become proclaimed as the 'New Messiah'. Now Ramaswami had become a collaborator in her campaign for Home Rule for India which was already well into its first year. Jim was pleasantly surprised and pleased to see that Mrs Besant and he had reconciled. In due course Jim entered into a life-long friendship with C.P.

A new phase in the history of the Theosophical society was beginning.

Spirituality was being generated through the arts and on 5 December 1915 the Arts League was formed at Adyar. The formal opening was held on 16 December, Mrs Besant presiding. Gretta played and Jim sang. Both the President and Mr Jinarájadása[42] spoke. Initially the form was mostly western in flavour. Soon indigenous music was gradually introduced along with Eastern painting. In this way Jim was becoming involved in the arts of India and this aspect of his life continued to develop strongly in the years ahead, including a long-term friendship with Rabindranath Tagore,[43] whose seminal work the Gitanjali was prefaced by WB Yeats.

Two of Gretta's early excursions she found delightful. First she accompanied Mrs Besant to a political Conference at Palghat, Malabar, in the South West. This was on the subject of Home Rule and for the first time she observed the skills of her leadership, this little white-haired lady. She heard and saw her superlative oratory with which she held an audience spellbound and presented a unity of vision to them. The second excursion was to Poona (Pune) situated on the uplands east of Bombay (Mumbai). This journey was taken alone. It was arranged in order that she could take her seat as a member of the first Senate of the new Indian Women's University founded through the vision and devoted labours of Professor D.K. Karve.[44] He had, having come from extreme poverty, devoted his life to raising the standard of education for women. Gretta's initial contribution was to add comparative religion to the curriculum of the University.

---

42 **Curuppumullage Jinarajadasa** (1875 – 1953) was an author, occultist, freemason and theosophist. Jinarajadasa was one of the world's foremost Theosophical authors, having published more than 50 books and more than 1600 articles in periodicals during his life. His interests and writings included religion, philosophy, literature, art, science and occult chemistry. He was also an accomplished linguist, who had the ability to work in many European languages. In 1916, Jinarajadasa married the English feminist Miss Dorothy M. Graham, who founded the **Women's Indian Association (WIA)** on a suggestion by Margaret Cousins in 1917.

43 **Rabindranath Tagore** (1861-1941) was a native of Calcutta, India, who wrote in Bengali and often translated his own work into English. He won the Nobel Prize for Literature in 1913—the first Asian person to receive the honour. He wrote poetry, fiction, drama, essays, and songs; promoted reforms in education, aesthetics and religion; and in his late 60s he turned to the visual arts, producing 2,500 paintings and drawings before his death.

44 **Dhondo Keshav Karve** (1858 – 1962), popularly known as *Maharishi Karve*, was a social reformer in India in the field of women's welfare. In honour of Karve, Queen's Road in Mumbai (Bombay) was renamed Maharishi Karve Road. Karve continued the pioneering work in promoting **widow's education.** The Government of India awarded him the highest civilian award, the Bharat Ratna, in 1958, the year of his 100th birthday.

## Unsettling OUT

Some five months after their arrival news came of the 1916 Easter Rising in Ireland. Jim, who was editing the war cables for New India newspaper, was extremely shocked at what he read. Apart from tragedy for Ireland there was news of a more personal tragedy. For Mrs Besant there was great sadness, as she had publicly declared that 'three-quarters of her blood and all of her heart were Irish.'

Jim writes:

"The news of the rebellion in Ireland came with shocking suddenness and poignancy to us. Press reports during our interval in England had told of plots and counterplots, of labour agitation and rival volunteers. But in an unarmed country there was, we thought, little danger of any large-scale violence or anything more sanguinary than drama and eloquence. Æ had written to me six months after we moved to Garston saying, "You are well out of Dublin these times. It is the most undrained swamp of humanity I ever heard of." Now I was reading of the probable first victim of the rebellion, my collaborator and afterwards my successor in editorship of "The Irish Citizen." On the third evening of the outbreak Frank Sheehy-Skeffington went down town to try and use his influence to keep them from mob violence and threatened looting.

He was not part of the organisation of the rebellion; but, as a pro-nationalist publicist, he was on the black list of Dublin Castle. He was recognised, arrested by the military and summarily shot. Then came the name of others who had met the same fate, with whom I had been associated in literary and humanitarian activities; Pádraig Pearse, educational idealist; his brother William, who had acted in one of my plays; James Connolly, labour leader and historian of labour in Ireland; Tomás MacDonagh, teacher and poet. And then, there was Countess Markievitz, feminist and actress, who escaped death by being a woman, and lived to be the first woman elected to the British Parliament but refused to take her seat until she could do so in the free legislature of her own country; and a man who also escaped death because he was found to be by birth an American, Éamon De Valera, a name then unknown to me but destined to become world-famous."

Only a month later circumstances forced another change. Both Gretta and Jim had come via England to offer service to India in their various capacities. They did not now foresee returning to Ireland except perhaps on furlough for a short time.

Jim began to feel that his role as sub-editor of New India was becoming a drain on the finances. He felt change was wafting on the wind. He heard a whisper that George Arundale, who had been principal of the Central Hindu College at Benares, founded also by Mrs Besant, was coming to resume service under her work of agitation for Indian Home Rule. In fact he would now be joining the staff of New India. Jim concluded that this could only happen by his own replacement. The job did need someone more *au fait* with politics, which Jim was not. Politics had never suited his temperament or indeed his ideals.

It was not, therefore, too great a surprise when Mrs Besant, shortly after Arundales' arrival, called him into the office one day and explained that his services would no longer be required from the end of the month (June 1916). She added, of course, that their return passage to England would be fully paid. There was nothing he could say. He had seen it coming. Jim did explain to Mrs Besant that they had come to serve India and that they would use the money until they found some new ways of service. She agreed with their joint decision.

Both he and Gretta had shut the door-of-return to the beloved Motherland and were now determined, more than ever, to seek new pastures of service within India, a land they had fallen in love with, its peoples and its culture.

# CHAPTER FIFTEEN

## NEW PASTURES
The Scout Movement – Indian style
A School Parliament
Indian Women's Suffrage on the horizon
The spontaneous beginning with Gretta as the catalyst

### New pastures

Life went on much as usual at Adyar. Meantime Jim found a vacant lectureship in English at a Missionary College in northern India with a decent salary, accommodation, status, vacations and a future for their security. Just as he was about to sign the contract, Ernest Wood, who carried out Mrs. Besant's educational plans, heard of his probable departure from Adyar. Jim was asked if he would consider taking a post in a new Theosophical College in Madanapalle, founded by Mrs Besant. He felt relieved at the thought of staying within the Theosophical 'bubble', breathing the air of freedom from orthodoxy rather than facing the prospect of becoming hemmed in by the 'stuffy atmosphere of religious propaganda'.

Next day he met with Mrs Besant who agreed to this proposal. He was offered a salary of 100 rupees monthly, plus an extra R50 on the understanding that Gretta would agree to teach English in the High School from which the College had been developed. She was willing and so they both moved to live at the College in Madanapalle, a city some 160 miles from Adyar.[45]

Dr. Annie Besant

Prof. Ernest Wood

The Besant Theosophical College –Today

---

45 **The Besant Theosophical** College started on 19 July 1915. It was affiliated to Madras University. In 1917 when Dr Annie Besant led the agitation for 'Home Rule', this institution, which became a centre of nationalist activities, was obliged to dissociate itself from the Madras University and became part of the newly organized **National University**. Dr Rabindranath Tagore became its Chancellor.

The open animosity of the English Principal of the school to Mrs Besant's agitation for political autonomy for India led to his dismissal, or, as it was called, 'early retirement.' The Vice-Principal, Mr C.S. Trilokekar, who had served with Mrs Besant in Benares and fully shared her ideals, was promoted to Principal. Gretta was moved up to Vice-Principal. She became 'mummy' for the girls at the school. Each day began with 'dedication', ten minutes of short prayers of aspiration by students from various faiths; Hindu, Zoroastrian, Buddhist, Christian and Muslim. Day by day the Besant ideal of an all-round education for the body, mind and spirit was organically growing and becoming increasingly practiced.

Gretta and Jim were by now fully sharing in the ideals of the Theosophical Society, the ideal that all religions should be included and that an open and rounded education was fundamental for both sexes. Also they believed that both Ireland and India should be permitted to have autonomy and their own elected legislature. To this end Annie Besant, faithful to her universal ideals often said that:

"There were two great Movements which stood for Universal Brotherhood. One was the Theosophical Society ... and the second, the World Boy Scout Movement."

**The Scout Movement – Indian style**

Lt General Baden Powell

Lady Olave Baden Powell

Lt General Robert Baden-Powell had founded the International Scout Movement in 1907 as a result of his own experiences of serving in the British Army in South Africa. His seminal work 'Scouting for Boys' outlined the principles and aims of scouting mostly by out-door activities aimed at developing character, citizenship and personal fitness among male youth. The whole programme was designed to develop a high degree of self-reliance, initiative, courage, helpfulness, integrity, sportsmanship and resourcefulness. Scouts should be helpful; understand their society, their heritage and culture; have respect for the rights of others; and be positive role models as leader-citizens. The Movement was open to boys of all faiths and cultures. Later his wife, Lady Olave Baden-Powell became totally involved in the Girl Guides, eventually becoming Chief Girl Guide. The Movement itself was run on parallel lines to the Boys.[46]

The first Movement of Boy Scouts in India was due indirectly to Mr C. W. Leadbeater, who had spoken highly of their training programme. He had shown General Baden-Powell's book to his private secretary, Ernest Wood. When Wood became Hon. Secretary of the Theosophical Education Trust, he introduced scouting at the High School in Madanapalle, where the first Troop was started under the leadership of Mr Deobhankar.

About a year later Wood arranged with Frederick Pearce, Assistant Commissioner for Boy Scouts (B-P style) in Ceylon, to send a trained first class Troop. Stimulated by this success, other Troops sprang up in various places. These trained Scouts provided many services for the community, especially in sudden catastrophes, such as fighting fires, finding lost children and so on. During epidemics, such as cholera, scouts were always to the forefront, so much so that eventually the Government advised people to call the nearest Scout Master whenever help was required.

This type of Scouting developed as an Indian model based on the original Baden-Powell Movement. They had wanted it to be linked to the B-P Movement but requests sent by the Madanapalle Troop to B-P officials were either ignored or received unsatisfactory answers.

What did not sit well with Mrs Besant, was that the B-P Scout Movement in India was limited only to Europeans, Anglo-Indians, and a few Indian Christians, all under European Scoutmasters. It was not all-inclusive, which broke one of the cardinal principles of Theosophy - inclusivity.

---

46 **Lady Olave's** first offer to help the Girl Guides in 1914, was turned down. The Girl Guide Movement had started following pressure from girls who wanted to become Scouts; the Movement was set up by Robert Baden-Powell and his sister Agnes Baden-Powell. After the reorganisation of the Girl Guides in 1915, Olave again offered to help, this time successfully, and she started organising Guiding in Sussex. She became the County Commissioner for Sussex in March 1916. Later she became the World Chief Guide.

So, in 1917, The Indian Boy Scouts Association took shape at Madanapalle under the guidance and inspiration of Mrs Besant, with George Arundale, Lieutenant Tarini Sinha and Mr Sanjiva Kamath as the chief organisers.

## A School Parliament

Another front in the development of educational programmes at the College was a 'School Parliament.' Jim became Speaker for the first year. The purpose was to introduce the more senior pupils to the techniques of debate. Thus, in their own way, they 'settled the affairs of India once a week with remarkable earnestness and oratory'. Along with the College Parliament went a College Jury for the trial of 'offences'. Their services were not often required but, when they were, findings and awards were well-grounded and seriously observed.

Soon the first wave of the Gandhian non-cooperation movement spread to Madras. The powers behind the college were at one with Mohandas Gandhi in his desire to free India from external domination, but they disagreed with his methods of agitation even though peacefully done. Students were allowed to attend rallies but advised not to take part in the politics. Observe and learn was Gretta's advice to them.

Jim and Gretta both continued teaching. Jim proceeded to introduce drama as a means of education, leading to confidence and skilled expression. Many graduates of the College went on to trusted posts in various disciplines and professions.

## Indian Women's Suffrage on the horizon

The various activities of life at Madanapalle College and the ethos of Adyar, as well as the implementation of the Theosophical principle of inclusiveness and universal brotherhood, were not giving Gretta as much satisfaction as her heart craved. She could not pin-point any particular thing as being wrong. Life was pleasurable and had its interests. Yet, somehow deep inside, she was looking for a challenge. She began to yearn for something more human, more creative than the donkey-work of correcting student's essays in not very clear writing and in very rudimentary English.

Subconsciously, it would appear, that her previous life in Ireland, with its childhood urge to seek equality for women and men was beginning to fight its way back to the surface. This unuttered prayer was soon to be answered. She writes:

> "One day, Jim, with his customary intuition of my mental states, asked me. "What about Votes for women?" "In a hundred years we may begin to think about it." I answered. My estimate was based on

a western notion of the age-long subjection of Indian women to their men-folk, and their consequent backwardness."

College life impinged on that of the local town, Madanapalle, with its 7000 inhabitants[47]. Gretta's memories of 'Irish hospitality' led her to begin inviting the ladies of one family and another to afternoon tea, a function which, under the title of 'light refreshments,' did not impinge on any 'caste'[48] restrictions. Then one of the lecturers, a Brahmin, conceived the idea of having a similar function, to which he invited other staff members and their wives. Strangely, nothing like this had been heard of in Madanapalle before. The newness and the uniqueness of such an event added that extra piquancy, that zing to the pleasure of tea, homemade sweets and savouries. Of much greater importance was the social significance of this spontaneous demonstration of equality of the sexes. Normally the men-of-the-house would be served at home by their wives. This tradition was written in stone!

Gretta again:

"At the party everybody served everybody else under the leadership of our Brahmin host. Something was happening though I did not know what. The tea-parties moved to various residences. I recall one as typical. One of our lecturers, a smart-brained and highly vocal Brahmin, had brought his slim young wife to settle down with him near the College. Our host and I were chatting on the cloth-covered floor of the small general room when the young lady entered. She had never been in the company of Europeans before, and she passed like a shadow on the wall to a position of obscurity behind her husband. This was the beginning of our acquaintance. In the thirty years between then and the writing of our life-memories, I saw her develop from self-effacing timidity to becoming a confident, informed, executive women, a graduate of our College, a Senator of two Universities, a member of a District Board, and an Honorary Magistrate.

She was one of a great company of Indian women who, unknown then to me, were awaiting the signal of emancipation. …. So none

47 **Madanapalle** has a current population of some 190,000.
48 **The Caste System**: The four classes were the **Brahmins** (**priestly** people), the **Kshatriyas** (who were **rulers**, administrators and **warriors**), the **Vaishyas** (merchants and **tradesmen**), and **Shudras** (**artisans**, farmers and labouring classes). The lowest caste was the – **Untouchables** – also called **Dalit**, formerly **Harijan**, in traditional Indian society. The **former** name for any member of a wide range of low-caste Hindu groups and any person outside the caste system. It was a pyramid of people with the lowest of the low at the bottom and literally untouchable.

of my own ideas could interfere with whatever was arising out of the inherent genius of Indian women-hood. I simply reacted to the life around me, and my first reaction was to follow up on our tea-parties, which had shown men that Indian women were just as human as myself and as interested in one another. I brought them together to see what would happen.

What did happen, after some preliminary meetings that created enthusiasm in those who attended, and criticism in those who stayed away, was a society which called itself the **Abala Abhivardini Samaj:** 'The Weaker Sex Improvement Society', an inferior title that took me some time to get used to. Anyhow my repugnance to avowed inferiority had only to stand trial for a year and it quickly became obvious that it was a misnomer. It was soon to change."

Some of the members were outstanding characters. One, called affectionately 'Auntie,' whose Brahmin heart was as big as her amazing brown legs. She arrived in a trotting bullock cart which was the Rolls Royce of the town. Sadly her exceptionally large physique did not prevent her from succumbing to the influenza pandemic of 1917. In her dying moments she called for Gretta, whom she called 'Sister Margaret'. She died shortly afterwards in the arms of her younger Irish sister – which was an utterly unorthodox thing to do. The touch of anyone outside her own caste was conventionally a pollution. Love, respect and confidence have a way of driving bullock carriages through outworn shibboleths.

Soon after, Gretta took a trip to Burma and, while there, happened on a small local industry of ratten-weaving[49]. In a flash Gretta saw the possibility of developing this into a useful and practical skill back home for the women and children of the Samaj.[50] She immediately learned the skill and then, upon returning home she instructed the ladies at Madanapalle. Everyone was enthused and soon they were reproducing baskets for fruit and flowers and plates for carrying offerings to the temples. It was not long before 'ratten weaving broke out in many places.'

It appeared that the wind of change was blowing stronger. Gretta could not possibly have imagined that within ten years the 'All-India Women's Conference' would have had its christening in Pune.

News of Samaj developments soon reached the ears of Dorothy Jinarájadása at Adyar. She immediately took the Samaj model for a **Women's Indian Association.** The Samaj dropped its 'weaker-sex' name and became one of

---

49 **Ratten:** The thin-jointed stems of a palm tree
50 **Samaj:** A society; a congregation;

the first branches of the new WIA. Annie Besant became its first President (in absentia). It was now July 1917 and they had seventy members. From its inauguration Gretta was Hon. Secretary until her transfer back to Adyar from Madanapalle in 1922.

Rumours had been circulating in early June suggesting that Mrs Besant had been interned because of her agitation for Home Rule for India. Then on 17 June the news reached Jim and Gretta that she had indeed been arrested, along with two of her collaborators, George Arundale and Bahman Wadia. In fact they were under house arrest. She was released in early September of that year when Gretta organised a protest meeting in Madanapalle. Gretta comments:

"The internment of Mrs Besant was an entirely political move, and entirely foolish, as it immediately aroused all India, and gave her campaign for Home Rule more publicity in a few days than it would have got in years of constitutional agitation. Mrs Besant's activities on behalf of women and children, her work for education, her help for the depressed of all grades and religions, had made her a legend of benevolence. They revered her as Ammaji (Great Mother), and became indignant at the disrespect shown to her in shutting her away from the humanitarian activities that were her life."

The College Assembly for prayers was taking place in Besant Hall on the morning of 18 September when word came through that Mrs Besant and the others had been released. The assembly exploded with excitement. A holiday was declared and a procession announced for 1pm, which would walk through the town. The flames of joy were doused, briefly, by the arrival of a Police Inspector to inform them that the event could not be permitted as it might lead to a breach of the peace. Jim explained that it was simply a school outing. It was not a protest march. He guaranteed peace as they were simply showing their happiness that their 'Mother' or Ammu was now free. Jim promised to marshal the procession himself. The Inspector agreed and so, for the first time in the history of Madanapalle, a band of 50 Indian women and girls in bright saris, with jasmine flowers in their plaits led by Gretta, took their place in a public procession.

All went well – and the 'joy' was shared with the general population.

# CHAPTER SIXTEEN

## Deputation to the Viceroy and the
## Secretary of State for India

One day, during the latter half of 1917 Jim noticed in his daily newspaper an announcement that the Secretary of State for India, Edwin Montagu, was coming from England to join the Viceroy, Lord Chelmsford, in a country-wide survey of conditions throughout India. This was to advance Queen Victoria's long-announced goal of self-government for India. He handed the paper to Gretta, and after she read it he asked: 'What about votes for women?

This simple question subsequently led to all Indian women fully exercising their right to vote on equal terms with men. It would seem that Gretta was now, at last, finding her true destiny in India. Jim by asking that same question back in Ireland had triggered the setting up of the Irish Women's Franchise League. Now this same question bore the germ of an idea with colossal future historical consequences. Gretta takes up the story:

"My reaction to Jim's question was to put out feelers in different directions. I wrote to Professor Karve of the Indian Women's University in Poona (Pune) about the possibility of getting up a deputation to the Secretary of State and the Viceroy, and had an encouraging reply. In the middle of October 1917, after much wiring and writing, I got an application for a deputation signed by a number of leading women in various parts if India and dispatched it to the organisers of the Montagu-Chelmsford tour. Then came an interesting turn of events which indicated that something in the cosmos had a bigger Idea of the immediate future of Indian womenhood than the most forward amongst us. Our application, which was initially for an opportunity to state the claim for an extension of girls' education (that was all, though at the time it was a revolutionary idea), was declined as being outside the terms of the enquiry which was limited to purely political considerations.

Jim was my intimate adviser and encourager in all things. When I showed him the application he repeated his previous question, "What about votes for women *now*?" There was no alternative to the direction of fate. Again wires and letters, anticipations, 'stone walls' – jungles of discouragement so dark that you couldn't see either the wood or the trees, then rays of heart-lifting light, refusals, promises – and then at last on 28 November 1917 a wire saying that a deputation of ladies on the subject of women's suffrage would be received on 18 December."

Gretta was in no doubt of the huge importance of this opportunity. She could scupper the whole thing if the statement to be read out in front of the Secretary of State for India and the Viceroy himself was not carefully crafted.

"I can tell anybody who wants to know, that to have your finger on a turning point in the history of a vast country is no matter of light refreshments. A month in Holloway Jail and another in Tullamore seemed, in retrospect, rest cures compared with the brain-racking job of having to formulate a demand without precedent in the long history of India, a demand well past the understanding of all but the minutest fraction of those for whom it was being made and likely to have their opposition, as well as that of men of orthodox and conventional mind. Opposition didn't scare me. What worried me was my ignorance of the colossal reality of India. I was a mere two years in the country."

She was under no illusion that she must strike a balance between her own fighting spirit and the Indian 'quietism' when she came to the point of preparing the draft of this first request for votes for Indian women.

"I had bad times over it, for it wouldn't come, or move when it came. At last, after squirms and blanks and a half formed resolve to throw it to a real writer, like Sarojini Naidu, who has to be on the deputation, it came. I sent a copy to each of the expected members of the deputation for suggestions and correctness. I expected elaborate amendments to be worked into a fresh statement. To my surprise, and to the saving of much time and expense, every member wrote or wired expressing approval."

The Montagu-Chelmsford inquiry into possible political reforms began in the north. Those chosen for the Woman's Deputation were ready to travel anywhere to make their presentation. Then news came that The Viceroy and the Secretary of State for India were both coming to Madras and that the Deputation would be received there.

When Gretta arrived from Madanapalle on 16 December at Madras Central Station she found that Sarojini Naidu had already arrived and was surrounded by a crowd of students.[51]

Mrs Naidu was taken to Adyar and that afternoon she, together with Gretta and Mrs Besant, had afternoon tea, ironing out points of procedure for the meeting. Sarojini Naidu was chosen to be leader and spokeswoman, as the voice of awakened Indian womanhood. Next morning Gretta met the other members of the deputation off the train and dispatched them to their various quarters. There was a last minute panic when the timing of the deputation was changed from early in the morning to 11am. Dorothy Jinarájadása's husband started out next morning and woke them

Sarojini Naidu
'The Nightingale of India'

all, instructing them to be at the rendezvous at Government House sharp at 11am. At 9.30am Mrs Besant took the Adyar contingent in her car to a studio where the whole deputation was assembled and an official photograph taken.

Gretta records her impressions of the historic meeting:

"At 11am on 18 December 1917 we were ushered into the dual presence and received with cordiality. The Viceroy struck me as a perfect gentleman, but not impressive in intellectual quality. The Secretary of State, Mr Edwin Montague, was obviously humane and

---

51 **Sarojini Naidu** (1879 – 1949) was a 'freedom fighter' and famous poet known as the 'Nightingale of India'. Her poetry includes children's poems, poems on nature, patriotic themes, and others about of love and death. She was born into a Bengali Hindu family at Hyderabad and educated in Chennai, London and Cambridge. She joined the Indian National Movement in the wake of the partition of Bengal in 1905. She came into contact with Gopal Krishna Gokhale (Senior Leader in the Indian National Party), Rabindranath Tagore (National Poet) Muhammad Jinnah (Founder of Pakistan), Annie Besant (President of the Theosophical Society and Educationist), Mahatma Gandhi (known widely as Father of the Nation), and Jawaharlal Nehru (Future Prime Minister of India). In 1915–18, she travelled to different regions in India delivering lectures on social welfare, women's empowerment and nationalism. She is commemorated in the names of many institutions, including Sarojini House (Head Quarters of the A.W.I.C), Sarojini Naidu College for Women, Sarojini Naidu Medical College, and Sarojini Naidu School of Arts and Communication, University of Hyderabad. Aldous Huxley, who met her in Bombay, once described her as: "A woman who combines in the most remarkable way great intellectual power with charm, sweetness with courageous energy, a wide culture with originality, and earnestness with humour."

Sir Edwin Montagu
Secretary of State for India

Lord Chelmsford
Viceroy of India

very intelligent and earnest. Mrs Naidu read the Address as if she herself was composing it as she went along. There was no reply, but four members of the deputation were given private interviews: I, being only the Secretary, was not one of them."

What follows is the substance of the historical document. Although it is quite long, it was at the core of the work Gretta did in India. It was composed by Gretta, approved by others, and then read to the Secretary of State and the Viceroy by 'The Nightingale of India,' Sarojini Naidu.

"We have asked for a portion of your valuable time because the women of India have awakened to their responsibilities in public life, and have their own independent opinions about the reforms that are necessary for the progress of India....We are in touch with the new outlook of Indian women, and we make bold, at this historic time, to lay before you women's views concerning the necessary post-war Reforms, as we believe them to be the necessary complement to the views of our men... Our interests, as one half of the people, are directly affected by the demand in the united Scheme (1.3) that "the Members of the Council should be elected directly by the people on as broad a franchise as possible", and in the Memorandum (3) that "the franchise should be broadened and extended directly to the people."

We pray that, when such a franchise is being drawn up, women may be recognised as 'people', and that it may be worked in such terms as will not disqualify our sex, but allow our women the same opportunities of representation as our men. In agreeing with the demand of the above-mentioned Memorandum that "a full measure of Local Self-Government should be immediately granted", we request that it shall include the representation of our women, a policy that has admittedly been successful for the past twenty years in local-Self Government elsewhere in the British Empire. The precedent for including women in modern Indian political life has been a marked feature of the Indian National Congress, in which since its inception women have voted and been delegates and speakers, and which this year finds its climax in the election of a women as its President. Thus the voice of India approves of its women being considered responsible and recognised citizens; and we urgently claim that, in drawing up all provisions regarding representation, our sex shall not be made a disqualification for the exercise of the franchise or for service in public life.

In order to fit ourselves and our children for future public responsibilities arising out of the foregoing considerations, it is absolutely essential that our educational system should be reformed. At present only one girl out of every hundred, and only thirteen boys out of every hundred, are educated…. We bring the urgent necessity for immediate action in educational matters before you now because the granting of facilities for education is a section of Indian Administration definitely under the control of the Imperial Legislative Council and the Government of India, and it must be made as far as possible a uniform policy throughout all British India.

We therefore ask:

(1) That the Government shall make a pronouncement in favour of Compulsory and Free Primary Education, and immediately set to work to bring this into being area by area, as is being done in several of the Indian States.

(2) We ask that during the time elapsing before the completion of this reform, the Government shall immediately devote as much attention to the education of girls as it is now giving to boys, and provide as equal number of school facilities for them, and thus remove the unwise differentiation which provide facilities for ten times as many boys as

girls, a policy which defeats its own ends, as the uneducated wives of these boys later hold back their progress.

In order to provide teachers for this wide spread of education, we ask the Government to provide a largely increased number of Training Colleges for Indian Women teachers and also to establish a number of Widow's Homes for this purpose, supplemented by the grant of scholarships to widows and those anxious to be trained as teachers. Several travelling scholarships should be made to assist Associations which are now so widely attempting to continue their education of married women outside ordinary school hours and curricula.

As a better physical standard is also essential of Indian progress, it is necessary to have educational means by which to cope with the disastrously high rate of mortality and the high death-rate of young married women. We therefore press Your Excellency, and you, Sir, to urge the Government to establish more Medical Colleges for women and institute short Maternity Courses, giving certificates to duly qualified persons, in connection with local hospitals in the large towns throughout the country and to encourage women to attend them by means of bursaries.

We deal with all these matters now, because, unless action is taken with regard to them, all other reforms will lose their full efficacy."

* * *

After the historical meetings in the morning, whose consequences would, they all hoped, make radical changes in the way in which women on the Indian subcontinent would be treated, they celebrated and relaxed later in the day.

"That afternoon we had a great 'At Home' in Gokhale Hall. I made a life-friendship with an admirable lady, Miss (Dr) Joshi of Bombay. My diary says; 'I like her'. I have never ceased to do so, and have watched with admiration her development into one of the foremost women of India as Rani Rajwade.

It is interesting to note that Gretta's initial assessment of Dr Rani Laxmibai Rajwade was subsequently proved to be extremely accurate. She was born in 1887. She and her three younger sisters were sent to the local convent school where English was used as the medium of instruction. Later they attended Degree Colleges in Bombay in spite of social opposition. Rani Rajwade passed her matriculation from Calcutta University and thereafter joined the Grant Medical College in Bombay. Winning a number of scholarships, she earned the degree of L.M.S. with distinction after which, she proceeded to England. There she met Emmeline Pankhurst. Rani Rajwade practiced medicine in Bombay (Mumbai) for fourteen years and took active interest in the work of the All India Women's Conference. Later, she was elected secretary for two years, and thereafter became its President. Jawaharlal Nehru appointed her as the head of the section of Women's Welfare, Education and Advancement under the National Planning Committee.

Rani Rajwade finally passed away in 1984 at the ripe old age of 97.

# CHAPTER SEVENTEEN

## THE BOARD OF NATIONAL EDUCATION
### Jim goes east & Gretta goes west
### Headmistress of Besant Girl's School in Mangalore
### Getting to know the Collector

After the high point of the appeal to the Viceroy and the Secretary of State for India on the 18th December, Jim left Madanapalle for Adyar to spend a few quiet days with Gretta before they took the forty hour train-journey to Calcutta (Kolkata) for the 33rd Session of the Indian National Congress presided over by Mrs Besant. This would be less than quiet!

Jim records:

"A great crowd saw the President-elect of Congress off at Madras Station and at stations all along the line groups of people of all grades presented her with flowers. Something of the national importance of the occasion had got into the consciousness of the people. A tremendous welcome awaited at Calcutta: a vast cheering multitude waited outside the crowded station…. Sir John Woodroffe[52] met us with cordial friendship, and motored Gretta and myself to his commodious and artistic home."

Prior to the official opening of the 33rd Session of the National Congress, the first official meeting of the Board of National Education took place. Jim continues:

"To us personally a most important part of the visit was the first official meeting of the Board of National Education. It was most impressive to be among a large and animated gathering of leaders of culture in Bengal and elsewhere in India, and to feel the growing sense of understanding and approval of the scheme of the proposed University as it was propounded by George Arundale standing at the side of Mrs Besant, who was elected to the Chair. The Board took charge of both school and college education. The Theosophical Educational Trust merged itself in the parent body of the new scheme, the 'Society for the

---

52 **Sir John Woodroofe** (1865-1936). Was enrolled as an advocate of the Calcutta High Court in 1890. Was appointed Standing Counsel to the Government of India in 1902 and two years later was raised to the High Court Bench. In 1915 he officiated as Chief Justice. After retiring to England he was appointed Reader in Indian Law to the University of Oxford for seven years.

Promotion of National Education'. The establishment of a National University was formally accepted. At an adjourned meeting on 30 December 1917, Sir Rabindranath Tagore was elected Chancellor, Mrs Besant was elected Chairman of the Executive Committee of the parent body and Mr Arundale elected Registrar of the University. Gretta and I were asked to become members of the Council. Later we were put on the Senate."

While Jim continued his travels around India on the theme of education as well as the arts, Gretta's work at the College in Madanapalle continued as usual.

The historic Deputation on 18 December still showed no signs of yielding any fruit whatsoever. Gretta was becoming more and more frustrated about the urgency of women's suffrage. She kept witnessing the cultural cruelty and violence both physical and emotional by men towards women.

"I was revolted by the slavery and indignity put on women-hood by the inconsiderate domination of men, and there grew within me a determination to do all I could to forward all circumstances calculated to bring women into public and particularly legislative life so that this evil and others might be rectified."

Gretta clashed in opinion with Mrs Besant, who was currently focused almost totally on Home Rule for India. She refused to make 'votes for Indian women' a plank on the platform of her Home Rule League. This seemed to parallel what the Irish Parliamentary party had said that the Votes for Women issue would have gone against their main thrust which was Home Rule for Ireland. Gretta wrote a pamphlet on the urgent need for suffrage but it faded like a damp squib.

* * *

Later in 1918 news came through of the Armistice signed on 11 November. The Great War, to end all wars, was over. Millions had been senselessly slaughtered. A holiday was declared for the College.

Some five months later Jim was invited to go to Japan. As a result of collusion between Sarojini Naidu and Yone Nagichi of Japan, two widely known and respected poets, Jim was invited along as a third. They were offered Guest Professorships in Modern English Poetry for one year, in the first modernized university in Japan, the Keiogijuku of Tokyo. As the slow boat to Japan was 'taking off' from Calcutta Jim took the opportunity to visit his close friend Rabindranath Tagore at Santiniketan.

Gretta writes of their emotional farewell at the station:

"I kept as brave a face as I could until the train, bearing my beloved comrade away to Japan for a whole year, had left and I said goodbye to the friends of all castes who had seen him off, and got back to my room at Adyar with its poignant sense of vacancy."

She was cheered up by a short holiday to Ootacamund, where she relaxed and focused on 'suffrage correspondence'. But she could not wait any longer. There was continued 'shuttling hither and thither' organizing public expressions of demand for votes for all Indian women, especially as Mrs Besant's Government of India Bill was shortly to be given its first reading (July 1919). Gretta arranged a public meeting in Madras where a number of eminent South Indian women came together, and who were destined to become powerful in the political life of India. Women such as Rukmini Lakshmipathi and Dr Muthulaksmi Reddy attended.

Rukmini Lakshmipathi [53]     Dr Muthulaksmi Reddy[54]

Gretta sent a protest letter to the press on the omission of women voters in the Reforms.

"It went all over India. I sent information to England for publication. Curiously enough, though I had the backing of some of the best women in India, I was the one voice publicly explaining and proclaiming the suffrage Cause; not because I had any special fitness, but simply because the women-hood of India had not yet found its authoritative voice."

53 **Rukmani Lakshmipathi**, (Dec 1892 – Aug 1951) was an Indian independence activist and politician belonging to the Indian National Congress.
54 **Dr Muthulakshmi Reddy** Social reformer, women's rights activist, writer and eminent medical practitioner and social reformer. She was the first female legislator in India being appointed to the Madras Legislative Council in 1927.

It is important to emphasise that the services Gretta, and Jim for that matter, gave to India were a multitude. They fell into two main categories: **votes** for Indian women and **education** for Indian women and men. In Ireland it focused only on woman's suffrage. Education played little part. Now the huge task of giving Indian women a proper education, after franchise was won, became much more important. Educating women was then Gretta's devotion for the rest of her life through the medium of the All Indian Women's Conference, which was yet to be born. She still had that driving urge to see women's equality with men. She did not forget what she felt way back in Boyle when yet a very young lady:

"I saw that it was counted a kind of curse in those days to be born a girl. One of my missions in life, equal rights for men and woman, was finding me."

### Gretta goes west to Mangalore

This passion for educating women lends more importance to the immediate task given her by Mrs Besant. Gretta's obligations to the educational movement cut across her suffrage activities for the next year. During Jim's absence in Japan, Madanapalle College was run by Gordon Pearce. As Mrs Besant was starting a Girl's School in Mangalore, on the west coast, it needed a Head Mistress. Gretta accepted her request to transfer to Mangalore, some 500 miles to the west, just as the monsoon season was approaching. (May 1919). Her time there was far from easy but taught her a lot about the education of girls.

"It took some time to assemble my new world. For a while I had to live from hand to mouth, sans husband, sans deputy husband (my piano!), sans home, sans spiritual friendship, and deprived of a sight of myself, as no mirror was provided. I found the work of a Head Mistress more invigorating than the grind of essay-checking in Madanapalle High School. In my position of responsibility, I had to be everywhere at the same time, all of the time. The making of time-tables and syllabuses gave me great pleasure. It had something of musical composition about it... I had to move into a larger bungalow more suited to my work. My baggage, except piano, arrived from Madras, although some articles had been stolen.

I had never learned anything but the most rudimentary physical exercises in my school days and now behold me at forty installed as drill mistress of the senior girls....

I got into my larger bungalow on 26 June 1919 and unpacked the baggage from Madras. Nearly all the china was smashed. Just enough things for personal use were saved from the wreck. I found the damp and greyness depressing. Nothing could be put out to dry. There was a heavy wet fog each morning and no sun. Under the thickening monsoon the compound became a lake three inches deep. After ruining two pairs of shoes going to and fro from the school I tried sandals, but they gave up the ghost. Bare feet were the last resort.

The piano duly arrived, in good tune notwithstanding the long journey, the rain, and the treatment to which it had to submit to get it into place….

Sports were a disappointment. When the first race was run, the spectators ran along with it! Some of the teachers viewed the event superciliously. The older girls would not take part. It was "undignified to run after you are twelve!" This was a social inhibition based on sex. I privately made up my mind to help to break up such obsolete superstition….

The trials of principal-ship began, after a couple of months, to get on my nerves. The aesthetical life was far below the beauty that Jim and I gathered and created for ourselves. Music had failed me, as many notes on the piano had stuck with the damp. All the same the demands on me brought out latent ability, goodness knows for what purpose. At one time an unexpected lecture had to be given on the deepest aspects of philosophy; at another a tough problem in algebra had to be solved; then the devising of physical culture exercises, and methods of teaching infants; the laying out of a garden-scheme; and the preparing of materials for rattan work, that needed navvy's hands instead of a pianist's….

School-work went on, and my busy days made up in friendship and kindliness for Sundays and holidays. Occasionally there came a crash. I found that a number of objects of art were missing, but the chief item that appeared to have been 'lost' was the prison-brooch that Mrs. Pankhurst had pinned on my breast at a public meeting in memory of my imprisonment in Holloway. Questions and denials only darkened the atmosphere. Enquiries were not helped by the torrential rain. This created appalling damp. My books were ruined. Boxes were blue-moulded inside and outside. My underclothes never dried; some split in pieces. The smell from these, and from the constantly wet bedclothes, was disgusting."

The inauguration of periodical visits by students to their temples brought Gretta up against the caste system. Non-Brahmin girls could not go. Brahmin girls could only go after changing their clothes, as mixing with lower castes among the students and staff had 'polluted' them. On the first visit, the favoured fifty came *en masse* to get her 'blessing' but she refused to let them come near her, "you might pollute me!" This was just an Irish twist, but she saw it brought a realisation to some of them, the stupidity of caste restriction.

The September space between the summer and winter monsoons dried up all Gretta's belongings, wearable and playable, and her philosophy turned more optimistic.

### Getting to know the Collector

Gretta felt it her duty to pay a call on the new Collector of their District, a Mr. Ellis.[55] She found him to be a hearty County Tyrone man whose mantra was 'there was no country like Ireland'. They shook hands on it, and chatted about places and people they knew, parting with promises of further home-sick friendly meetings.

Her little home became a magnet, especially for gentlemen visitors whose lives appeared to be enriched by a little feminine company of an intelligent kind. Gretta's small supply of books for loan was not equal to the demands. She was advised by 'those who know' that, as a Theosophist she would never

Lord and Lady Willingdon

---

55 **A District Collector** is the foremost Indian Administrative Service Officer in charge of revenue collection and administration of a district in India. Since District Collectors also have executive magisterial powers, this post was also called District Magistrate.

get any contact with Catholics or Protestants. Despite this warning she found *them* coming to her. The secular head of a Protestant mission confessed to being an avid reader of Evelyn Underhill, and was thrilled when she lent him her latest book.

A visit by Lord and Lady Willingdon[56] brought Gretta a number of invitations to various functions. Mr Ellis, the 'Irish' Collector, asked her to dinner with their excellences. For the sake of the school she was happy to accept this invitation but had qualms about appearing in her rather drab dress when all the world would be in full evening dress. There were difficulties too about gloves and shoes, but an English artist lady-friend helped her out in every way. There were twenty-four diners, all Europeans, of which seven were ladies. Gretta was embarrassed given the prominence of being placed close to Lady Willingdon and the Collector, who had a twinkle in his eye that might have been interpreted in various ways. Lady Willingdon talked quite a lot during dinner. Gretta was asked why she was vegetarian. She manufactured a number of reasons besides the original one. There was quite some difficulty over 'her' votes for Indian women. Lady Willingdon did not believe in women's rights. "Their influence was sufficient— backstairs", she said. Gretta kept silent.

After dinner the Collector asked her to play. The piano was jingly-jangly, as all west coast pianos could hardly fail to be, because of the interminable damp. However Chopin's Fantasie Impromptu seemed to go off all right, and encores were demanded.

She had good fun with His Excellency who obviously enjoyed repartee. They passed lightly from point to point and person to person and finally landed on "that terrible old lady who has given me infinite trouble." This was an unveiled reference to Annie Besant.

"Not half as much as Your Excellency has given *her*." Gretta rebounded.

They both parried phrases with laughter. He looked at her quizzically.

"I believe you will be just as dreadful."

"Probably—when I'm also72," she retorted.

"Then I will have to put you on the top of that hill[57] when you are 72."

After a thought he added: "Will you play for me then?"

"Of course I shall, to so appreciative a jailer. But if I do, perhaps you will want to keep me there longer." Even when saying good-night, he said, "Remember—top of that hill at 72."

---

56 **Lord Willingdon** (1866-1941) was governor of Bombay (Mumbai) (1913-1919) and then Madras (Chennai) (1919-24). He later became Governor General and Viceroy of India (1931-1936).

57 Reference to the **Ootacamund Prison** for political prisoners where Gretta did actually end up!

"And what age will Your Excellency be then?" He paused and made a mental calculation. "A hundred and twenty." "Then I promise." Gretta had the last word.

The result of the dinner was her establishment in society, for which she cared nothing, but it would, hopefully, be good for the work.

Not far from half way through their 'year of Japanese separation', towards the end of October 1919, the 'The Hindu Festival of Lights' (Dewali) in Mangalore gave her a new glimpse of the religious life of Hindu India. A group of Scouts invited her to go with them on a tour of the town to see the decorations and illuminations. The atmosphere of good-will was tangible. She was presented with a splendid bouquet by a patron of the school. At other shops, while pausing to admire them, she was given a garland, or a sweet-meat, or a sprinkling of rose-water. She noticed that there was, not surprisingly, total absence of women.

"On one Sunday I dictated an article in my bedroom to an orthodox Brahmin, had tea out with Hindu lady-friends, came home to give tea to some of the leading local Indian Catholics, went to the Protestant church and revelled in the rich Dublin brogue of the new padre whose sermon contained a funny story and such flavorous phrases as "surely to goodness." I was, I gathered, quite an enigma to the various local sections. The Catholics couldn't understand how an Irishwoman could be both a Protestant and a Home Ruler. The Protestants couldn't understand why I was not a missionary. The European club couldn't understand how I could be so jolly and yet be a vegetarian—**and** a follower of Mrs. Besant.

Then came the beginning of the victory of the Indian agitation for votes for women—23rd November, 1919. I was hurrying to get through the harrowing end of Lady Constance Lytton's book, 'Prisons & Prisoners,' with the description of the cruelties inflicted on her when she was thought to be a plain working woman, when this devilishness of the British Government made me throw the book across my room. I had to pace up and down to quiet my surging emotions of pride in martyred womanhood, joy in having belonged to their band and sickness at the awful things they had had to endure at the hands of supposed civilised men. Just then the post came in with an amazing group of related matters. First came a long affectionate letter from my old fellow-culprit, Emmeline Pethick-Lawrence. Then letters and papers, three weeks delayed, from Mrs Tata in London, telling me, of the progress of the agitation to get votes for women into the

Indian Reforms some way or another; and then (what a climax!) the announcement in the Press that, without any time restriction:

> "If any Provincial Legislative Council decides by a resolution in favour of woman's franchise, women should be put on the register of that Province."

What a vista of activity opened up? Bombay was sure to give the vote soon. It was also stated that "the franchise for the University seats is to be extended to **all** graduates of over seven years 'standing' which, of course, included women.

Then a letter of 22 January (1920) brought Mrs Besant's consent to my joining Jim in Japan. She said she felt it was right that I should do so. She did not feel it reasonable that we should be separated so long. "Thank you for all you have done in Mangalore." The consent shook me almost as much as a refusal would have done. My poor little will had a hard job to get me through the day between the ecstatic anticipation of recapturing a husband who was the ideal completer of my life, and the heart-breaking calls on me from both Mangalore and Madanapalle not to desert them.

On 28 February I received a second letter from Mrs Besant that put all my machinery, as motorists would say, into reverse.

> My dear Margaret,
> I would be delighted if your husband came back: then we could continue the College which is otherwise hopeless after Pearce leaves. If you agree, let me know his address and I will cable. Or better, you cable and let me know the cost. Then you can take your holiday together, and return to Madanapalle. It will much relieve my mind.
> Ever yours, Annie Besant."

Gretta immediately cabled Japan. Just as she sent the cable she received both her passport and passage to Japan! Instead of dreaming eastward, she began searching for rooms in a hill-station in Ceylon (Shri Lanka) for a month's holiday with Jim. She reached Colombo six hours after Jim's arrival at 2am on 18 April 1920 and was piloted to the pier in order to meet him.

"How well my beloved looked, and what a joy it was to feel that both ends of life had come together again. A day and a night and part of a second day put a baddish dream behind us, and brought us back to our old habit of visiting local schools, Buddhist ones this time, and making sage remarks to students who didn't understand a tenth of what we said. But education was not just then our enthusiasm. We wanted one another, and next day camped in a hotel at Kandy, the old seat of the last of the Kings of Ceylon. The scenery around a lake and into the surrounding country, including the fascinating oriental garden at Peridenya, was entrancing, perhaps more so than usual in response to our joy in one another's company. After three days in the little paradise we went higher, through tea plantations, to a Government Rest House at Patti-pola, at 6,200 feet. Here, after some adjustment to the rarefied air, we revelled in six-mile walks in the major directions of the compass for ten days. A further week went in a delightful visit to a new friend, Wilfrid Stott, an English tea-planter, obviously an expert in the mysterious processes of transforming green leaves of stubby bushes into fragrant cups of Moolgama tea. Nature on his estate was at its loveliest; especially exquisite after dark when moonlight was criss-crossed by fireflies and pervaded by perfumes.

We got down from Moolgama as a result of a hair-raising drive followed by a tiresome train-journey and a roly-poly crossing in a small steamer, to the landing port in India."

At Madura, 8 May 1920 they broke journey to gratify local Theosophists by attending the death-anniversary of Madame Blavatsky, called 'White Lotus Day'. A group of Brahmins from the great temple chanted from the Sama Veda, and thrilled them with the intimate touch of an ancient tradition. They left Madura the next day, the thermometer registering 102F, and reached Adyar next morning. They both spent twenty-six wonderful days within the Theosophical 'bubble' of peace and tranquillity. By 6 June they were back at Madanapalle, driven by a friend from the station which was just eight miles from the college. The long stretches of land, with backgrounds of picturesque hills and the coolish air were most refreshing to them after the extreme heat of Madura.

# CHAPTER EIGHTEEN

Forces of division increase
A chance meeting with the Maharaja of Kumar
Difficulties with the implementation of Votes for Women
Sad news from Ireland
Famous visitors to Adyar – artistic heights
Unannounced visit of Rabindranath Tagore

Realisation was beginning to dawn that the Madanapalle Theosophical College founded by Annie Besant was doomed. A number of forces were operating making its closure inevitable. In 1920 the satyagrah [58] movement, of which Mahatma Gandhi was the initiator and the inspiration, developed into an all-India boycott of the British Government under the term non-cooperation.

As part of the movement, students were called out of Government and Government-aided schools and colleges, and alternative educational institutions were opened. Public media focused on the apparent personal animosity between Mahatma Gandhi and Mrs Besant. In reality there was no animosity, although they disagreed as to the method of achieving Home Rule for India. This was yet another example of agreement with an ultimate goal but disagreement on the precise path to follow in order to reach it, as it had been amongst some of the suffragette movements in Ireland and England.

Jim and Gretta both felt this move would unleash an incalculable force for ill. The nationalising of Indian education should, they felt, be brought about by consultation and demonstration, not by fanning the young into emotional excitement. Jim was in a quandary when he began to receive requests for printed matter and details of their scheme for National Education. His quandary was made worse when he was invited to preside at the opening of a non-cooperation school. He discussed the matter with Mrs Besant, but her reply was typical of her approach. Of course he should accept the invitation, for "What does it matter who does the work so long as it is done?" She put principle before the fact that the Gandhian movement was deflecting students from their schools.

Another **force** operating against them was, curiously, the opposite. Their National University degrees, now not being officially recognised, would not

---

58 **Satyagraha** is the concept of nonviolent resistance ('fighting using peace') started by Mohandas Gandhi, known as "Mahatma" Gandhi. He used satyagraha in the Indian independence movement and also during his earlier struggle in South Africa for human rights.

take students into other colleges, such as law, medicine or engineering, or even into Government jobs. The result of these 'pulls' from different directions was the reduction of the roll at the National University. Student numbers fell to about thirty.

Still another force was the objection of Madras University to a Government-recognised and an unrecognised college being run within the same premises by the same staff!

Finally, yet another negative force affected the High School at Madanapalle. While in other parts of India students were being drawn away from schools and colleges connected with the British-controlled educational authorities, parental fear in Madras and Madanapalle set about creating a rival High School. Part of their premises was commandeered for its beginnings while its own buildings were being put up on the opposite side of the town. Disunity was polluting the air. The fear thus generated was obvious, that the Theosophical High School would be closed by the Department of Public Instruction, and local children would have nowhere to go for their schooling that led on to degrees and official jobs.

## A chance meeting with the Maharaja of Kumar

A month's tour during January 1921 to the Sind[59] with Gretta, yielded additional interests in nature and humanity. Having her keen pair of eyes, that had a way of noting and remembering local changes of dress, was something Jim did not possess.

At Udaipur, on their way to the train departing for Delhi, Jim was quick to notice a festooned and decorated elephant at the entrance to the royal tombs. A majestic figure was sitting on an ornamental chair. He recognised the figure as the heir to the throne of Udaipur State. Jim waved from their car. Fortunately the train was delayed. An official approached their carriage and announced that His Highness the Kumar had come to the station and wished to see Mr and Mrs Cousins.

His Highness, young and bright, greeted them with a cordial smile. He had already known of their brief visit. He read in the papers what Mrs Cousins was doing for education in raising the status of Indian women, and what Mr Cousins was doing for Indian art and culture. He was very happy they had taken Udaipur into their purview and gave them a cordial invitation to return for an extended visit, when the Maharana would be at home. They could then spend some days at his up-country Palace in the midst of solitary peace and beauty. They thanked him profusely hoping they might return at a more convenient time. After shaking hands they returned to their delayed

---

59 **Sind** was a province of British India from 1936 to 1947.

train, pondering the 'whims of destiny' that oscillated between the thatched huts of villages around Madanapalle to the stone and marble palaces of the senior Prince of Rajputana, a land of almost unbelievable heroism, and of an archaeology that soared back to the 3rd century.

Once they arrived in Delhi they were put up in a room on the roof of the Indraprastha Girls School. The view was streaked across by monkeys on their marauding rounds from roof to roof. Their afternoons and evenings were pleasantly filled by attending lectures in the Girls School and the Hindu College, as well as the Lady Hardinge Medical College where Gretta gave a piano recital. They finally reached Hyderabad, Sind, on the afternoon of 17 January 1921, and were immediately absorbed in a programme of lectures. Gretta's 'Man's responsibility to Woman' drew a great crowd in the very large Theosophical Hall, which was the cultural centre of the city.

## Difficulties with the implementation of Votes for Women

The general election for the new legislatures, constituted under the Montagu-Chelmsford Reforms, was approaching and much depended on the attitude of the candidates to woman suffrage. Agitation and organization had to be quickened and spread. The area was enormous, the workers were few.

The Women's Indian Association was as yet the only body that took on the responsibility of the approaching situation—the establishment of parliaments in which members were elected on a franchise wider than anything known in India's history.

Sadly the implementation of votes of women was contaminated and caused disunity as a result of the "Communal Award"[60] that emphasised social and religious differences, and was therefore calculated to impede the development of an All-India consciousness, and even to engender attitudes of communal antagonism. But the point of special importance to Indian women was the statutory authority given to the new parliaments, when formed, to grant votes to women by a majority vote of the members after the General Election on November 30, 1921.

It became necessary to direct attention to the widespread and serious demand of Indian women for direct legislative representation. The Madras Parliament being our nearest objective, Gretta shuttled between Madanapalle and Madras (180-miles) helping with the organisation of a representative

---

60 **The Communal Award** retained separate electorates and gave weightage to the Muslims in various provincial legislatures. The Bombay session of the *Indian* National Congress held in October 1934 decided that its attitude to *the Communal Award* would be neutral. There was, however, a powerful section among the Congressmen known as the Congress-Nationalists who were bitterly opposed to the **Award.** Mahatma Gandhi's famous fast to the death of September 1932 against *the Communal Award* is, of course, well-known.

women's meeting. This came off successfully on 28 December 1921 in the Senate House of the University, with an audience of five hundred influential women.

"I asked Mrs. Besant if she, as President of the Theosophical Society, would permit me to work for woman suffrage publicly from Adyar, where I wished to reside, and where my husband would teach in the School and College at Damodar Gardens on the Society's estate. In her reply she indicated that, while the Society had no doctrines, it was bound, by its First Object, to help all movements that worked for the brotherhood of humanity. No movement in this direction was more essential than the freedom of the women of India. I would be most welcome to join Mrs Jinarájadása who was already working at Adyar for the Women's Indian Association. A month later I went with Mrs Jinarájadása to the Council Chamber. Here we saw Mr Krishna Nair, a Malabar lawyer, who was to propose the granting of the vote to women in Madras Presidency next day. The resolution was to be seconded by the Raja of Ramnad, landlord of a large estate in South Madras.

To this day I retain the memory of the deep thrill of pride that went through me when I heard or read the speeches of the various members of the legislatures from firstly Madras in 1921 to finally Bihar in 1929 in support of woman suffrage. No gibes or cheap jests, such as one became accustomed to at Westminster, marred the sincerity of the speeches, that might all be condensed to the simple argument: How could we refuse our mothers and sisters and wives the portion of freedom that we have won for ourselves?

Outside British India certain of the Indian States preceded and followed the Provinces. The little State of Rajkot in the North-West brought women into legislation; Travancore in the extreme South appointed a woman as head of the State Medical Service, and granted votes to women. Mysore State, in April 1922, after a day's debate, which was hardly a debate since it was all praise of women on the highest level, unanimously gave the vote."

After **votes for women** was permissible for each State Legislature, as we have seen, the process took from 1921-1929 to achieve full agreement by all States. **Membership of women on State Legislatures** was a different matter, and required a lot of effort.

Gretta again:

"Much of my time went into travel on behalf of this logical and essential advance. I went from town to town and village to village, and everywhere found women of all ages and social ranks full of interest and intelligent response to the cause; everywhere men, young and old, acted as escorts and interpreters. But time had to pass before the legislative machinery could move."

## Sad news from Ireland – December 1921

Gretta records:

"The creation of the Irish Free State was announced 6 December 1921 with the signing of the Anglo-Irish Treaty. But our first joy in the freedom of the major part of Ireland was clouded by the further announcement of a split between those who accepted the Treaty with Britain as a step towards ultimate complete freedom, and those who insisted on an All-Ireland Republic. Civil war soon broke out and the antagonism that had been concentrated against the seven-century foreign destroyer of Irish culture, economics and social organization, was, alas, turned by one group of Irishmen on another. We were torn with grief. We knew that dear friends would, like the combatants at Kurukshetra,[61] be on opposite sides of the controversy. We could do nothing to help. We could only await inevitable events."

## Famous visitors to Adyar – artistic heights

Towards the end of June 1922 they were back at Adyar. Day shade temperature was 102F. However they were too busy to worry about bodily discomfort. Sunday afternoon tea with Mrs Besant set matters off. The 100th Anniversary of Percy Bysshe Shelley's death resulted in Jim delivering a talk to the students on 'Shelley's Idea of Citizenship,' and on 8 July 1922 a public lecture entitled 'Shelley & World-problems,' at which Mrs Besant presided and, at the end, presented the audience with a masterly spontaneous summing up. Percy Bysshe Shelley was Jim's favourite poet and greatly influenced his own work as an Irish poet.

---

61 The **Kurukshetra War**, also called the **Mahabharata War**, described in the Indian epic Mahabharata. The conflict arose from a dynastic succession struggle between two groups of cousins, the Kauravas and Pandavas, for the throne of Hastinapura in an Indian kingdom called Kuru. It involved a number of ancient kingdoms participating as allies of the rival groups.

Sarojini Naidu arrived in August of 1922. She was recuperating from illness so she rested in one of the seaside bungalows as a guest of the President. A morning delight for Jim and Gretta was to watch the white-haired old mother (AB) go slowly by their windows in her car, with a tray balanced on her knees bearing the paraphernalia of coffee and dainties for the patient. During her stay at Adyar, Sarojini Naidu was a magnet for all the local leaders from various departments of life. During the many chats that Jim and Gretta had, her nimbleness of mind and scintillating repartee disguised the fact that she was getting over illness.

Percy Bysshe Shelley[62]

Henry Eichheim
Composer & Conductor

The intended visit of Henry and Ethel Eichheim[63] from America came to fruition in August 1922. Mrs Besant made the Eichheims and their daughter Ethel her honoured guests, because of their international service as eminent

62 **Percy Bysshe Shelley** (1792 – 1822) was one of the major English Romantic poets, regarded by some as among the finest lyric poets in the English language, and one of the most influential. Recognition for his poetry grew steadily following his death. Shelley was a key member of a close circle of visionary poets such as Lord Byron, Leigh Hunt, and his own second wife, Mary Shelley, the author of *Frankenstein*. Shelley is perhaps best known for classic poems such as *Ozymandias, Ode to the West Wind, To a Skylark, Music, When Soft Voices Die*, and *The Masque of Anarchy*. Shelley's theories of economics and morality had a profound influence on Karl Marx; his early writings on nonviolent resistance influenced Leo Tolstoy. Shelley became a lodestone to the subsequent three or four generations of poets, including Robert Browning and Dante Gabriel Rossetti. He was admired by Oscar Wilde, Thomas Hardy, Bertrand Russell, WB Yeats.

63 **Henry Eichheim** (1870–1942) was a Chicago-born composer, conductor and violinist who made five trips to Asia between 1915 and 1937. He was the first American composer to combine western musical instruments with **gamelan cultural music from Java**. A passionate collector, Eichheim took photographs, notated music he heard in the streets and in the theatre, and collected musical instruments on his journeys. Eichheim began his musical career as a violinist in the Boston Symphony Orchestra.

artists. At a recital they gave in Headquarters Hall, to a packed audience of eastern and western residents and visitors, she had them garlanded with the gold-and-silver-thread garlands that she reserved for special appreciation.

During their visit Jim took Henry into Madras for a private recital of Carnatic (Hindu) music of which the Muslim singer, Abdul Karim, was a famous exponent. After two or three short pieces, Eichheim whispered:

"Jimmy, I can't get the hang of this music. It has no time." Jim asked the singer to show him. Abdul Karim sang an air in his soft high voice. It was beautiful as a melody, but still did not present a recognisable time-rhythm to Eicheim. Then the singer repeated it, counting out each phrase (bar), with a clap on his knee for the vocal swarams (notes) and a flick of his hand in the air for the blanks between each accumulating phase of the 'bar':

1 (blank): 1, 2 (blank): 1, 2, 3 (blank): 1, 2, 3, 4 (blank). That made 10 sounded notes and four blanks. After a second count, the long-trained leader of the Boston Symphony Orchestra looked at Jim with wide-open eyes and said:

"Jimmy, I've found a new world of rhythm."

### Unannounced visit of Rabindranath Tagore
A month later, 29 Sept 1922, Jim and Gretta were only two thirds through siesta at Leadbeater Chambers, when a young friend put his head through their open window and whispered hoarsely, "The Poet has come!" They only just had time to make themselves respectable when Rabindranath Tagore entered their living room, which was curtained from their sleeping accommodation by hand-printed Masuli-patam cloths. The great figure in the doorway was in his usual fawn-coloured robe and high biretta-like cap. Above his longish grey beard and the nose of aristocracy he smiled through his clear brown eyes. In his high voice he began a literary and intellectual give-and-take that lasted for about two hours.

The Saraswati puja, prayers for the culture Goddess, was to be held at Chambers at 4 o'clock. Mrs Besant was to attend in the dining-room a couple of doors from theirs. Jim hurried to her. "Mother, Rabindranath Tagore has come. May he greet you now?" "Don't trouble him to come to me," she said, "take me to him."

Sitting on the floor of their room the two great luminaries met, with the eminent admirer of the poet, 'Charlie' Andrews, in the background.[64] One of the subjects of their former chat had been the necessity for a magazine, at least quarterly, to disseminate the ideas of the International University that Tagore was founding at Santiniketan. He was as hesitant over the proposed magazine as Andrews and Jim were keen on it.

On 8 October 1922, a week later, Rabindranath and Charlie came to a conclusion on the matter of the magazine. It was finally agreed and the "The Visva-Bharati Quarterly" began to be published.[65] The first edition was circulated in 14 April 1923. It is still published quarterly today – 2018.

---

64 **Charles Freer Andrews** (1871–1940) was a Church of England priest. As a Christian missionary, educator and social reformer in India, he became a close friend of Gandhi and identified with the cause of India's independence. He was instrumental in convincing Gandhi to return to India from South Africa, where Gandhi had been a leading light in the Indian civil rights struggle. He was affectionately dubbed *Christ's Faithful Apostle* by Gandhi, based on his initials, C.F.A. For his contributions to the Indian Independence Movement Gandhi and his students named him *Deenabandhu*, or "Friend of the Poor".

65 **The Visva-Bharati University** was a public central government funded university located in Santiniketan, West Bengal. It was founded by Rabindranath Tagore who called it *Visva-Bharati*, which means 'the communion of the world with India'. Until independence it was a college. Soon after independence the institution was given the status of a university and was then named Visva-Bharati University. It grew to become one of India's most renowned places of higher learning, with a list of alumni that includes Nobel-winning economist Amartya Sen, globally renowned filmmaker Satyajit Ray and the country's leading art historian, R. Siva Kumar, to name but a few.

# CHAPTER NINETEEN

## THE FIRST NON-INDIAN WOMAN MAGISTRATE IN INDIA
### Madras Presidency Legislative Council election – 31 October 1923

During October 1922 an unexpected event occurred of another historic nature. Their friends the Gallettis, then stationed at Madras, where he was Collector of Chingleput District, came for dinner with Gretta and Jim 'for a chat'. After dinner they adjourned to the piano-room, and were joined by some of the residents at Adyar. As usual at such gatherings, Gretta played. Just as she was about to sit down at the piano, in answer to a request for an *encore*, Arthur Galletti's incisive voice asked:

"Mrs. Cousins, would you like to be a magistrate?"

The question was the first of its kind in the history of India. Never had a non-Indian women been invited to such a post. The date was October 16, 1922, and the beginning of a new era in the administration of the law. But the utterly unexpected question gave her such a shock it upset her music. Jim later explained to Gretta what had happened as she had been too dazed to recollect much of it:

"'Phew!' Then there was silence. "Not for myself, as I have as much in hand as I can cope with. But if it would open the magistracy to Indian women, then, yes." Mr. Galletti said: "It has occurred to me only now. I have been appointing women to various offices, and I have just thought that women should have a voice in the cases brought before the bench in which women are involved. I shall put it before Government. They can only say, there *is no* precedent for it, or, there is no precedent against *it*. Let us hope they will give the right answer."

Gretta takes up the story:

"On 8 November 1922 I received the formal invitation to become an Honorary Bench Magistrate. On my birthday the previous day, my book, "The Awakening of Indian Womanhood" had been published. Who can unravel the mysteries of the calendar? On 19 February

The first non-Indian woman magistrate in Indian history

1923 I was received on the bench of Saidapet Courthouse at what was, surely, one of the most unique and flavorous ceremonials. The bench consisted of a retired Brahmin Magistrate as Chairman, a non-Brahmin, a Muslim, an Indian Christian, and an empty chair to which I was conducted as the first woman Magistrate in Indian history under British rule. Rose garlands were distributed.

Prisoners awaiting trial in a back-room were filed into a space on one side of the Court-room as witnesses of the event. Advocates at the bar made short speeches stressing the historical importance of the occasion, and emphasising the humanitarian purpose that was intended to influence the strict procedure of the law. When this ended, the prisoners were taken back to the guard-room to await trial under the new regime; visitors went their ways; and the day's work proceeded as usual—with the ceremonial difference that, in token of the occasion, statutory sentences were cut in half!

A year after my being "invested with power" as a Magistrate, as the official notification put it, I was asked by The Times of India to write an article on my experiences. I think I told of a group of prisoners, charged with fighting in a village, who, when they saw a woman on the bench, fell on their knees and penitently implored pardon for offending against Amma (Mother). I probably also told of the family jars[66] in a village because of the deficiency in a dowry that was delaying a marriage, and how, in an adjournment of the case,

---

66 **A jar:** a state or manifestation of discord or conflict

Dorothy Jinarájadása and I saw the parties in the village, and made up the deficiency ourselves; whereupon Kalyan[67] music broke out from oboe and drum.

I remember clearly my expression of loneliness as the one woman on the bench in a vast country, and my hope that my loneliness would be broken soon. Not long afterwards the Government appointed a woman magistrate from each of the cultural divisions of Bombay. Their example was duly followed elsewhere. An age-long inhibition on the activity of women in the service of the country was broken."

### Indian General Election Day – at last – 7 November 1923
Gretta observes the General election.

"I was in the thick of it, delighted to see so many women voting. We had a jollification over it on 7 November in Gokhale Hall; and as this was my 45th birth-anniversary, there was tea, and a lovely gift of a Satsuma porcelain coffee set from S. V. Ramaswami Mudaliar; and deep affection from "AB." (Mrs Besant). On the strength of the occasion I toured some of the big cities of the south-east-coast, trying to bring the future of women into a more accessible place than the past. That is - into the present."

---

67 **Kaylan:** Marriage music

# CHAPTER TWENTY
## EUROPE BETWEEN THE WARS

In 1925 Gretta and Jim had the opportunity to travel to Europe. It is interesting to see how, on this extended tour of Europe, they were both very much 'together', sharing while satisfying their different passions for art and music. Gretta was also seeking any opportunity to advance the cause of women's equality in all things. Together their search for true beauty was, perhaps their deepest passion of all. Beauty in art, beauty in music and beauty in all religion in the broadest sense.

They left Madras on March 28 1925, courtesy of travel agents, Messrs Cook, reaching Rome in April. On the ship prior to docking they had been looking at war-torn villages along the coast of Italy over the taffrail,[68] one of the passengers, an Italian, threw up his hands and with agonised fervour exclaimed "No more war! No more war!!" This according to Jim was a prayer, not a prophecy. At another time, on a train from Milan to Paris, an old Frenchman shook his fist towards Germany and viciously cursed it and all its people. This was, according to Jim a prophecy, not a prayer.

This was Holy Year, when a usually closed door in St. Peter's was periodically opened. Arriving late in the day, and, after a change of clothes and dinner, they went for a stroll which took them to St. Peter's Church, the centre of Roman Catholic Christianity. The following forenoon gave them another view, when they spent nearly four hours in the Vatican Museum pouring over the sculptural and pictorial treasures of antiquity, but especially those of the Italian Renaissance. They visited the 'strong and overcrowded paintings' of the Sistine Chapel, on the morning of 26 April, and in the afternoon chose to attend a special papal benediction[69] in St. Peter's for a crowd of Americans. Jim describes the occasion:

" The vast church was crammed. His Holiness was carried the length of the church on a throne above the shoulders of Cardinals. His entrance was the signal for an undisciplined stampede by the multitude to get a share of the blessing that the Holy Father was radiating to all parts from his oscillating right hand. When the procession came opposite our wing, the crowd sprang to its feet, and climbed up on the benches, blocking the view of all behind them. They too climbed, but we kept

---

68 **A taffrail** is the handrail around the open deck area toward the stern of a ship or boat.
69 **Pope Pius XI** was the current Pontiff.

our seats. Then paradox suddenly appeared. I put the curved handle of my umbrella round an ankle of a large woman, intending to give her a civil hint as to good manners. But I might as well have tried to fell a tree. I desisted before the umbrella might lose its head. I caught Gretta's eye, and through the unholy hubbub collected words that, confirmed later, said: "A sight for the Gods! An Ulster Protestant trying to get Catholics in St. Peter's in Rome to behave!"

Next evening they arrived in lovely Florence. After dinner, their friends Genaro and Pauline D'Amato took them on a night walk to catch a flavour of the city.

News of the Cousins presence reached the Lyceum, and they were invited to share an hour and a half between them. Gretta's forty-five minutes was on women's affairs in India, then Jim on Indian painting. Their talks were translated into mellifluous Italian by a large good-humoured Countess. Everyone expressed pleasure at their extended knowledge of India, and they both hoped that their evenings' presentations had contributed towards international understanding.

Next afternoon, 1 May 1925, they arrived in Venice and were taken to their waterside hotel by gondolas, crafts in black mourning. Next day, during their sight-seeing, they came on a small middle-aged Italian woman behind the counter of a shop which they had entered. After Jim introduced himself she said:

"It was told me you might call. Dr & Mrs Arundale also called. When Mrs Arundale walked along the streets, people looked at her with reverence and said, 'the Dark Madonna.' Then she asked "What have you seen so far in Venice? Now, we shall see something that tourists don't see!"

She piloted them through lanes and narrow streets, into shops, among fruit-sellers, and brought them to a kerb-stone cafe, where they drank delicious coffee from a man in the street. They then returned to the ladies' shop. "What is your plan for tonight?" she enthused. "Dinner and bed probably," was Jim's reply. She opened a drawer and retrieved two tickets.

"These are for an opera tonight, 'Nativity'. There is nothing to pay."

Opera came their way again next evening in Milan. Toscanini was conducting Verdi's 'Falstaff' in La Scala theatre. They were especially struck by the way in which Toscanini got every movement and gesture into rhythmical concord with the music.

Next morning they had one of their most deeply artistic and uplifting experiences so far on their trip. Jim describes:

"A look through Leonardo da Vinci's sketches took us off the ground; but we reached the apex of artistic 'levitation' in the refectory of St. Mark's when we saw his 'Last Supper.' We were familiar with plain and coloured reproductions of the immortal masterpiece; but half an hour in the presence of the original gave us a sense of artistic achievement that the passing of time has not dulled. What depiction of a dozen different ways of asking a question 'Is it I?' drawn out by the declaration, "One of you shall betray me!" How difficult it was for the eye to believe that the space of the supper-room and the landscape through the back window were illusions created by genius with brushes and colours on a flat surface!"

Thence to Paris for a varied week as full as they could imagine. Towards the end an unexpected visit was arranged to 'the last of the French Impressionists.' They were invited to visit Claude Monet at his home in Giverney. This was situated some distance outside Paris by train and carriage. Jim again:

"The short, well-built artist, in roughish tweeds and frilled cuffs, was about eighty. One eye had failed him, also half of the other. But, with quarter-sight, he went on painting in the spotty style that he had developed in order to give pictorial effect to his theory that what is seen is not the real object, but the light reflected from surfaces. Now he was a stay-at-home; but, if he could not go to his subjects, he could get some to come to him. So, in a pool in his garden, he had grown superb water-lilies, and these he painted at various hours and from various angles. It had become a habit for everything painted by Monet to be a masterpiece, hence expensive. Our visit was in this connection.

A millionaire friend had established the convention of giving his wife an expensive wedding present annually. One year it was a mansion, this year it was to be a Monet masterpiece at any price. We chose one of the latest water lilies. There was no bargaining: he would sell no work under 30,000 francs. In addition to his big studio and its accompanying hanging-rooms, Monet showed us many of his paintings he had hung all over his home. A glimpse through a slightly open door drew an exclamation from me. Seeing my interest he opened the door, and we entered a room hung from ceiling almost to floor with Japanese prints. I identified a number, and wondered why such things should have interested him. He painted light: they ignored light-and-shade. 'This is my religion,' he confessed; and he summed up his evaluation of his collecting since he was a boy, with the declaration, 'They were great artists.'"

Although Jim had indulged his passion on this trip Gretta's passion for music was not neglected. Within ten days they saw three grand operas, the climax being Debussy's 'Pelleas & Melisande'. But the most impressive, from the purely musical point of view, was a Sunday morning service in the Russian Orthodox Church. The unaccompanied choral singing had a richness they had not heard before, especially in the deep tones of the bass.

By the evening of 18 May 1925 they were in Rotterdam staying at the home of an old Theosophical friend, which had a real Dutch interior, such as they had seen in paintings by the masters. Fatigue and weather laid Gretta low for some days. Meanwhile Jim had excursions in various directions— to The Hague and the Peace Palace, in Amsterdam; to Amersfoort and an International School of Philosophy where Jim spoke on *"The Philosophy of Beauty"* mostly according to India.

He then circled back to Rotterdam and the picturesque lodging on a dike and was reunited with his recovering patient. They were then off to Brussels on 23 May. Jim records:

"Here our supreme happiness was the instantaneous affiliation of our thought and imagination with two of the world's master artists, one in the flesh, one in the spirit: Jean Delville[70] the Belgian painter, and Alexandre Scriabin[71] the Russian musician. As the end of my lecture on 'Eastern thought on Western Problems' I found an intelligent listener in a man of distinguished bearing, bearded, about sixty, simple in dress, but with the

---

70 **Jean Delville** (19 January 1867–19 January 1953) was a Belgian symbolist painter, author, poet, teacher, and Theosophist. Delville was the leading exponent of the Belgian Idealist movement in art during the 1890s. He held the belief that art should be the expression of a higher spiritual truth and that it should be based on the principle of Ideal, or spiritual Beauty.

71 **Alexander Nikolayevich Scriabin:** (1872-1915) was a Russian composer and pianist. He developed a substantially atonal musical system. He associated colours with harmonic tones and was influenced by Theosophy. He was considered one of the most innovative and yet most controversial of early modern composers. The *Great Soviet Encyclopedia* said: «no composer has had more scorn heaped on him or greater love bestowed.» Leo Tolstoy described Scriabin‹s music as «a sincere expression of genius.» Scriabin had a major impact on the music world over time, and influenced composers such as Igor Stravinsky & Sergei Prokofiev.

touch that revealed the artist. He immediately showed an understanding that was more than intellectual of my exposition, and specially responded to my inclusion of artistic creation among the essentials of real living. He said he, Jean Delville, was a painter. He had been the first General Secretary of the Belgian Section of The Theosophical Society when it was formed in 1911. To see something of his art and simultaneously to exchange ideas, he suggested showing us over his mural paintings in the Palais de Justice next morning. These, we learned from friends, were masterpieces, finished in 1914 just before the Germans invaded Brussels, and saved from ruin because, not being in metal, they served no war-purpose, and remained undisturbed until after the war.

Fortunately next morning was Sunday, and we were free to go where we pleased in the Palais de Justice under the guidance of the artist, whose eminence we had begun to realise. The murals were in the Criminal Court, and to see them intimately we climbed into all sorts of unofficial, occasionally dizzying, positions around the balcony. The murals were, like all great murals, significant, not simply decorative. They depicted the development of criminal law from its savage original, through the ruthless stage of: 'An eye for an eye,' up to the Christ-ideal of compassion, and thence to a psychological conception in which the details of an offence were of less importance than the causes of it. In this mural (to indicate only one) a criminal crouched at the feet of a lawyer. The lawyer had closed his book of jurisprudence, and was looking intently into the eyes of the criminal. The dead letter of the law had been set aside; the mystery of human evil had struck him with revelation. We were stirred at being given so intimate a touch of greatness in skill expressing vision of the highest order. A master-artist had taken over the prophetic office."

Then came an even more amazing and historic experience that evening (24 May 1925). Deville, invited them for dinner. An upright piano, past its prime, shared the small sitting-room with them. Gretta asked: "Who was the musician?" There was none, but there had been one, whose touch had immortalised the instrument – Scriabin. When he was composing his "Poem of Fire" he used to dash in to play over a theme that had come to him, or a revision of a former theme.

They begged Delville to tell the whole story, even if it took half the night.

"In 1905 Delville (38) and Scriabin (34) met at various art-functions in Belgium. Both had reached considerable eminence in their arts.

Delville had won prizes, including the Prix de Rome, and exhibited many paintings. Scriabin had composed from his fourteenth year, and had become famous for sonatas and symphonies somewhat after the manner of Chopin. Delville was earnest but balanced; Scriabin was equally earnest but temperamentally uncertain. Scriabin asked what it was Delville had that he hadn't. He wasn't sure of himself; he didn't see where his work was moving, while Delville had some centre of intellectual and emotional calm. Could he explain it? Delville produced his two volumes of 'The Secret Doctrine' by Madame Blavatsky, and suggested that if Scriabin studied them and set them to music he might find what he wanted. The composer took the volumes to his rooms, and went 'aflame' with their amazing knowledge and outlook. The result was the completion in eight years of his 'Poem of Fire,' that expressed a revolution from his early lyricism to a kind of hypnotic suggestion through sound of a vast interwoven life, warmed and lighted by what the Hindus had called Agni, the personification of the universal element of fire. As a complement to this, Delville engaged to paint 'The Secret Doctrine' in the form of Prometheus descending from heaven bearing an iridescent globe. It took him four years to do this in a studio raised like a tower, to accommodate the immense painting."

After the illuminating discussions with Delville, they arrived at Victoria Station, London, at 11.30am on 27 May 1925. They had taken the boat train from Rotterdam, and were now conveyed to friends at 'Kelmscott' north of the Thames. A hectic ten days of renewing old friendships began a realisation that they had both 'grown' in the last ten years of their life in India. After all they had both been immersed in Theosophy, food reform, art, religion, philosophy, yoga, poetry, social reform and, of course, Indian women's suffrage and working especially in the field of education for equality. With this spiritual and material immersion it seemed that they had transformed and were continuing to transform.

They now had the opportunity of sharing with others their experiences of art, culture, and aspects of Indian life. They lived on a diet of lectures, at homes, garden parties, press interviews, lunches, concerts and poetry recitals.

Through the kind offices of their friend Henry Eichheim, who was visiting London at this time, they were given seats at a chamber music reception by the American millionaire and pianist, Elizabeth Coolidge[72], who spent her spare cash supporting musicians who had not yet received the recognition

---

72 **Elizabeth Sprague Coolidge** aka **Liz Coolidge** (1864 – 1953), was an American pianist and patron of music, especially of chamber music.

they deserved. For this occasion she had invited Maurice Ravel[73] for whom Gretta had huge admiration. A specially chosen audience of music-lovers thoroughly enjoyed an evening of great music.

On another side of their varied interests came notice of the Whitsun Convention of The Theosophical Society in Britain. They attended as plain members, but found themselves hoisted to the presidential chair because Dr George Arundale failed to arrive on time. The main meetings were held in the large hall of the Central Station Hotel at Kings Cross. The meetings were full of the friendliness of the First Object of the Theosophical Society, 'without distinction of any kind'. As they were about to leave, a tall, thin, man said he wanted to go to Adyar and join the Brahmavidya Ashrama. His name was Lieutenant Colonel Call. He had joined Kitchener's army in the war. Jim continues:

"He did come to Adyar for the opening of the fourth session (October 1925), and volunteered to say the Buddhist prayer at the opening of each day's work. On a call at my study he looked around my bookshelves. "You seem to be keen on Shelley. You have quite a number of books on him. I notice you often quote him in your lectures. But there is one book I don't see and that's the 'Last Days with Shelley'

"Oh!" I said, "I can get a copy of Trelawny's book any day for sixpence." "But you can't get a first edition. I'll send you mine when I go home." "How come?" I replied surprised by this extremely generous offer. "You remember Trelawny[74] had a daughter?" "Yes, and she declined to marry while her old father lived. But she married after his death, isn't that right?" "Well, I'm her son!"

I touched his hand, which had touched his mother's hand, which had touched his father's hand, which had touched Shelley's hand."

---

73 **Joseph Maurice Ravel** (1875 –1937) was a French composer, pianist and conductor. He is often associated with impressionism along with Claude Debussy. He liked to experiment with musical form, as in his best-known work, *Boléro* (1928), in which repetition takes the place of development. He made some orchestral arrangements of other composers› music, of which his 1922 version of Mussorgsky's *Pictures at an Exhibition* is the best known.

74 **Edward John Trelawny**, (Nov 1792 - Aug 1881), English author and adventurer, friend of Percy Bysshe Shelley and Lord Byron. Trelawny was a handsome, dashing, and quixotic personality from an old and famous Cornish family. In 1822 Trelawny met Shelley and Byron in Pisa, and, after Shelley drowned at Livorno on July 8, he supervised the recovery and cremation of Shelley's body. Later Trelawny vividly recounted his friendships with the two great poets in his *Recollections of the Last Days of Shelley and Byron* (1858).

Among various personalities they met while in London in their numerous lectures and meetings of various artistic and feminist groups, a handful stood out. They had lunch in the House of Commons with Fred and Emmeline Pethick-Lawrence, renewing their deep friendship from the Suffrage days. They found themselves the focus of attention, as Frederick had attained political fame a couple of years previously by beating no less a lion than Winston Churchill in a general election, by a majority of 4,000.

Lord and Lady Astor gave an 'At Home' at which Viscount Philip Snowden[75] and his wife were the chief guests. Jim again:

"In a crowd of distinctive men and women, sitting and standing, absorbing all sorts of tantalizing and unnecessary refreshments, Lord Astor stood out with a natural bonhomie radiating from breeding and ancestry. Lady Astor was everywhere dispensing bright-eyed hospitality, flavoured by verbal dexterity that came from a clean-shaven mind. The two chief guests presented a remarkable contrast. Philip Snowden looked small, asymmetrical and delicate. In such an assembly one could note his reserve, his keen eye, his air of intellectuality, showing that he was somebody. He had, in fact, passed his peak as Chancellor of the Exchequer. As he stood beside his seated wife, one felt it should have been the other way round. She was full-sized, vital, not phlegmatic but unfussed, observant; and the occasional wafts of a low bell-like voice through the hubbub of conversation confirmed, as far as the oral side of expression was concerned, her reputation as a platform speaker."

A short break in Wales followed for Gretta and Jim as well as a five-day tour to old haunts in north-west England. During a visit to Southport Jim saw one of the very early 'aeroplanes' circle and land on the seashore.

"I sensed a possible joy-ride to compensate for a cancelled flight from Belgium to England, and we ran for it. The pilot took a pound for ten minutes in the air. But before we got into the tandem seat he asked for five minutes to do a little repair to the engine. He produced a piece of wire such as in our early days was used for fastening corks on lemonade bottles. "I think that will do" he said. Encouraging for one's first flight! We thought we were going to rise into the blue ; instead, the blue stayed where it was, and city and seashore fell slowly below us, and

---

75 **Philip Snowden, 1st Viscount Snowden**, (1864 –1937) was a British politician. A strong speaker, he became popular in trade union circles for his denunciation of capitalism as unethical and his promise of a socialist utopia. He was the first Labour Chancellor of the Exchequer, a position he held in 1924.

moved first to left, then to right, then right about, and after another turnabout was just where it was when we began."

By 3 July 1925 they were back in Dublin, their first visit in ten years. These had been ten years of revolution, civil war, and party animosity within the once united patriotic group. But their visit had its social side with renewed friendships. Jim describes their various renewals with old friends.

"This took us to receptions, family parties, exhibitions by new and old painters, excursions, drama recitals and the Abbey Theatre. Our first touch with the new political circumstances was a Celtic concert in one of the large theatres. Twenty five years ago, under the cloud, perhaps the stimulus, of foreign government, Dr Douglas Hyde's[76] 'Twisting of the Rope'[77] had untwisted the rope of cultural domination and set the imagination of Celtic Ireland free to express itself in its own tongue.

There he was Dr Hyde in a royal box. At the interval we pushed our way round to the box, and to our deep delight were recognised and welcomed by him. Our next gather-up of the threads of history was an assembly of the Dail Eirean in the concert hall of the Royal Dublin Society, where we had enjoyed recitals by master-musicians. We were sponsored by William Sears, now a member of Parliament, but no longer red-bearded. He put us in seats in the visitors' gallery, and after some account of history took his own place. Here Gretta was thrilled to be hearing for the first time a speech by a woman member, and this in the Parliament of relatively free Ireland: two freedoms for which we had both worked, and for one of which she had borne all the obloquy and suffering that unregenerate man knew how to dispense. The woman speaker (after President Cosgrave and Dr Hyde) was Alice Stopford Green,[78] herself a specialist in the history of Ireland. It took us

---

76 **Douglas Hyde** (1860-1949), was an Irish academic, linguist, scholar of the Irish language, politician and diplomat who served as the 1st President of Ireland from June 1938 to June 1945. He was a leading figure in the Gaelic revival, and first President of the Gaelic League.

77 **Twisting of the Rope**: A short story by WB Yeats

78 **Alice Stopford Green** (1847 – 1929) was an Irish historian and nationalist. In the 1890s she became interested in Irish history and the nationalist movement as a result of her friendship with John Francis Taylor. She was vocal in her opposition to English colonial policy in South Africa during the Boer Wars and supported Roger Casement's Congo Reform movement. Her 1908 book *The Making of Ireland and its Undoing* argued for the sophistication and richness of the native Irish civilisation. She supported the pro-Treaty side in the Irish Civil War and was among the first nominees to the newly formed Seanad Éireann in 1922, where she served as an independent member until her death in 1929.

some time to get our eyes dry enough to seek out friends in the lobby.

Next afternoon, 8 July 1925, I managed to get an invitation to an 'at home' by President Cosgrave at his official residence outside the city. Compared with the colour and variety of dress at any gathering in India, it was dead in its dullness and uniformity. The only funny item was Yeats in a frock coat and tall hat. The others one accepted, but WB, in velvet jacket long lock of hair and glasses on a long tape, looked as if he had been dressed-up for the occasion.

We spent an evening with Yeats along with Æ, Gogarty, Lennox Robinson and Dermot Coffey. I was surprised at the poverty of the conversation, with such eminent talkers present. But I felt that each cock would only crow his best on his own dunghill; and I looked forward to an evening at Æ's, remembering past outpourings from the mystical and intellectual giant between 8pm and 4am. Times, alas, had changed. Instead of the gang, overflowing from chairs on to tables and the floor, the only person present when I arrived was Padraic Colum, and no more turned up. People had moved away, interests had gone into other things than ideas, Æ had been heroically critical in a time of tragedy and tension, and such a time does riot make for stability of appreciation. We did not keep the immortal poet long from his reading, and walked towards the parting of our ways pondering local and personal history."

Lunch at a house outside Dublin brought them quality of noble womanhood. Charlotte Despard and Maud Gonne, with her niece Isolda, were living in a place they had made into a refuge for sufferers from the bad times. Mrs Despard had no room for any more lines on her wise face than she had had eleven years previously when Gretta presided over her in Liverpool. Madame Gonne had moved from the queenliness of years before in to stately age. Both were full of anecdotes and prophecy.

Jim called on Éamon De Valera at the office of the Republican Party which was developing towards the future. He was quietly confident that he would come into power, which he did for 20 years, until defeated through the entrance into general electioneering in 1948 of that little boy, recollected from 1912 in France, the son of Maud Gonne and Major Mac Bride, Sean McBride[79].

They ended their brief visit to Dublin with a suffrage party and next day on 22 July 1925 they were in Boyle, with Gretta's parents: Jim records.

---

79 Gretta and Jim had met Sean as a young boy while visiting Maude Gonne on holidays in France

"Nature was at its summers best, and walks, 'we two together' and in groups, also boat-tea parties down at the lake, in the 'official' two dry days to three wet, were daily delights, with old abbeys turning up at intervals on excursions to prevent our forgetting that there was such a thing as a historical past. One such excursion was to Rosses Point on the coast of Sligo. All the paraphernalia of poetry was at its best, as in the sensitive days of Yeats, the rolling Greenlands, with yellow granny's pockets in fragrant hollows; the long ridge of Benbulbin against the blue and white sky, making a terrestrial pathway for the celestials and an entrance to immortality for such mortals as had earned the knowledge of the way thereto; the Flash Pool that glistened with verse in the "Celtic note" and with Wordsworth's other light. I found a deep hollow where I was unseen by the others and their happy but distracting talk was inaudible to me, and got down ideas for a lyric expressing my joy at being in a free Ireland and my hope that it would attain unity of purpose.

## IRELAND AFTER TEN YEARS

Land of my birth! Again I greet
Thy grey-wing sky, green earth, sweet air;
And, passing hence, lay at thy feet
The tribute of a simple prayer,

That, since thy long red saga's wave
Beyond thy dreams' edge sinks from view.
Thy children, one in heart, may brace
The splendid hazard of the New;

Yet, for the spirit's deeper thirst,
From ancient, wise, enchanted springs
Drink, that thy Last be as thy First –
A glory sought by saints and kings.

*Rosses, Sligo, July 1925*

I sent the twelve-line poem to Æ for his agricultural and cooperative weekly. He published it, and much to my surprise sent me a guinea! But the peak of pleasure, just under the high satisfaction of having written

136

the verses at all, came from a copy of a London weekly, 'The Sketch,' then edited by Clement Shorter. My poem to Ireland was admirably reprinted, and with it an editorial note to the effect that, while the magazine had ceased publishing poetry, it couldn't resist the temptation to copy the following from Æ's paper for some complimentary reason that I have forgotten."

Leaving Ireland they both embarked from Birkenhead heading for Colombo in Ceylon (Shri Lanka) on 19 Aug 1925. Coming past Gibraltar Jim was haunted with day and night dreams of making plans for a new and unusual university, and then tearing them up. A few days after they had arrived back in Adyar news came that the founding of a World University had been announced at the Theosophical 'Star Camp' at Ommen, in Holland. Jim's name had been mentioned as having laid the foundation of it in the Brahmavidya Ashrama[80] which he had shared in founding in 1922, and of which he was Director of studies currently on leave.

---

80 **Brahmavidya Ashrama** was an institution established by the Theosophical Society (TS) on 2 October 1922, with the aim of bringing under the light of theosophy all branches of knowledge. It had a staff of twenty lecturers at the beginning, with James H. Cousins as the Registrar of the Ashrama and director of studies. It aimed to respond to the following **needs:**

1. that of a body of earnest workers, mainly in India, who are strong in intuition and abstract thought, but lack the definition and intellectual power which are derivable from a synthesized knowledge of modern culture in its aspects of thought, artistic and social activity;

2. that of scattered persons in various parts of the world, who have been reared in a scientific and commercial atmosphere, but who feel the need of a clue to the apparent maze of life, and an attitude of human comradeship and cooperation based on a sound understanding of the real nature of things;

3. that of certain students in India and elsewhere who, having finished their ordinary education, and being without urgent need to engage in professional or business life, require a course of all-round scientific, cultural and spiritual training.

In 1922, 176 lectures were conducted on mysticism, religion, philosophy, literature and drama, arts and crafts, and science.

# CHAPTER TWENTY-ONE

## THE BIRTH OF THE ALL-INDIA WOMEN'S CONFERENCE

The three years between their return from Europe in August 1925 and setting out in April 1928 on what expanded into a world tour, were crowded with activities that worked out the details of Movements already set in motion. Gretta recollects:

"I had full scope for my feminist energies in the General Election of 1926. Kamaladevi,[81] that pearl of Indian womanhood, 23 years old, decided to contest the seat in her home District, Mangalore, on the West Coast, for the Madras Legislature, to which, for the first time, women were to be admitted. I spent five days canvassing for her, generally continuously from nine to three, in all sorts of vehicles, from Malabar jutkas[82] upwards. There was an obvious weightage of custom and influence against her, as her opponent had held the seat, and was locally powerful. But there was nothing personal in Kamaladevi's candidature. She wished to establish a custom of women coming into political life, and to demonstrate the growing political consciousness among women in general. She was, as expected, defeated, but the custom of women candidates was established, and went on to the appointment of women Ministers and Ambassadors in the work for the emancipation of women.

The climax in these years was the creation of the All-India Women's Conference. From what simple and unconscious circumstances great

---

81 **Kamaladevi Chattopadhyay** (April 1903 – October 1988) was an Indian social reformer and freedom fighter. She was most remembered for her contribution to the Indian independence movement; for being the driving force behind the renaissance of Indian handicrafts and hand looms in independent India; and for the raising of the socio-economic standard of Indian women by pioneering the co-operation. Several cultural institutions in India today exist because of her vision, including the National School of Drama, Central Cottage Industries Emporium, and the Crafts Council of India. She stressed the significant role which handicrafts and cooperative grass-root movements play in the social and economic benefits of Indian people. To this end she withstood great opposition both before and after independence from the power centres. In 1974, she was awarded the Sangeet Natak Academy Fellowship, the highest honour conferred by India's National Academy of Music, Dance & Drama. She was conferred with Padma Bhushan and Padma Vibhushan by Government of India in 1955 and 1987 respectively.
82 **Jutka**: A small covered wagon drawn by a donkey or such animal.

things may grow! An elderly Englishman, passing through Calcutta, remembered that his daughter had been Principal of the Bethune College for women in Calcutta, and thought he would visit, and take news of the election back to her, then Mrs Huidekoper of Karachi. He happened on the prize-giving function, when the English Director of Public Instruction in Bengal called on Indian women to: "Tell us with one voice what they want, and keep on telling us till they get it.'"

Mrs Huidekoper took up the challenge and wrote to 'Stri Dharma,' the Journal of the Women's Indian Association. Gretta, taking up this suggestion from Mrs Huidekoper, once again acted in her established role as a catalyst.

"The organising and carrying out of the answer of the women of India fell to my lot. In the autumn of 1926 I sent out an appeal to women to form local Committees and organise Constituent Conferences in the Provinces and the States. These constituent Conferences were to draw up a series of resolutions on education from the point of view of women in two main categories, local and all-Indian. It was an inspiring, if somewhat exacting experience, to collate and condense the remarkable number of expressions right out of the hearts and minds of the women of India, and, with the help of such wise stalwarts in the cause of women's advancement as Dorothy Jinarájadása and Dr (Mrs) S Muthulakshmi Reddi, to put them in order for discussion at the first session of the All-India Women's Conference. (1927)"

The approach of the First Session raised the matter of a President. They were a democratic body meant to represent all the people, from highest to lowest. They needed a leader of social eminence and experience, as well as a keen interest in the women's cause. She should have ability and personality. The triumvirate of Gretta, Dorothy Jinarájadása and Dr Muthulaksmhi Reddi,[83] suggested Her Highness the Maharani of Baroda. She graciously accepted their invitation, and cancelled a visit to Burma in order to do so. The possible venue for the Conference seemed to arise out of Gretta's past visits

83 **Dr Muthulakshmi Reddi** (1886 – 1968) was an eminent medical practitioner, social reformer. She was the first woman legislator in India. She was appointed to the Madras Legislative Council in 1927. For her, this nomination marked the beginning of her lifelong effort to "correct the balance" for women by removing social abuses and working for equality in moral standards. She was one of the women pioneers who stood for the cause of liberating India from the British. She was the first female student to be admitted into a men's college, the first woman House Surgeon in the Government Maternity and Ophthalmic Hospital, the first Chairperson of the State Social Welfare Advisory Board, the first woman Deputy President of the Legislative Council.

to the Indian Women's University in Poona (Pune). Teachers and students were enthusiastic and they were offered every help with accommodation and hospitality.

All was ready, after considerable organisation and frenetic activity, for the inauguration of what they felt, rightly, would be an historic occasion.

Ferguson College in Pune had been generously placed at the disposal of the Conference. Its capacious galleried theatre made a dignified setting for the inaugural meeting. Twenty two Constituent Conferences, with 5492 members, not to mention twice the number of sympathisers, sent 58 elected delegates. This was an open session, and drew a packed audience of both men and women. The Rani of Sangli, in her address of welcome as Chairman of the Reception Committee, stated:

> "This is a unique occasion, as this is the first time when an attempt is being made by Indian women to formulate their views on a subject of grave national importance, namely, the education of the present and future generations of children in this country."

The President of the session, The Maharani of Baroda, arose to the occasion and raised up the whole audience as one. She confessed:

> "I have spent many years of thinking over the problems of Indian womanhood, and accepted the invitation to preside as a duty which any woman should be proud to have placed upon her."

Fergusson College, Poona (Pune), venue for the inaugural meeting of the AIWC

She allowed no politeness of place, due to her status, to interfere with her straight attack on positive evils and the darkness from which Indian women, particularly those in purdah, had to be released. The Maharani continued:

"Our honoured patriots have been straining every nerve for political emancipation. They have relegated social advancement to the background. They have to be painfully reminded of the question raised by the poet Shelley, 'Can man be free, and woman be a slave?' Without woman's elevation, the progress of man, politically, socially, and even economically, can only be lop-sided and insecure."

Her Highness shared the vision of present needs and future responsibilities as demonstrated in Resolutions passed by the first session of the All-India Women's Conference on Educational Reform. **Education** was their only remit at that time.

## The Resolutions:
It may be apposite to state all the resolutions made at this first and most historic of the AIW Conferences. (5th- 8th January 1927)

(1) This Conference defines Education as training which will enable the child and the individual (adult) to develop his or her latent capacities to their fullest extent, for the service of humanity. It must, therefore include elements for physical, mental, emotional, civic and spiritual development. The courses of study arranged for these purposes must be so flexible as to allow for adaptation to the needs of the individual, the locality and the community.

(2) Moral training, based on spiritual ideals should be made compulsory for all schools and college (3) Compulsory physical training (4) Compulsory medical inspection.

(5) Ideals of motherhood and beautiful homes should be kept uppermost in all education of girls.

(6) This Conference deeply deplores the effect of early marriage on education, and urges the Government of India to pass legislation making marriage **under sixteen** a penal offence. It demands that the age of consent be raised to 16.

(7) & (8) Asked for proper facilities for girls in purdah educational institutions, and for some better way than examinations for testing knowledge.

**The Resolutions on Primary Education** recommended:

(1) That it be made compulsory for all boys and girls.

(2) That preparatory vocational and manual training should be included in the curriculum suited to the child's needs and daily experience.

(3) That the salaries of teachers be raised.

(4) That special schools for defectives be established.

**The Resolutions on Secondary Education** recommended that the vernacular should be the medium of instruction. English being a compulsory second subject, with Hindi or Urdu in a group of classical languages of which one should be compulsory.

That fine Arts took their place in alternatives for girls not going on to College, and sex hygiene in schools and colleges.

In **College education**, Resolution I, II, recommended the addition of Fine Arts, Domestic Science, Journalism, Social Scheme and Architecture to the optional subjects; and special encouragement was added by scholarships to women students in Law, Medicine, Social Science and Fine Arts.

Adult education was also recommended.

Thus ended in triumph the first All India Women's Conference on Educational Reform, which still holds an annual conference today. The Maharani of Baroda was the First President. Sarojini Naidu was voted the 4th President in 1930 followed by Dr Muthulakshmi Reddi in 1931. Gretta herself was President in 1937 for one year.[84] This 11th Session of the Conference was held in Ahmedabad 23-27th December 1937.

---

84 **Author:** During visits to India in the 1990s my wife and I met some of the more recent past-Presidents. Mrs Shobana Ranade, the current President, came to Ireland and was invited to meet the then President of Ireland Mary Robinson. Mrs Ranade unveiled a plaque at Gretta's birth Place in Boyle, in Rosscommon - **16th September 1994.**

# CHAPTER TWENTY-TWO

## THE 2ND AIWC SESSION – DELHI
### The Child Marraige Act

After the inaugural AIWC Session in Pune a triumphant Gretta headed for Adyar by way of Bombay, Nagpur and Delhi, 'trailing clouds of conference glory'.

What made her especially happy was that the Conference had agreed to meet annually, although it was planned initially to be a one-off statement on education.

What excited them all was the current attention paid to their resolution number (6) which stated:

> "This Conference deeply deplores the effect of early marriage on education, and urges the Government of India to pass legislation making marriage **under sixteen** a penal offence. It demands that the age of consent be raised to **16**."

The Age of Consent Bill was being sponsored by Sir Hari Sing Gour, who had taken a special interest in the subject for quite some time.

Historically, in 1891 the 'Age of Consent Act' had established that the minimum age of consent within marriage for girls should be **12 years.**

Then in 1922, Rai Bahadur Bakshi Sohan Lal proposed that the age of consent should be raised from 12 to 14. This motion was defeated.

Another attempt in 1924 by Sir Hari Singh Gour brought the age of consent issue back into the Legislature with a similar proposal to raise the minimum age from 12 to 14 years for girls. After amendments and the appointment of a select committee, Gours Bill was passed and thus raised the age of consent to **13 years** for girls in 1925.

Sir Hari again appealed in **March 1928** for the importance of accepting the standards of modern clinical psychology and pointed out the emotional problems of early marriage, such as the incidence of polygamy. As husbands grew older many decided they desired more compatible partners. Occurrence of suicide and generally marital unhappiness for both partners was on the increase. It was not passed at that court but subsequently, on **28 September 1929,** the 'Child Marriage Restraint Act' was passed and fixed the age of marriage for girls at **14 years** and boys at 18 years, which was later amended to **18 years** for girls and 21 for boys.

\* \* \*

The year 1928 began with an intensive continual preparation for the second annual session of the All-India Women's Conference to be held in Delhi.

"In addition to directing its organisation I had to find the ideal President. The Maharana of Baroda had been a pillar of strength and a fire of inspiration at the First Conference. Could I find another leader of equal eminence and equal brightness? There was no one religion in the Conference. We had been led by a Hindu before: Why not a Muslim this time? So on my way to Delhi, I made a stop-over for a day at Bhopal, hoping to get an interview with Her Highness the Begum Saheba, and hoping also to induce her to be President of the Delhi session. We chatted happily for an hour and a half, and I left on my toes with her promise to do what was wanted.

The work of the Women's Conference began in Delhi on 6 February. Sarojini Naidu came to the meeting of the Standing Committee; and I saw a future prospect for the presidential chair.[85] She made a good start by presiding over the Delegates Session on 7 February, when we had a most impressive opening in a big cinema hall. Next day, at our two crowded open sessions, the choice of the Begum of Bhopal as President thoroughly justified itself. Her personality, so like that of Mrs Besant (short, sturdy, white-haired, calm but energetic) her fine command of the English language, and her big ideas for womanhood in the future life of India gave the cause a great fillip. I was no toady, but I recall a touch of pride when at one of these open sessions I counted eight royal ladies on the platform. We were out to liberate and raise what Tagore called 'the poorest, the lowliest and the lost.' It began in a solid manner at the morning gathering on the fourth day, when a call for a fund brought an immediate response of R.30000 amid great enthusiasm.

A Standing Committee, meeting under trees at the Qutab Minar,[86] was environed by history, art and nature. A number of us attended the final debate in the Legislative Assembly in Delhi on the Age of Consent Bill, and had the experience of seeing a man-run parliament turn it down. Some of our members wanted to cry, others to break loose."

The final morning and evening sessions on 9 February were wonderful occasions of inspiration for work. Gretta hurried around and escorted Mrs

85 **Sarojini Naidu** did become President in 1930.
86 The **Qutub Minar** is the tallest minaret in the world made of bricks. It is now a UNESCO World Heritage Site in Delhi is a 73-metre tall tapering tower of five storeys, with a 14.3 metre base diameter. Its design is thought to have been based on the Minaret of Jam, in western Afghanistan.

Besant to the closing meeting. She gave one of her inspired extemporaneous speeches. Gretta describes the scene.

"It was a sight for the Goddesses, and any Gods who cared to look on, to see the two venerable old ladies, the Begum and Mrs Besant, full of years of experience and fun, walking hand in hand down the passage to the exit, between hundreds of charming, intelligent, free-minded Indian girls and women who saluted them, some in the Hindu way of palm to palm, some in the Mohammedan way of palm to forehead. At tea I had a good talk with Her Excellency the Vicereine, Lady Irwin, and laid out the scope of work and the methods of the Conference. Anything that smelt of politics at that ancient time was suspect. I think she was relieved to find that it was non-political. It included women of every shade of religious belief and political opinion in a sisterhood of cultural and social service. It didn't, I may here say, always remain non-political and united. By and by it came out on the side of Indian freedom, but without alliance to any political party; and the development of Mr Jinnah's campaign[87] took away a number of Muslim members. A picturesque garden party and dinner at the Lady Hardinge Medical College put a happy finish to the second session".

Gretta left Delhi for Adyar at night. Next morning, 13 Feb 1928, she stopped off at Baroda to report progress to their first President, the Maharani. She was escorted on a visit to the music school and a big art gallery before lunch. The discussion with the Maharani took more than two hours, such were her penetrating questions from someone with such an acute and comprehensive mind. Gretta was shown all over the Palace, ended up viewing the Zoo.

---

87 **Muhammad Ali Jinnah** (Dec 1876 – Sept 1948) was a lawyer, politician, and the founder of Pakistan. Jinnah served as the leader of the All-India Muslim League from 1913 until Pakistan's independence on 14 August 1947, and then as Pakistan's first Governor-General until his death. Jinnah rose to prominence in the Indian National Congress in the first two decades of the 20th century. In these early years of his political career, Jinnah advocated Hindu–Muslim unity, helping to shape the 1916 Lucknow Pact between the Congress and the All-India Muslim League. He became a key leader in the All India Home Rule League, and proposed a fourteen-point constitutional reform plan to safeguard the political rights of Muslims. In 1920, however, Jinnah resigned from the Congress when it agreed to follow a campaign of *satyagraha*, which he regarded as political anarchy. By 1940, Jinnah believed that Muslims should have their own state. Ultimately, the Congress and the Muslim League could not reach a power-sharing formula for the subcontinent to be united as a single state, leading all parties to agree to the independence of a predominantly Hindu India, and for a Muslim-majority state of Pakistan.

Once back at Adyar she and Dr Reddi reported back to a large gathering of women in Gokhale Hall[88] about the proceedings of the Conference.

A month later Gretta's pride in Dr Reddi was greatly increased by observing the skilful manner in which she pushed a resolution, in favour of the Child Marriage Bill, before the Central Government through the Madras Legislative Council after a debate of some three and a half hours.

---

88 **The Gokhale Hall** was founded as the Young Men's Indian Association Hall by theosophist and Indian independence activist Annie Besant in 1915. She announced the formation of the Home Rule League in 1916 at the hall. It was later renamed as Gopal Krishna Gokhale Hall after Indian leader Gopal Krishna Gokhale. In later days, Gokhale Hall served as a venue for music concerts.

# CHAPTER TWENTY-THREE

## THE 2ND WESTERN TOUR – 'GIRDLING THE EARTH'
### Meeting with Sir Patrick Geddes at Montpelier
### An observer seat at the League of Nations for Gretta
### Meeting Paderewski

April 1928 was a month of anticipation before their second western tour, which was extended to North America. Gretta had to settle such problems as finding enough weavers for the Samaj. Her five years as Honorary Bench Magistrate had now expired. Various groups, realising that she and Jim would be away for some months, laid on farewell parties with lots of excessive eating and drinking - non-alcoholic - and speech-making, all of which they appreciated immensely.

On 9 April they celebrated their silver wedding anniversary, helped with an enormous rich-in-calories wedding cake brought by their friend, S.V. Ramaswami Mudaliar, business man, art collector and idealist. Another good friend, Appa Rao, Registrar of the High Court of Madras, gave a dinner-party in their honour on the flat roof of his house, to which he invited a number of prominent Indian men and women. The day before departure Gretta was presented with the Founders' silver medal of The Theosophical Society as a tribute for long service.

As a farewell treat Annie Besant laid on an afternoon tea.

They left Madras by steamer on 29 April 1928, via Colombo, and by 21 May they were in dock at Marseilles. After five days of sight-seeing, Jim left Gretta with friends, and paid a visit to Sir Patrick Geddes[89] in his College at Montpelier. From his arrival at 11am the only time they stopped talking, until eight o'clock that evening, was for meals and a much too short siesta. He took Jim six miles into the country to Château d'Assas that he had bought with a view to future extensions. Jim stayed overnight. Discussion began again at eight next morning, but had to end by three as Jim needed to start back for Marseilles.

---

89 **Sir Patrick Geddes** FRSE (Oct 1854 – Apr 1932) was a Scottish biologist, sociologist, geographer, philanthropist and pioneering town planner. He was known for his innovative thinking in the fields of sociology and urban planning. He introduced the concept of "region" to architecture and planning and coined the term «conurbation". Geddes had an abiding interest in Eastern philosophy which he believed more readily conceived of 'life as a whole'.

"The subject of conversation was his work for international understanding. The centre round which our conversation moved was his desire to build up a biological view of life that would take in all the proven facts. At the end of our sixteen hours of one-sided conversation, he invited me, much to my surprise, to join him in his work at Montpellier. He wanted a mystically minded and imaginative person, such as he felt I was, to help him to complete his scientific work. But why, I asked, bring woolly headed mystics into a scientific thesis? He replied that, as he neared the apex of his research, he found he could not

Sir Patrick Geddes, Biologist, geographer, pioneering town-planner & philanthropist

leave out, however he tried, the mystical and occult aspect of life: his argument would be incomplete without it. It was not possible for me at the time to accept Sir Patrick's invitation; but, with his permission, I passed on the diagrams and a precis of his scheme to a scientific friend who had also found himself compelled to add occultism to his studies as a professional ethnologist. Time passed; so did Sir Patrick. He died four years later in 1932."

Jim re-joined Gretta in Marseilles, and they moved on to Geneva for a month of pleasurable artistic activities. They were guests of friends, Durga and Jack Selleger. The Stokowskis[90] had taken a house round a corner, and, it was a privilege to meet him. At another time they had tea with Sir Atul Chatterjee,[91] when plans were made for a lecture by Jim on 'Indian Architecture and Sculpture,' with slides, before the Anglo-Genevese Society in the Atheneum. The arrangements were perfect. The hall was crowded with representatives from all nations, to whom India was then little more than a name. Sir Atul Chatterjee presided. Jim was in good form, and his intimacy

90 **Leopold Anthony Stokowski** (April 1882 – Sept 1977) was an English conductor of Polish and Irish descent. One of the leading conductors of the early and mid-20th Century, he is best known for his long association with the Philadelphia Orchestra and for appearing in the film Fantasia.

91 **Sir Atul** was born in Calcutta (now Kolkata). He was educated at Presidency College in Calcutta and then at King's College at Cambridge University, where he graduated in 1896 with an honours degree. In 1896, he stood for the Indian Civil Service examinations. From 1897 to 1906, Chatterjee served as an ICS official in the United Provinces, eventually rising to the office of District collector. He represented India at the International Labour Conference in Washington in 1919.

with Indian architecture and sculpture appeared to make the slides not merely illustrations but living demonstrations of the creative imagination and skill of the ancient artificers. Hopefully, they thought, this was yet another step towards international understanding through art.

Through the efforts of Dr Anna Kamensky, who had taken her doctorate in the University of Geneva with a thesis on the 'Bhagaved Gita,' and who was appointed Professor of Comparative Religion, Jim was invited to give a lecture in the auditorium of the University on 'Oriental Idealism in Education.' The Rector found it difficult to agree to Jim speaking owing to his Theosophical leanings. He did chair the lecture however, but gave him a somewhat frigid introduction.

"I was told that as I proceeded the Rector became more and more interested. At the end he put his revised feelings into a phrase that got into public print, and that I quote, not as a garland for the lecturer but as indicating the illumination that a presentation of the idealism of the East was capable of giving to the West: "The Chairman, in thanking the lecturer on behalf to the University and the audience, said the lecture was not only *on* education but was itself *an* education and a compendium of a course of lectures on a most important subject."

Gretta did her bit in culture-spreading at lunches and with lectures on *The Awakening of Asian Women.*[92] She was cock-a-hoop when the 'wireless' reported that British women had at last got equal franchise with men, twenty-two years after Gretta had worked for it in Ireland and England. Indian women had got it in eight years.[93] One Sunday she preached the sermon at St. Gabriel's Liberal Catholic Church in Geneva. Her subject was 'The World Mother.' Many were impressed by the power and conviction that she put into her appeal for the bringing of the feminine influence into life more fully than it had been.

They passed from Geneva to Rotterdam then to the Theosophical Centre at Ommen - 2 July - to attend a meeting of the 'Order of the Star'. Krishnamurti was present but illness prevented a scheduled start. They remained at the camp for several weeks and listened intently to many lectures by Krishnaji.

During early August Gretta returned to Geneva to find a locale for an

92 **Gretta's** book: 'The Awakening of Asian Women' had been published in Madras in 1922.

93 **The Representation of the People** (Equal Franchise) Act 1928 was an Act of the Parliament of the United Kingdom. ... The 1928 Act widened suffrage by giving women electoral equality with men. It gave the vote to all women over 21 years old, regardless of property ownership.

International Theosophical Centre near the League of Nations and the Swiss Section of the Society. As editor of 'Stri Dharma', the magazine of the International Theosophical Society, she also got a place as an observer at the 'League of Nations Assembly'. Most of a month went by in attending sessions of the League and sitting on special Commissions. She was included in a 'Women's Deputation on Disarmament' representing Ireland, feeling it an historic honour to be so closely involved with the first event of its kind.

Meantime Jim began a period of shuttling between England and Ireland, with much talking, music, drama, and sight-seeing. During his foray to Ireland an evening at Æ's in Dublin showed clearly the passing of time. Dudley Digges,[94] now grown corpulent, turned up on one of his annual vacations from the Theatre Guild of New York. A French lady was announced as "the historian of the Abbey Theatre." Jim's name was new to her. At an appropriate moment Digges fell on my shoulder and chanted: "O Seamas! Isn't it grand to come to a country where you are not known?"

Once back in England again Jim spent an afternoon - 27 Aug 1928 - in a music hall in London, together with a friend, to see how far the professional Irish Players had progressed. Between items a screen was illuminated and announced:

**"The Kellogg Peace Pact was signed at 3.50"**[95]

The audience broke into spontaneous applause. Jim composed a poem to celebrate the occasion, "Peace, an Anticipation." Sadly it was not to be, even when Germany was one of the signatories.

From 1-24 October 1928 Jim fulfilled a private hope to mount an exhibition of Indian paintings in the heart of London, which had rarely shown examples of Eastern art. A society which called itself 'The Faculty of

---

94 **Dudley Digges** (1879 –1947) was an Irish stage and film actor born in Dublin. He became acquainted with drama enthusiasts William and Frank Fay and took an interest in acting. He joined Fay's Irish National Dramatic Company, along with others such as Máire Nic Shiubhlaigh, James H. Cousins, Fred Ryan and Máire T. Quinn. Their first production, *Cathleen Ni Houlihan*, with Maud Gonne in the lead role, and *Deirdre*, was on 2 April 1902.

95 The **Kellogg–Briand Pact (Pact of Paris)**, officially **General Treaty for Renunciation of War as an Instrument of National Policy** was an international agreement in which signatory states promised not to use war to resolve «disputes or conflicts of whatever nature or of whatever origin they may be, which may arise among them». Parties failing to abide by this promise «should be denied of the benefits furnished by [the] treaty». It was signed by Germany, France, and the United States on 27 August 1928, and by most other nations soon after. Sponsored by France and the U.S., the Pact renounces the use of war and calls for the peaceful settlement of all disputes.

Arts' allowed him its fairly large hall somewhere behind Piccadilly Circus. A few artistically minded people trickled in and out. Laurence Binyon[96] went around the collection in silence, and departed with a sign of pleasure. While packing up the exhibition an enthusiastic man demanded a look over the dismantled pictures. He came at the request of the Editor of 'The Illustrated London News' who had wanted Jim's advice whether any of them could be reproduced in colour in the Christmas number. The visitor was R. H. Wilenski, a prominent art critic. A week later Jim was called up by the Editor to view a group of the paintings. From these he selected half a dozen, which duly appeared, and gave Indian Art an unexpected boost of publicity.

Jim then joined Gretta in Geneva and was just in time for her birthday. They spent a happy afternoon with congenial friends in the garden of the Villa Deodati, where Byron had lived and Shelley had visited (1816). Jim read some of Shelley's poems. On another day they found an excuse to call at the Hotel Angleterre where Shelley had stayed, such was Jim's deep love and respect for the famous romantic poet.

## Hearing Paderewski play

The 27 November 1928 brought them to one of the highlights of their musical lives. Gretta came home, breathless with excitement. She had seen a 'window bill' announcing a piano recital by Paderewski[97] in Lausanne Cathedral that night. Jim describes their dash to a once-in-a-lifetime opportunity. Gretta, you will remember, had heard Paderewski play in Dublin before she even met Jim.

> "We just must go, snow or no snow. Tram services had stopped. We ploughed through slush to the railway station. The Cathedral was crammed but we got seats. A platform had been made at the rose-window end for the grand piano and stool and some kind of pot-plant. A notice on each pillar commanded silence; but at the end of the

96 **Robert Laurence Binyon**, (1869 – 1943) was an English poet, dramatist and art scholar. His most famous work, *For the Fallen*, is well known for being used in Remembrance Sunday services.

97 **Ignacy Jan Paderewski** (Nov 1860 – Jun 1941) was a Polish pianist and composer, politician, statesman and spokesman for Polish independence. He was a favourite of concert audiences around the world. His musical fame opened access to diplomacy and the media. Paderewski played an important role in meeting with President Woodrow Wilson and obtaining the explicit inclusion of independent Poland as **point 13** in Wilson's peace terms in 1918, called the Fourteen Points. He was the Prime Minister of Poland and also Poland's foreign minister in 1919, when he represented Poland at the Paris Peace Conference. He served 10 months as prime minister, and soon thereafter left Poland, never to return.

first item, silence hid itself in tumultuous applause. "He's an archangel," Gretta averred."

When they returned to their flat in Geneva a telegram awaited them. Jim read it with 'growing palpitations', but said nothing to Gretta until he got his breath back, then he handed it over. She read it and went off in a wild dance around the drawing room, chanting to various melodies. "Oh! Jim!! Lunch with Paderewski!" Unknown to Gretta Jim had sent him some of his sonnets and gathered later

Ignacy Jan Paderewski

that, after reading them silently over and over, stated, "We must have him to lunch to-morrow!" It seems he had said to his family "The man who wrote that poetry must have a nice wife, and she must be with him." Hence the telegram had read:

"WILL YOU AND YOUR WIFE LUNCH WITH US TOMORROW AND GIVE ME THE OPPORTUNITY OF THANKING YOU FOR YOUR LOVELY POETRY. MY CAR WILL MEET YOU AT MORGES STATION AT 1.20PM. PADEREWSKI."

"When we arrived at his house, looking across the lake to Mont Blanc, he welcomed Gretta with a hand-shake, and then gave me his hand with, "Here is my poet." At once he entered on a discussion of form in poetry as in music, the artist losing thought of the sonneteer or the subject.

Lunch was at a big table round which artists and literary persons were placed in affinities. Paderewski took Gretta in, and I, with Madame Paderewski on my arm, was placed opposite. Madame was unwell, and a charming niece was seated on one side of me to keep me in chat. I don't remember at what stage of the proceedings I grew inattentive to my chatty partner, and could only afford her one ear, as the other was intent on the opposite side of the table. Politics had come up: the age-long struggle for freedom between groups of humanity; Ireland freed into civil war; then Poland. "Yes, Monsieur," Gretta said, sotto voce, but not sufficiently sotto to miss my ear, "When the newspapers brought word to Adyar that Poland was free, I ran down to the music room and played Chopin's polonaise for freed Poland." I don't know what flashed through Paderewski's mind, but his big hand went out to Gretta's and enveloped it; he turned various shades of emotional red, and with deep feeling said: "Thank you, Madame, thank you." The afternoon went in pleasant conversations, and a visit to the chicken-run and vinery of which Paderewski was proud. At tea he carried plates of rich cake around the outside of the table trying to induce his guests to ruin their digestive apparatus—and succeeding! When we said good bye he gave us a warm invitation to look him up if our paths crossed in America."

They left Geneva soon after this historic encounter and travelled to London. After two days of seeing Members of Parliament on Irish Franchise League matters, Gretta sailed for Ireland to see friends, while Jim laid preliminary plans for their trip to America.

# CHAPTER TWENTY-FOUR

## ACROSS THE 'POND', BUT
## NOT A SMOOTH RIDE
### Meeting Nathalia Crane, a young American poet
### Experiencing a Quaker meeting
### Meeting an old friend, Dudley Digges
### Gretta kept awake by a nearby slaughter house

On 16 Jan 1929, during a snowstorm, they boarded the Homeric at Southampton (34,000 tons). Gretta was none too impressed at the size. Not being the best of sailors the increasing wind and, the incessant twisting and rolling of an 'immense thing that should have known better', kept her well and truly in her bunk in their second class cabin. By the fifth day of a seven day voyage they had only covered four days' distance. Even this immense liner had to slow down a number of times and face vast waves that sent foam against the lounge windows some eighty-feet above sea-level.

They finally reached New York on 25 January. A deputation of friends arrived as they disembarked which consisted of an American Major who, out of a family fortune, was guiding schools for native children in Africa; an Englishman, who had been a ship's captain and had retired to create railways in India; an Irish actor; an Indian making a living in America; and to Jim's great delight, the poetess, Nathalia Crane,[98] then sixteen years old.

Nathalia Crane as a teenager

Four press-men headed for Jim who had been rumoured to 'be somebody' from India which was a popular subject at the time among American press men. Jim side-stepped them to deal with customs while Gretta regaled them with all sorts of news about the advance of women in India. None of them produced a

---

98 **Nathalia Clara Ruth Crane** (1913 – 1998) was a poet and novelist who became famous as a child prodigy after the publication of her first book of poetry, *The Janitor's Boy*, written aged 10 and published two years later. Some of her poetry was first published in *The New York Sun* when she was only 9 years old, the paper unaware that she was a child. She was elected to the British Society of Authors, Playwrights, and Composers in 1925 and later became a professor of English at San Diego State University.

notebook or a pen or even a pencil. They were simply not interested.

They were taken to the home of Mr and Mrs Robert R. Logan, descendants of city pioneers, at Eddington, outside Philadelphia. It was good to get a steady night's sleep, and to rise next morning to gasp at the beauty of snow. They dressed warmly and ran down to the edge of the Delaware River to watch great blocks of ice floating by. In the afternoon they were driven to Philadelphia, as guests of the Duchess of Hamilton for a dinner-party given by a prominent judge. On the way they had their first experience of Quaker culture. Jim was invited to give a talk to the young 'Friends'. He was conducted to a seat on the platform. Gretta was invited to sit in a pew on the floor of the meeting-house which was a square shaped undecorated room with none of the usual outer signs of a church. It was simple and bare.

"Jim had been as curious as myself, and asked the usher why he was given so prominent a position. He presumed he was on a speakers' platform. Correct. "But I didn't know you anticipated speeches. I thought you waited for the spirit to move a speaker." "So we do, usually, but on this occasion we are hopeful that the spirit *will* move you." And it did. After some men and women had spoken briefly of personal spiritual experiences he stood up, moved by something, and gave a short talk on his favourite text, "Stand still and see the salvation of the Lord," a plea for repose and meditation as a means of realizing, rather than just mentally understanding, one's real nature and the nature of the larger life on which this life depends."

They left Philadelphia for New York where a series of Sunday evening talks for the Theosophical Society was held in the large hall of a hotel.

These were given during the time of arctic conditions, a heavy overcoat being essential. At the last of the lectures Jim laid his coat on a chair at the back of a hall. At the close of the meeting he went to pick it up. It was gone! Someone had felt that the 'donation' of such a 'warmer' was necessary in order to face the sub-zero temperature. The hall was stuffy, being fortunately well-heated. Outside, however, the temperature was indeed arctic. They had to cross the city in an unheated tramcar to attend an Irish *ceilidh* in the home of Dudley Digges. Some kind of warm coat was therefore essential.

A bright idea struck the lady cloakroom-attendant. An overcoat had been left by accident two years previous and had not been claimed. He could have a 'loan' of it. It reached to the ground and even farther. He waddled to a tramcar like a penguin, ignoring any odd looks from passing strangers. Digges himself opened the door. "'*Céad Míle Fáilte' mo chara*"[99]. Taking a

---

99 '*Céad Míle Fáilte' mo chara*' - a hundred thousand welcomes, my friend.

second look he asked, "Dressed up for a charade or a movie?" Jim explained what had happened. "Don't worry." said Digges, "I'll give you an overcoat that will fit you exactly." "But what about yourself? Won't you freeze to death?" "I have one that I wear every day. The other I haven't put on for two years, Heaven knows why."

While Jim was collecting overcoats and hobnobbing with the Poetry Society Gretta made a four-day visit to Washington to link up with the splendid work for equal rights by the 'Women's Party'.

"My admiration for the devotion of Alice Paul[100] to the cause of womanhood and for her unique gifts of foresight and organization had grown immensely since our first meeting at Geneva. I saw in her a front-rank leader at the Pankhurst level, but with a less steely temperament. We talked incessantly for hours, and I was uplifted by meeting a number of women of first-class capability, clear mentality and firm determination. My visit coincided with the birthday of George Washington. I heard a speech of his read in the Senate Hall, and made the chance discovery that the reader was a far cousin of my own"

Gretta visited Pittsburgh and especially the steel district. A talk at lunchtime to the 'Hungry Club' of 300 well fed men was ironic and she found it hard not to make obvious jokes. She was more at home, subsequently, in a drawing-room meeting of women of the Jewish Council, and in an assembly of the Pennsylvania College for Women. Everywhere the call on her was for first-hand information about India, especially about the conditions of life and the status of Indian women.

"It was not always easy to convey the reality of a largely open-air life, with huts and cottages in the 700,000 villages of India as places of retirement for sleep, and not always so when the thermometer indicated anything from 80F to 100F+, to people whose life moved by car between office and flat, and to whom familiarity with nature was an occasional treat glimpsed between advertising boards along car-lined

---

100 **Alice Stokes Paul** (1885–1977) was an American suffragist, feminist, and women's rights activist, and one of the main leaders and strategists of the campaign for the Nineteenth Amendment to the U.S. Constitution, which prohibits sex discrimination in the right to vote. Paul initiated, along with others, carefully organised events such as the *Woman Suffrage Procession* and the *Silent Sentinels*, which were part of the successful campaign that resulted in the amendment's passage in 1920. Decades later she won a large degree of success with the inclusion of women as a group protected against discrimination by the Civil Rights Act of 1964.

roads. We came upon exceptions to this when we got disentangled from the large cities of the eastern States and emerged into the towns and open spaces from the 'mid-west' to the 'coast' which meant the Pacific. But that was not yet. I had to talk many times to Theosophists, women and the general public in the handsome city of Cleveland. In Detroit I had a similar crowded programme, into which I crammed a visit to the Ford motor works, to give thanks for the funny car I had been given years before in Madras. The nearest I got to Henry the 'Fordth' (as Jim called him behind his back) was his wife at an impressive meeting of the 'Women Voters' League'."

Back in New York, Anna Hempstead Branch,[101] a prominent poetess, saw possibilities in the coming together of the three poetical **C**'s in New York at this time, Joseph **C**ampbell, Padraic **C**olum and James **C**ousins, and gave a reception in Christodora House, with recitals of their own poems by the guests of honour. This was a happy ending to their visit to New York for Jim and Gretta.

On 2 April 1929 Gretta detoured to Madison, Wisconsin, to give talks in the University that held 5000 female students, while Jim went to Evanston, near Chicago, and hung Indian paintings under the auspices of the North Western University Guild in a hotel ball-room. At a big dinner party Jim gave an after-dinner talk on 'Hindu Conceptions of Beauty.' Next day he spoke on Indian Culture for the Renaissance Club of the University of Chicago.

Once back together, they dined at Hull House,[102] the community centre of Jane Addams, whom they had met at Adyar, when she was touring the orient. She headed the table, but did not contribute much to conversation. Jim took a late train for Iowa while Gretta slept at Hull House, or rather didn't sleep.

"I was awakened and kept awake by the awful blood-stench that the wind brought from the stock-yards, and the noises in the street that were associated with the traffic in animal slaughter. The agony and

---

101 **Anna Hempstead Branch** (1875 –1937) was an American regarded as a major poet during her lifetime. William Thomas Stead called her «the Browning of American poetry». 102 **Hull House** was a settlement house in the United States that was co-founded in 1889 by Jane Addams and Ellen Gates Starr. Located on the Near West Side of Chicago, Illinois, Hull House opened to recently arrived European immigrants. By 1911, Hull House had grown to 13 buildings. In 1912 the Hull House complex was completed with the addition of a summer camp, the Bowen Country Club. With its innovative social, educational, and artistic programs, Hull House became the standard bearer for the movement that had grown, by 1920, to almost 500 settlement houses nationally.

murder, the brutalising of the murderers, that the proximity to the vast slaughter-yards brought so close to me, aroused a flaming indignation in me, and an intense despair for the future of humanity while such fiendish barbarity was considered necessary to its well-being. I was sick all next day from the shock of realization of the sub-human level on which all but a handful of so-called civilized people lived. One touch of consolation was that my beloved and I had made our peace with the animal Kingdom, and would never, under any circumstances, be a party to the stupendous evil that would have to be atoned for before the alleged human race would attain a level of humanity. All the same, I got through a packed meeting of the Women's International League for Peace and Freedom, and a fine gathering of the Women's Republican Club. India was the subject for both."

Passing through Los Angeles overnight they arrived next day in Santa Barbara and the exquisite home of the Eichheims. Their garden was a horticultural show without being too excessive. Afternoons and evenings were given to musical at-homes, with Elizabeth Coolidge and Ethel Eichheim dividing accompaniments to Henry with his superb violin recitals. An at-home in their honour was a social, musical and literary occasion of a high order. Santa Barbara, was the 'the city of millionaires,' who came and filled the big drawing-room, through whose immense window the rhythmical outline of the mountains blended well with the music being created. It was magnificent, Gretta's contributions being warmly applauded. Jim, as joint guest of honour, recited some of his own poems, again received well by the appreciative guests.

A Hollywood friend drove them to the dock at Los Angeles on 7 September 1929. The six day journey to Honolulu was dull and stormy. On the morning of the thirteenth they were in sight of the Hawaiian Islands. A wireless telegram came from Mrs Swanzy.[103] inviting them to lunch. Jim describes their stay:

"I had heard of her from Padraic Colum, who had been her guest when on literary work in the islands. She was regarded as the hostess of Hawaii, and we replied accepting the invitation provided no other engagement had been made by friends with whom we were to stay during our four days between steamers. No other engagement had

103 **Mary Swanzy** (1882 – 1978) was an Irish landscape and genre artist, noted for her eclectic style. She painted in many styles including cubism, fauvism, and orphism, and was one of Ireland's first abstract painters.

been made, and our friends fell in with a little plan for us to stay in Mrs Swanzy's house on the top of Mount Tantalus, looking down into a happily extinct crater.

In addition to the small Theosophical group in Honolulu, a Lodge had been formed in the Schofield military barracks some miles into the country by a road that was mainly bounded on one side by sugar-cane and on the other by pineapples. The Commanding Officer was President of the Lodge. His Chief of Staff was Secretary. Among the membership of twenty or thirty were the chief Chaplain and several padres. We were driven out for an informal visit; but the lodge had set out dinner (all-vegetarian in a military camp of 14,000). After the meal there was an artistic and talkative get-together. Gretta played. We were driven home terribly late for respectable people, full of good food and heartiness, in bewitching moonlight."

# CHAPTER TWENTY-FIVE

### The conception of an All-Asian Women's Conference
### Home again, home again – jiggety jig
### Gretta launches the All-Asian Women's Conference

Among the occasions that came their way while still in Hawaii, one stands out which was to span hemispheres. They were invited to attend a sessional meeting of the 'Pan-Pacific Union of Women' in Honolulu prior to their departure for Adyar. Two hundred representatives of countries bordering that somewhat large stretch of water had gathered to discuss problems of human organisation, and had invited the Cousins as delegates, albeit unofficial ones. After all they hailed from a land that, not geographically within area, had much in common. Gretta noted a significant difference between the joyful and uplifting atmosphere of AIWC gatherings and what she was observing here:

> "There was nothing that led, no vision, no ascension, only efforts towards horizontal ameliorations in response to material necessity; all quite good, but inadequate because they omitted the raising of the quality of human life on which the quality of its organisation ultimately depends.
>
> I longed for a touch of the reverence, humanitarianism, the grace and beauty of Indian womanhood. Hence a thought: "Why not a Pan-Asian Conference of Women, in India?" Why not, indeed? It only needed some person or association to announce the idea and then organise the assured response. The idea became a fixation that turned itself into a slogan: 'The First All-Asian Women's Conference'."

After a generous farewell and much kindness they boarded the 20,000 ton 'Taiyo Maru' in the afternoon through a barrage of struggling passengers, coloured paper streamers and musical and unmusical 'alohas.' Soon they left Honolulu behind and headed for Japan.

On 27 September 1929 in the afternoon they had passed the lovely shapes of the coast on the edge of ceaselessly moving waters, and were welcomed at Yokohama. They were soon taken by train to Tokyo, where they were briefly put up in the Station Hotel.

Further travels brought them to Singapore. It was here that the press, the paparazzi of the day, were on their tail. The timing of their planned arrival preceded them. Both were sustained with lunch in a local Temple, seasoned with talk on religion and philosophy. There followed a lecture given by Gretta to a group of spiritually-awake women in which the subject and the possibility of an **All-Asian Women's Conference** was mooted.

Their continued journey brought them Malaysia at Penang – 25 October – where they docked for six hours. This was mercifully short in the steamy heat, and being from sunset to midnight there was no temptation for either of them to go ashore. As compensation an immense blue-black thunder-cloud formed above olive-green seas, with reds and golds around its edge. This was a magnificent site and set Jim off on one of his most colourful, imaginative and profound poems, 'The Fan.' [104] They finally arrived in Colombo harbour in Shri Lanka at 4.30am on the morning of 31 October 1929. Gretta realised that they had put –

"'A girdle round the earth,' not in Ariel's forty minutes, but in nine rich and picturesque months. Two days later, fourteen years from our first arrival, we were back in Adyar with the complex feeling that we had never been away and had just arrived for the first time."

\* \* \*

Two months later a call from America asking Jim to repeat his previous tour was answered and he left Madras on 28 April 1930. Gretta, having left her beloved on the steamer, began to throw herself into political agitation but at the same time felt impelled to push ahead with the launch of the 'All-Asian Women's Conference'.

Further agitation had become necessary as no progress had been made towards Home Rule and most Indians were finding it financially difficult to make ends meet. The process of non-cooperation initiated by Gandhi continued and peaked at a point when Gandhiji led the 'salt march' to the sea in order to separate salt from sea-water. This was symbolic, showing that Indians were prepared to produce their own salt rather than pay exorbitant prices charged by British India. Many goods in India were being taxed or imported and sold at high prices, cloth and salt were only two. Hence the enormous efforts made to produce home-spun cloth called khaddar. [105]

Gretta received a letter from Sarojini Naidu on 22nd May 1930.

---

104 'The Fan' – p.341 Collected Poems of James H Cousins. Available on the internet.
105 **Khadi** or **khaddar** was hand-spun, hand-woven fibre cloth from India, usually woven from cotton and may also include silk, or wool, are all spun into yarn on a spinning wheel called a *charkha.* It is a versatile fabric, cool in summer and warm in winter.

"My dear Gretta,

Tomorrow I shall probably be going to jail for a long or short period—who knows? I am sending you a word of greeting. I shall of course be useless as regards the Women's Conference for the present, but I am sure you will all carry on and make the year's record one of signal success. As for the Pan-Asian Conference of Women, do go on with its preparations. I am looking forward to it, and I hope I shall be free to attend it and to preside over it also."

Sarojini Naidu was indeed arrested the very next day and was in jail for several months. She had been arrested along with Gandhiji, Pundit Malaviyaji and Jawaharlal Nehru for taking part in the salt marches. Subsequently as a member of the Indian National Congress she participated in the 2nd Round Table Conference in London, along with Gandhi, (7 Sept -1 Dec1931).

During all the political hubbub Gretta had been carrying on her work as one of the secretaries of the 'Women's Indian Association' and as editor of its monthly magazine, "Stri Dharma". Feelers put out to women in various parts of Asia began to attract favourable responses for the creation of an **All-Asian** Women's Conference. Some months hence the annual session of the **All-India** Women's Conference would be held. It seemed sensible, then, to hold the All-Asian Conference while the machinery and personnel of such meetings were well-oiled and raring to go. The first step towards an All-Asian Women's Conference was a circular dated 12 March 1930 setting out the circumstances that made such a coming together not only desirable but necessary. The dates suggested were from 19 Jan to 25 Jan 1931, between meetings of the Pan-Pacific Women's Conference in Honolulu in August 1930 and the same in China in 1932. The invitation was signed by fourteen eminent Indian women, including: Sarojini Naidu, Dr Muthulakshmi Ammal, Dr Poonen-Lukhose, Lady Abdul Quadir, Mrs Rustomji Faridoonji, Lady Hydari, and Rajakumari Amrit Kaur.

Rani Lakshmibai Rajwade took up the secretary-ship, while Gretta had her hands full with the preceding **All-India** Womens Conference, booked for Lahore that year. The first **All-Asian** Conference took place 19-25 January 1931 also in Lahore. Sarojini Naidu had been elected President *in absentia*, she being still in prison. With her temporary absence it was agreed to have a different President for each day.

| | |
|---|---|
| Lady Bandernaike, | Ceylon |
| Mrs Kamal-ud-din, | Afghanistan |
| Miss May Oung, | Burma |

|                         |            |
|-------------------------|------------|
| Mrs Shirin Fozdar,[106] | Persia     |
| Dr Muthulakshmi,        | Madras     |
| Miss Hoshi,             | Japan      |
| Begum Hamid Ali,        | North India|

Gretta later quoted from the report she wrote after the Conference had ended.

"Thousands of men and women attended the opening ceremony of the Conference. The reception address was given by the premier Princess of the Punjab, the Maharani of Kapurthala; and the exchange of greetings in many languages, and the speeches of noted men as well as women, made a veritable synthesis of Asian kinship in the artistic surroundings of the unique event ... An immense pandal[107] beautifully decorated with palms and foliage, and the unfamiliar and colourful dresses of the visitors from abroad as well as the bright turbans of the Punjabis and the brilliant colours of the ladies saris, made an unforgettable scene . . .

The Resolutions were led by a delegate asking the women of Asia to preserve a high standard of spiritual consciousness uninfluenced by modern materialistic trends. Another expressed the opinion that, in order to promote a spirit of religious tolerance, the lives and teachings of great religious leaders should be taught in schools, and a comparative study of the great religions of the world should find a place in College curricula. No whisper of the conditions in India was allowed; but a Resolution was passed saying that, in order that every individual and every nation may have the unfettered right of self-expression for the enrichment of the human synthesis, the Conference considered it imperative that each country shall have full responsible self-government. . .

So potent was the seed sown, and so psychologically right was the moment of its planting that even on its second day of the Conference was enabled to wield international influence of a powerful kind, for the cables that it sent to the Japanese and Persian members of the Council of the League of Nations, asking them to vote for the reconsideration of the unequal nationality rights accorded to women in the Draft of the international codification of laws, turned the attitude of the Council in favour of the request of world-womanhood, and secured the

---

106 **Mrs Shirin Fozdar** was a well-known member of the Baha'i Faith from Persia (Iran) who was particularly interested in equality for men and women in all things, one of the core principles of her Faith.
107 **Pandal**: A marquee.

establishment of the first 'Committee of Women' called by the League of Nations to submit women's views on matters directly affecting their interests.

Among other pioneer Resolutions was that a woman should have the same right as a man to choose her nationality, and that marriage should not compel her automatically to take her husband's nationality.

A second session of the All-Asian Women's Conference was planned for 1935 in Japan or Java, but circumstances prevented this, and later the matter was taken up by a group of fine forward-looking women in western Asia. I had a private weep of satisfaction over the extraordinary success that had come out of my dreams along the east coast of Asia a little more than a year previously.

# CHAPTER TWENTY-SIX

## Gretta observes the increasing agitation for Home Rule Crisis call to the USA because of Jim's ill-health

Prior to the first All Asian Women's Conference in Jan 1931, Gretta had observed the development of increased agitation for Home Rule. During April 1930 Gretta, together with a lady friend, attended a meeting on Madras beach not intending to speak, but just to feel what was happening in the emotions of the masses.

> "And such a crowd! Immense, quiet, orderly, dignified. The crush was so great that the full number of speakers could not make their way to the platform. To keep the attention of the multitude engaged I was asked to say something to them. There was no loud speaker then, but what I said was heard over a large area and well received. My friend and I started for our car to get back to Adyar. We walked through the crowd without the least trouble. Just as we got into the car, a posse of mounted police turned on to the beach road. I felt they would incense the people with their show of force. And so it happened.
>
> To safeguard a few Europeans, who were taking the air in their cars by the edge of the beach, the police were ordered to disperse the crowd. In that wholly unnecessary process, as we learned next morning, four people were killed and many injured. This brought individuals and associations into the struggle for freedom of speech who otherwise would have kept aloof. The authorities put a gag on the city for fourteen days."

In these developing circumstances Gretta found her own position delicate and difficult. One of the stock arguments against the increasing part that Indians were taking in the political movement was that they only did so because Gretta led them.

> "Because of this my name was not wanted among the signatories to telegrams of protest to the Viceroy and the Governor of Madras by the Women's Indian Association, which was non-political. The press and the telegraph offices were gagged. Mr Rajagopalachariar,[108] one of the

---

108 **Rajagopalachariar** was the last Governor-General of India, as India soon became a Republic in 1950. He was known affectionately as Rajaji.

political leaders, had been arrested on April 30. The news of this was brought personally by courier to Madras, as it was not allowed to appear in the press."

The arrest of Rajagopalachariar was followed on 5 May 1930 by the arrest of Gandhiji.[109] All India was aroused to demonstrations of protest. The criss-cross of feeling was shown two days later when the crowd on the beach recognised Mrs Besant driving that way as usual. She had become unpopular through her temerity in opposing Gandhiji's breaking down of respect for authority. The crowd, knowing nothing of the principles of the matter, and of her strong-unity with him in ideals, although not agreeing with his tactics, insulted her and tried to prevent her from driving along the Marina. Tension was rising and things were beginning to get out of hand.

Gretta records:

"On May 12 Rukmini Lakshmipati was the first woman to be sentenced in Madras for sedition. She had a 10 minute trial which ended in 12 months simple imprisonment. Four days later my beloved 'spiritual daughter' Kamaladevi became the second woman victim, with nine months simple imprisonment. Sarojini Naidu on May 23 was the third. Even before that men would come to me in a kind of secret way and tell me how their lives were made miserable by shadowing and suspicion. Some of them were starving, and it hurt me that my own circumstances in Adyar did not permit my giving them anything to eat, as I was not in a house of my own. One such caller just came for sympathy. An ashram[110] in which he was a resident had suddenly been surrounded by police and all present were put under arrest, and were later scattered over thirty or more houses. A vakil (lawyer) was arrested while saluting the unofficial flag of India. I had greatly admired his Krishna dance which he also performed in front of the flag. At his trial he told the court that the 'dance' had called to the artist in him—which was worthy of India's best idealism. And there were other touches that lightened the darkness of tyranny. While Kamaladevi was in the lock-up in Bombay awaiting trial, one of her permitted letters was to me, and she began it with: "Today I lay forward my claim to be your spiritual daughter and disciple." What an honour for me!'"

---

109 Gandhiji was a more familiar name showing respect and love for the person. In this case Mohandas Gandhi. Apparently he did not like being called Mahatma – meaning Great Soul.

110 **Ashram:** a hermitage, monastic community, or other place of religious retreat.

The Women's Indian Association was roused into action to organise a meeting, which was really a bid for free speech. For some days it was not known whether it would be prohibited or permitted. Even the planning of such a meeting gave quite an upsurge of popularity for the WIA. Gretta spent much time hunting for speakers without much success. There was plenty of appreciation for their courage in even attempting the meeting. In order to keep within the rules they had to limit themselves to talking on Dominion Status[111] and the Round Table Conference and refrained from speaking Satyagraha[112] though most of them were 'red hot inside' with the news that along with Sarojini Naidu 2000 other volunteers had been arrested after being beaten with lathis (rods). One hundred required hospitalisation. Gretta had been very angry at such mass injustice:

"Such treatment of unarmed and unresisting, patriotic people screwed me up almost to breaking point. I longed to protest in the most public way possible against the pain, shame, horror of the infamous treatment meted out by the foreign authority to people asking for the rudiments of human liberty and citizenship, and under the tutelage of Mahatma Gandhi offering no hand of defence against such treatment.

I do not recount these matters with any rancour carried over from that time, but as a frank indication of historical circumstances through which one nation passed in order to free itself from the unnatural over-lordship of another. The wrong that man has committed on man is due to a human failing. It can only be eradicated, I believe, by three generations of education directed towards international knowledge and sympathy through the culture of the individual, and by the influence of women at least on the same level as that of men in the affairs of life."

In spite of the restrictions put on the subject matter of the meeting of the Women's Indian Association, or perhaps as a reaction to them, it drew a fine platform of speakers and some straight speaking in showing why Dominion Status should be granted, and what the Round Table Conference[113] should set a goal itself for a self-governing Dominion. Gretta's own speech got an inch in the long reports in the press which said:

---

111 **Dominion status** was formally **defined** in the Balfour Declaration of 1926, which recognised these countries as «autonomous Communities within the British Empire», thus acknowledging them as political equals of the United Kingdom for example India.
112 **Satyagraha** – roughly translated as "insistence on truth", "loyalty to the truth" (*satya* «truth»). *agraha* «insistence» or «holding firmly to» or *holding onto truth*[1] or *truth force* – is a particular form of nonviolent resistance or civil resistance.
113 **The Round Table Conferences** of 1930–32 were a series of three conferences organized by the British Government to discuss constitutional reforms.

"The English people should voluntarily give up what was asked. After all they were not giving away anything that was theirs but only withdrawing from what they had seized."

Saying this at that time was verging on sedition. Through all her turbulence of mind Gretta felt support flowing to her from all sorts of people who read the straightforward things she had said in public. They felt she was being brave for them, but how was she to make them brave for themselves?

While these exciting and inspiring activities absorbed Gretta, letters from Jim in America indicated he was suffering from ill-health. She thought he was probably over-working. Concentration on the work in hand, no matter how trivial or remote from his own private interests, was his way of working. But the effect sometimes showed itself in a 'slump' in the level of his energy with some manifest signs of depression. Gretta was not sure that she wanted to desert India at this difficult time. Also financial concerns were a significant issue. On balance, however, visiting him would present opportunities to perform some 'scattering of facts' about India, information that did not get through the censorship.

She tracked down a cargo-passenger service, and secured a passage. On arrival in New York she spied Jim from the upper deck and her life was colourful again. It was 3 July 1931. Events continued both on the artistic front, the musical front and the women's equality front. All this time, however, there was anxiety and a hunger for detailed and real news from India and not the fake news filtering through.

They both remained in New York. Jim describes their ulterior motive.

"I was approaching sixty, five years beyond the retirement age for appointments in India. But India had shown no signs of wanting me at any age; and it was necessary to make some hay while the mental and physical sun shone. My year at the College in the City of New York would, barring unforeseen expenses, let me go back to India with a nest-egg with which to meet our financial destiny. And so we set out to make our composite room a social and artistic centre, as if we were to inhabit it for ever."

# CHAPTER TWENTY-SEVEN

## Setting off home to India with a detour to the League of Nations

In July of 1932 they left American soil and headed east-ward. Jim mused, which he did often in his poetic moments, sometimes for hours.

"And now, with funds sufficient to keep us for five years, as a result of my tour in the United States, we speculated on the possibility of my spending a year on the Island of Capri for the sole purpose of immersing myself in the myth, traditions and history of that romantic Island and writing whatever I was able to do in the time. With this in mind we got through the appalling scrimmage over baggage and landing at Naples, where nearly all of the 1742 passengers on the 'Augustus,' mainly Italians from the east side of New York on holiday, struggled and squeezed and gabbled and gesticulated, as if Italy might run away in five minutes and leave them marooned at sea.

We were at the home of our Dutch lady-artist friend, Emilie Van Kerckhoff,[114] at Anacapri by 9pm July 11. We were entitled to a collapse after eight hours of mental and physical tension. But the repose, the friendliness, the art, the piano, the ideal innocent supper, made it morning to us. Gretta played. We all talked in moonlight on the loggia until midnight."

Despite their desires to remain on this beautiful Island they knew that India was their true home. They left Capri on 8 August 1932 for the next stage of their journey, arriving in Milan soon after. Gretta became engrossed in activities on equal nationality for women. She survived five days of long committee meetings, while Jim went to Ascona to take part in the school of spiritual studies at the home of Madame Frobe-Kapteyn[115] on the edge of Lake Maggiore.

---

114 **Emilia van Kerckhoff** was a Dutch artist, born in Zwolle in 1867. In 1898 she settled with her partner, the sculptor Saar de Swart, in Laren (Noord-Holland). In 1918 they moved to Capri (Italy), where they had lived and worked for many years. Van Kerckhoff travelled to many North African and Asian countries. In her drawings and illustrations, she depicted the everyday life of Java, Bali, Japan, India and Egypt. She also painted flowers, birds and butterflies.

115 **Olga Fröbe-Kapteyn** (1881 – 1962) was a Dutch spiritualist, theosophist, and scholar who gained recognition in the 1920s.

On 1 September they were back in Geneva in the home of the Sellegers at Grand Sacconex. Their return had coincided, not by chance, with a meeting of the League of Nations.

Jim describes:

"Ireland, in the person of De Valera, head of the Irish Free State, was to be very much in evidence. He was to preside over the opening of the Council of the League of Nations, and at the assembly of the League was to hand over his Presidency to his successor. And, while Ireland was President of the 'world', we felt we should be there to gloat over the leader of a mere three million people telling the representatives of the rest of the world 'something' indeed 'anything'. Gretta had a still brighter idea. It was time that India, now where Ireland had been sixteen years previously, should make herself heard through free minds and voices instead of through muzzled and tutored officials. The idea found immediate response. An India Day was planned. Mrs Emmeline Pethick-Lawrence agreed to come from London for the occasion.

The Council of the League of Nations was to be opened on September 23, and we thought it well to call on the permanent Irish delegation to the League and put in our claim for admission. To our intense pleasure the permanent 'delegation', was in the form of one man. Sean Lister, though he had a southern Christian name, was a fellow Belfast man, on intimate terms with my brother Willie,[116] who was director of technical education in Northern Ireland. Permits were arranged and an invitation received for a reception next evening at the rooms of Sean.

We had a short chat with De Valera. Behind his tall dark clothing and his furrowed face, there was a radiation of human kindness, and an abstemiousness in smokes and drinks that was lighted up by humour. He was interested in Gretta's social work and my cultural advocacy in India, but the end of our chat was a request that we come home to Ireland.

Next day, 23 September, De Valera presided over the opening of the Council. Gretta and I waited at the stage door to greet him and his entourage, and then, duty done, scurry to our seats. There was no 'conquering hero' about the man who had been condemned to death by Britain for his part in the Irish rebellion of 1916, whose execution was cancelled when it was discovered that he was born American, and who was now in the highest seat of world honour. He walked slowly from

116 **Willie:** The author's grandfather, WD Cousins.

his car in his black hat and black clothes, as near the mournful garb of the Catholic priest as a layman could venture. But there was a friendly gleam in his eyes. Our seats in the Council Hall were amongst those of a bevy of continental women with whom Gretta was something of a lioness, as she had been made a member of the Women's Committee of the League of Nations.

In a talk with De Valera, Gretta raised the question of equal nationality of men and women. "It was very interesting," Gretta said to me afterwards, "to hear him unfold his character, narrow, formally righteous, clean principled, church ridden. He would not nominate me for the Committee on Equal Nationality for fear of criticism from his party followers; but he would support women's equality.""

Four days later a group of women waited on him as President of the League of Nations, on the subject of India. "A damp squib," Gretta reported. "He asked for no publicity, for reasons which were not given and we could not surmise."

India Day was celebrated on 6 October. Morning saw a business session when an International Committee for India was formed. From 15 countries 28 societies had sent 50 delegates. In the evening the big hall of the Salle Centrale was filled for a public meeting with Mrs Pethick-Lawrence as its central figure. There were a number of excellent speeches including one by Gretta. Then on 8 October she attended an emergency meeting of the Equal Nationality Committee. Next day she returned from a meeting of the League at which an Irish member opposed the women's resolution, thus causing its defeat.

Finally, on 11 October Gretta, after many eminent farewells and much packing, left for India full of missionary zeal for freedom, and accompanied by warm admiration for her initiative and her organising ability. What she was going to do was not yet clear. As for Jim, he had a feeling that the Celtic Gods would not be far away, and that the fourteen sonnets he had composed concerning the world situation would fulfil themselves in due course. He remained in Geneva.

# CHAPTER TWENTY-EIGHT

## GRETTA TAKES THE OVERLAND ROUTE TO INDIA
### Stopover in Haifa, Israel
### Meets the Guardian of the Bahá'í Faith

Gretta left Geneva for India on 11 October 1932.

She wanted to make personal contacts with the women of western Asia of whose fine qualities she had read in various magazines. She decided to travel by the overland route via the Persian Gulf. From Jaffa, on 17 October, she was escorted by two Jewish ladies to Tel Aviv, then throbbing with fresh life and anticipation. From there she was driven over bare hills to Jerusalem. Accompanied again by the same two ladies, she was taken on the next day to Old Jerusalem. They passed through narrow streets, displaying an enticing mixture of foods, smells and flies, before reaching to the Wailing Wall. Next she was taken to the Church of the Holy Sepulchre, the place of the Crucifixion, the Mosque of Omar, Gethsemane, Kedron, and finally to the Hebrew University. She ended the day with a successful meeting of the Jewish Women's Association.

The Shrine of the Báb at the Bahá'í World Centre in the port of Haifa, Israel
(picture taken in recent years)

"The New Jerusalem was not at all like my childish imagination of it, when I sang of it in the Methodist meeting-house in the west of Ireland; it seemed to be all shops and sales, with no golden gates or hosannas.

Next morning I had a drive to Haifa, some three hours away, and after eating a preliminary orange sitting in an Arab street, I lunched at the Labour Co-operative Hospital, and made a special examination of the maternity and baby wards. In the afternoon I went to see the house and prison of 'Abdu'l-Baha,[117] of whose life and sayings I had been one of the earliest readers in Ireland. On the way I stopped a driver from brutally whipping a horse. I slept overnight in the Baha'i home of purity and affection in order to have an interview next morning with the head of the movement, Shoghi Effendi.[118] He was thirty-five, a Persian exquisite, perfumed, manicured, dressing perfectly and with a lovely voice. One could see from his quick disposal of items that came and went, while we chatted on all sorts of things, that he was a born administrator."

A longer drive took her to Beirut. At a tea-party of some forty people in a private home she spoke of India and its women. The beautiful and clever Nazik al-Abid Bayhum then took her on foot to her own home, an Arabian Nights dream of artistic beauty. They had immediately taken a liking to each other.

Nazik was known as the 'Joan of Arc of the Arabs' and an activist for women's rights, as well as a critic of Ottoman and French colonialism in Syria. She was the first woman to earn rank in the Syrian Arab Army for her role in forming the 'Red Star Society', which was a precursor to the 'International Red Cross' and the 'Red Crescent Movement'. She was a revolutionary for national independence and women's right to work and vote in Syria.

Gretta spoke at several gatherings in Beirut, scattering knowledge about women's progress in India and its struggle for external and internal freedom.

Next she headed for Baghdad on 25 October in a big bus with seventeen other passengers, Gretta being the only westerner. She was repelled by the heat and dust of the desert. The fatigue of an all-day and all-night drive totally exhausted her. The only break in a 550 miles journey was breakfast at a rest-house. Grubbiness and fatigue were forgotten when she absorbed the

---

117 **'Abdu'l-Baha** (1844-1921) was the son of the Founder of the Bahá'í Faith, Bahá'u'lláh, who died in 1892. Shoghi Effendi was the Guardian of the Faith. The core beliefs are in One God, One Faith and One Human Race. Bahá'ís work for world peace and equal opportunity for male and female in all aspects of life, amongst many other principles. It has spread to every country of the world since its inception in May 1844.
118 **Shoghi Effendi** was the grandson of 'Abdu'l-Bahá.

excellent hospitality of the Standt household including a look over Baghdad with its unique costumes and customs. Dr and Mrs Standt were joint Heads of a school of four hundred boys. Gretta spoke to the school about her experiences with students in India.

On 27 October Gretta was received by the Queen of Iraq, accompanied by her two daughters and an English companion. They had a pleasant hour of chat on various topics concerning the place of women in the new circumstances within her country.

Her plans suddenly received an unanticipated extension with an invitation to a Women's Conference in Teheran, the capital of Persia (Iran). So, on 30 October she was up and ready at 4.30am for the long journey to Teheran. The car to take them at seven came at six. The next few days were, to say the least, harassing.

"On the edge of the desert we got a puncture. The flow of petrol failed sixteen times during the day. At night I tried to sleep in a small rest-house; but dogs, motor noises, cold, as well as a sore throat and mouth, kept me awake most of the night. Two of the ladies slept in the car. Next day we stopped at an American Mission hospital, and the doctor, on noticing my symptoms, strongly advised me to return to Baghdad. A good night's rest in a hotel and fresh morning air and breath-taking sky colours, reconciled me to returning in spite of the disappointment of not reaching Tehran.

I had a good talk with the Consul of Iraq in Kermanshaw, in Iran, and got my visa fixed up. I found a seat in a car for Baghdad. Time was lost by the usual puncture, also by a long wrangle between the driver and a fearsome armed soldier who insisted on getting a free lift. So we missed the train at the frontier, and I was faced with another night in my clothes with no sign of adequate accommodation, and no grasp of local language in which to express my bodily needs. Happily a Muslim woman offered me a shake-down in a corner of her home. It was probably the hen-house, as cocks and hens were roosted above a sheet that was stretched between them and me. Next morning the driver who had brought me thus far had no passport into Iraq. Luckily I was able to get a perch on the top of cotton bales in a transport lorry that would take me the seven miles to the nearest station within Iraq. Here I found myself in a queer tangle. I was challenged about vaccination. If I told the *exact* truth I could neither go forward nor backward. I decided on the lesser evil, and wrote less than the truth on the form in a language unknown to me. A dirty train took me over the desert back to Baghdad, for the last stage of my overland journey, from Baghdad to Basra."

After another twenty-four nightmare hours across the desert, smothered in dust, Gretta finally arrived at Basra at 6.30am. Thankfully she met a friendly face, Anis, who gave her a cordial welcome. She had known him in Adyar. All facilities for getting over fatigue and dirt were laid on. After tea there was a public meeting under the auspices of the Theosophical Lodge in Basra. Gretta pleaded with them for unity and friendship, and for a concerted effort to put women in the new Iraqi programme following the attainment of State sovereignty. This stirred some of the women present, who urged Gretta to draft a letter to the authorities. In the afternoon the letter was written and approved. She was then escorted to the steamer that was to take her to Karachi.

After a restful passage, feeling that she had done something useful on her journey through the middle-east, she arrived in Karachi on the morning of 10 November 1932. The Indian official refused to sign her passport, and passed it over to a young Englishman. After many questions and answers, she was permitted to land.

Gretta instantly sensed a change of atmosphere in the India she had left a year and a half previously. She met a large body of friends in order to report on her travels, but they were not as interested as usual. They seemed to have too much on their minds with regard to their own affairs to get excited about the affairs of others.

# CHAPTER TWENTY-NINE

## BACK IN BELOVED INDIA
### Into the thick of it – arrested
### Convicted and incarcerated in 'the prison on the hill'

When she reached Bombay (Mumbai) Gretta set matters in motion for a visit to Mahatma Gandhi in the Yerrawada jail, near Poona. By chance she saw Gandhiji's right-hand man, C. Rajagopalachariar, on the railway platform. Following a one minute whisper, out of ear-shot of anyone who might be listening, she managed to get his approval for her decision to defy the Ordinances against free speech and risk imprisonment herself.

On 20 November 1932 she had a sudden call informing her she could now visit Gandhiji. Remembering her own experiences of jail interviews twenty years previously she expected at least two warders present to listen carefully to everything being said, to try and catch a whiff of sedition. To her surprise they were alone in the courtyard and took turns at questions and answers.

"I told him what happened in Geneva at the League. He asked about the Women's Indian Association and sent his love to Dr Muthulakshmi Reddi. I told him of my intention to oppose the ban on public speech. He would not discuss this. It would be against his obligations as a prisoner. When I left him, after twenty-five minutes of happy give-and-take and the realisation of his unshakable rectitude, his secretary, Mahadev Desai, escorted me to the outer door, and told me this was the first item of a new regime, when Bapu[119] could see people quite alone.

From one jail I went to another at Belgaum to see my beloved Kamaladevi. I found her shrunken in body, but strong in nerve, and indomitable in will. With such brave and wise women as she and others in mind I faced southwards with determination and confidence. My first step after arriving in Madras was to seek out a lawyer of known Indian sympathy, Mr K Bhasyam, and plan the opening of a systematic attack on the Ordinances that had choked the expression of the people. Having come from the free air of America and Europe I was exasperated at the meanness of the British bureaucracy in extending

---

119 **Bapu** is a word for «father» in many Indian languages such as Gujarati and Marathi. The title was used to honour Mohandas Gandhi (1869–1948), officially known as 'Father' of the Nation.

rule by Ordinance[120] from three to ten months, then to five years, and, crowning evidence of the breakdown of foreign ruler-ship, the incorporation of what was at first said to be an emergency expedient into the law of the land....

At an enormous meeting on Madras beach, of which Kasturbai Gandhi,[121] wife of Mahatmaji, was the central figure, I was asked to make a short speech. I have no memory or record of what I said, but it gave me a mass contact that I was soon to follow up. Three days later, 3 December 1932, a public protest meeting was held in Gokhale Hall that Mrs Annie Besant had built for free speech.[122]

On 7 December destiny began to show its face. A thousand responsible people assembled at a meeting on the beach at which I was the chief speaker and urged the people to exercise free speech. I was followed by an Indian man who declared that he would defy the Ordinances. An English police officer ordered the speaker to stop. I broke in and said I endorsed all the man had said. The sergeant, after some hesitation, arrested me, and conducted me to Beach Road between lines of volunteers shouting slogans in my favour. He proceeded to hand me over to a superior officer, but was as much as told not to be a fool— and I was sent home to Ammu Swaminathan's."

Two days later at 7.30 am a notice was served on Gretta at Ammu's home by a plain-clothes policeman. It was preliminary to arrest, so she went over to Adyar to settle her affairs. She looked in at an evening meeting in the Headquarters Hall of the Theosophical Society when word came that two men, looking like policemen, wanted to see her outside. As she did not wish to have the Society mixed up with her personal activities, she politely asked the officers not to arrest her there and then, but to come to Mrs Swaminathan's. They agreed. Gretta was subsequently lodged in the penitentiary, where she had a sleepless night due to a bright light that kept burning.

"It is not necessary to go into the preliminaries of police formality leading up to my trial next day. From what I learned afterwards I got

120 **Ordinances** are laws promulgated by the President of India on the recommendation of the Union Cabinet. They could only be issued when Parliament was not in session. They enabled the Indian government to take immediate legislative action. The mechanism of implementing Ordinances in the 1930s is not clear. What was clear - they were prolonged **well after** their expected date of cancellation.

121 **Kasturbai Gandhi**, was a political activist and the wife of Mohandas Karamchand Gandhi. In association with her husband, Kasturba was involved in the Indian independence movement in British-ruled India.

122 **Annie Besant** died in September 1933.

press coverage that a successful boxer or a film star might envy. But the matter of personality did not count with me. The urge for freedom was born with me and any individual or group that tried to interpret its own freedom as freedom to tyrannise others brought the seven centuries' struggle of my beloved Ireland to a point of indignation that showed itself in action. It will suffice for this record if I include a condensed report of my 'speech from the dock' which I gave in reply to the magistrate's question asking me if I had anything to say:

"The fact that I am on trial in this court today is no accident. It is the result of seventeen years of intimate living and working with my Indian sisters and brothers. In moving freely with them in attempting to do constructive work, I and my husband learned how exploitation and injustice through foreign rule is crushing them down. I was a co-worker for Home Rule for years with Annie Besant, and took part in the agitation connected with her internment in this cause. I also shared in formulating the Commonwealth of India Bill. Government repression of organised Congress opinion, the largest representative opinion in India, has become ever more severe since then. I watched it in 1930-31. I reported what I had seen, in New York and Geneva during my visits there in the past eighteen months. In those centres of international opinion I laid bare the dual game Britain is playing; its pretence of making a Constitution to give India freedom, but its determination to hold tight to everything essential to India's self-government. I showed that its demands for unity and social reforms as necessary to swaraj[123] were conditions such as no country had ever complied with.

I proved that, instead of freedom, government by Ordinances was designed to break the spirit, ruin the health and cripple the resources of all the people of India who are determined to win the political freedom they want. Representative associations of eighteen countries have deputed me to tell the people here that they "sympathise with them, and that they denounce the rule of violence now imposed on India," as the New York protest meeting expressed it.

Now that I return, I find that the Ordinances have been turned into law for three years. This is a challenge to every believer in free speech, free political assembly, free press, free picketing and free

---

123 Self-government or independence for India.

peaceful self-expression. I adhere to everything I said in public. I reiterate that the Ordinance Bill and Ordinance Law should be made inoperative by everyone ignoring them by nonviolent defiance. Evidently the Government think me a valuable ally of the Congress when they priced my freedom by bail at thirty thousand rupees. If it is their intention to strike me dumb for a year, are we to deduce that their new Constitution is going to be so unsatisfactory that I must be locked up for all that time to prevent my criticism of it? If this is British justice and democracy, then I am proud to stand here in support of free speech and Indian national freedom, and I am ashamed that English idealism has fallen to the present depths of oppression and suppression."

At the end of the trial, on 10 Dec 1932, the judge decided that Gretta was to be sentenced to "simple imprisonment for one year" or until such time as she would execute a bond for Rs.10,000, and furnish two sureties of Rs.5,000 each to be of good behaviour for a year. She was then escorted to the Madras Penitentiary for two sleepless nights feeling anything but penitent. Dr Muthulakshmi brought her influence to bear on the Government and had her residence moved to the women's prison at Vellore,[124] some eighty miles from Madras.

On Monday at 1pm she was escorted, together with her baggage, by three police officers. They all boarded the train to Katpadi, where she was transferred to the Black Maria for Vellore, three miles away. She had been so meek and mild on the two-hour railway journey that her escorts were not prepared for a sudden impulsive move by this feisty Irishwoman, who had been reared on the backs of ponies and the front seats of country carriages. Gretta suddenly reverted to type.

"When my baggage was safely stowed away I suddenly climbed into the empty seat beside the driver, with the triple escort looking as if they didn't know where they were. I fancy one horn of their dilemma was that they didn't want to be made fools by creating a scene, and the other horn was that they could not spin out the necessary red-tape to have me dethroned by order. So they succumbed, and I assisted in driving them to Vellore Women's Jail, where I was welcomed at the gate by the Governor, Major Khan, as nice a jailer as anyone could wish for, who in the course of time suffered for acting on the unofficial idea that his prisoners were human beings."

---

124 **Vellore Central Prison** (Set up in 1830) is a prison for women.

Tea time came after admission when she was welcomed by a number of women political prisoners on a patch of green grass in front of her cell. Picketing foreign cloth shops and inducing people to go to shops where khaddar, both home-spun & woven, was sold, was their chief crime. For some unknown reason Gretta was given a second cell, which became her study and created a buffer between her bedroom and a condemned cell in which a young woman was awaiting execution for alleged murder.

The political wing, had a fair amount of communication with the outer world. Newspapers were allowed, and they learned, three days after her arrival, that the Corporation of Madras had been heroic enough to pass an adjournment motion protesting against her arrest.

Jim was still in Geneva on 10 December when the urgent cable arrived, sent by Ammu Swaminathan stating:

## "GRETTA SENT VELLORE. ONE YEAR. SIMPLE."[125]

The telegram had been swift. She was now in the 'prison on the hill'. The Italian press reported her as remanded in custody for "disseminating sedition." This had also been published in the London Times.

Gretta settled in and decided to help where and when she could to improve the lot of her fellow prisoners both political and non-political.

"I fell into a daily routine of rising at daybreak, ablution, meditation and chota hazri (breakfast). I walked a mile each morning, six times round the enclosure of the political wing. I spun a while, and conducted classes in civics, singing and needlework. For community exercise I succeeded in getting a piece of ground levelled and the equipment for badminton. The periods for this were later restricted by underlings on the grounds that we were much too happy for prisoners. Lock-up time was 6pm. A festivity the day before Christmas was the first birthday celebration of baby Meenu, a dear little person whom we all loved. The celebration was a meal of Indian preparation on the badminton court.

A fortnight after my admission I felt the need of some regular responsible duty. This I could only get under the term 'hard labour.' So I applied for hard labour, and was made superintendent of my block. I interpreted my labour as beautifying the place. I applied for seedlings to make a garden in a waste corner; and in due time we enjoyed watching tiny shoots developing into lovely flowers. I applied for a sand-box for children to play in, and got it and also a cane chair

125 'Simple' sentence meant straight forwards without hard labour, deportation or other conditions.

in which I could sit comfortably for reading the books that friends sent and that had passed the censorship of the ignorant office clerk.

There were festive occasions, admissions and releases that gave us chances of dressing up. We had been denied freedom of speech and movement; so we denied ourselves freedom from the need of a priest. At the festival of Pongal (harvest) in the middle of January, in a prison cell, we did puja (worship). Two babies were enthroned as representatives of deity. I as an Irish Methodist, was accepted as a kind of high priest robed in my best saree.

Routine was varied by visitors. My dear Dr Muthulakshmi, that great-hearted woman, brought a gramophone. K. Bhasyam brought welcome fruit and news of more arrests in muzzled Madras. A choice selection of four husbands was escorted from the men's jail to have a strictly guarded interview with their wives. I was not one of them, but I felt in my bones that my time would come.

Records of Indian songs were found in the jail office. I felt that the pleasure of playing them on the gramophone should not be restricted to the political prisoners alone and, after some official humming and hawing, I got leave to give a weekly recital to what we called 'our other sisters,' - women under life sentences.

The recounting of these incidents may sound as if imprisonment was a rest-cure. But there were clouds in the azure sky. I felt I was being viewed naked, when I saw one of Jim's letters, which were always at the very highest of perfect love, being read, before delivery to me, by the ignorant jail clerk. Through visitors I learned of letters that had not been given to me. Letters had come from friends and sympathisers in daily half dozen's. Even a request for the names and addresses of the writers was refused. But one letter from Jim brought me joy with seven of his best sonnets, showing that his mastery of that difficult form of verse was still with him. From Jim also I received a copy of 'The Story of San Michele,' which fascinated me with its revelation of strong personality and humaneness. But a snag was that press cuttings from Jim were thrown into the waste-paper basket. Later a concession was made and I was allowed to read letters addressed to me, but not to keep them."

Visitors got to know their way to Vellore, and soon enriched their tea-times with cakes and jams, almonds and raisins. Respect for Gretta and the other political prisoners rose perceptibly when an important Government official brought a number of gramophone records of classical western music for her special pleasure.

* * *

After some time Gretta was able to write to Jim in Geneva. The letter was partly redacted. In it she suggested with vaguely disguised phrases that he might return to India, as there *might* be something useful for him to do, suggesting also that he *might* 'summer' in North India. The reason behind Gretta's hint that Jim might return to India came in a letter from Madanapalle College appealing to him to return. His work would be that of general supervisor, designated Principal. He was asked to cable YES or NO to the offer to teach again. Next day he walked to San Michele during which he decided to make up his mind. Finally he cabled back – **YES**.

Things began to shape up towards the next phase of Gretta's future. She received word from Jim of his acceptance of the call to teach at Madanapalle College. Captain and Mrs Sellon and Professor and Mrs Wood came to Vellore, but it was not visitors' day and they were refused entry. A message was given to Gretta, however, to the effect that Dr Cousins' appointment as Principal of Madanapalle College had now received all the necessary official approvals.

In spite of these occasional pieces of good news it was tough going physically for Gretta:

"The brainlessness and heartlessness of my surroundings, and perhaps a state of irritability induced by the growing and inescapable heat of a tropical summer, gave me a bad time. We were not allowed to sleep out, though shade maximum temperature was 104F, and minimum was above the summer heat that gives sunstroke in England. I was so exhausted one evening that I fell asleep on the floor of my cell. I lost the urge to write. I had exhausted all reading matter."

On the anniversary of Gretta's wedding, April 9, her fellow prisoners wakened her with songs and flowers. In the afternoon they recited poems by Rabindranath Tagore and James H. Cousins, followed by a tableau[126] and dances. Prison staff were annoyed that all the prisoners seemed 'too happy', so more restrictions were put in place: badminton was stopped, drafts and ludo were withdrawn. Gretta wrangled over these idiotic restrictions with official visitors, and over restrictions in books and food. She discovered that it all came from the underlings, *not* from the Governor. Life was becoming boring. The heat burned the eyes. They had no exercise. Some respite came after rain, when she was able to plant a tree and weed the garden.

Diversion came with news of a threatened fast by Gandhiji. Gretta resolved to fast at the same time. However, 'Bapu' was soon released and called for a

---

126 **A tableau** vivant (often shortened to **tableau**) is French for 'living picture'. It's a static scene containing one or more actors or models. They are stationary and silent, usually in costume, carefully posed, with props and/or scenery, and may be theatrically lit.

cessation of Civil Disobedience for a month, and for the release of all political prisoners. Government refused his offer, and shadowy hopes of release were abandoned.

Then came Jim's first visit. His way to her from Capri via Sind and the Kangra Valley had been signalled by lovely poems and letters. Then, on 3 June 1933, at 2pm he was there:

> "He was thinner than when I left him in Europe nine months before, but in glowing health, while I had put on twelve pounds, probably for want of my customary energetic movements when free. Novelists have sentimentalised over love's first kiss. Few of them have shared the ecstasy of reunion under scrutiny in a jail office, after long separation and after thirty years of union in service to humanity. We were given an hour. Talk on politics was barred. But there was much to recount on both sides that was not 'seditious'."

Gretta added a course in First Aid to her skills. The details of this revolted her but she went ahead, sat for the exam and earned her certificate. She then began to experience a new and very upsetting symptom:

> "I became impatient for release. Imprisonment was, in my case, wastefully useless either as a punishment or as a deterrent. I would not rest while life lasted until India was free. But I had an almost overwhelming desire to scale walls and join my beloved in the solution of problems that were making the beginnings of his second term at Madanapalle not too happy."

At the end of six months thirteen of Gretta's fellow prisoners were released. Farewells to them were times for jollification, but she had a private sinking feeling of being left alone, 'alone in the arid and useless and enforced routine of a jail, in an atmosphere of suppressed criminality and official stupidity'.

She had visits from friends such as Lakshmi Gurumurti and V.L. Ethiraj, with a scheme for a 'Women's College' in Madras and ten lakhs of rupees (one million) as endowment promised. She was buoyed up to receive, via Jim, a message of appreciation and affection from Rabindranath Tagore.

> "Jim's sixtieth birthday, July 22, which promised to restore my spirits, was spoiled by torrential rain that flooded our cells. As a climax of misfortune I slipped and fell on the stone-floored veranda, luckily with no result but stiffness. My ulcerated mouth became a matter of

interest when it was found that six political prisoners were similarly affected; and still more interesting when a number of men prisoners complained of sore mouths. Bread was sent to be analysed. No verdict was vouchsafed to mere prisoners.

At long last, before the prisoners were awake, the young woman in the condemned cell was taken out and hanged. With this soul-sickening news of official and legal insensitiveness and depravity, from the High Court bench down to the hangman, came private word that she was brave to the last, and protested her innocence of the murder attributed to her in a passionate domestic outburst. Surely, I half hoped, India, in her coming days of freedom, would expunge this worst of savagery from the Swaraj[127] law-books."

For the first three weeks of September 1933 they were not allowed to see a newspaper. When at last a paper was allowed, it announced the death and cremation at Adyar of their spiritual guru and Grettas's long-time friend and mentor, Annie Besant. Through her the Cousins had come to India. All the services rendered by Gretta, and many by Jim, were due to the support and encouragement of this great lady. She had been eighty-six years old and had been out of affairs for three years.

"There is not a tear-drop of personal or conventional grief at the termination of her wonderful career in my diary. Jim and I had been so close to her in spirit and service for many years that she seemed always to be just round the corner. We felt that, if her 'yellow shawls' would be near her again in lives to come, we too would be there; and we were prepared to work on to the end of this incarnation, holding up her spiritual oriflamme[128] when necessary, and always living our lives, as near as possible, to the noble, pure and selfless pattern that she had laid before us with wisdom and humour and with freedom."

Ideas for a book came to Gretta, but the office refused to let her have writing materials on the grounds that she would be released soon, given her remission. However she kept badgering them till she got something to work with. She also managed to worm out of them undelivered letters from Jim, and a letter from Kamaladevi that had come four months previously.

127 **Swarāj** can mean self-governance or "self-rule" but the word usually refers to Gandhi's concept for Indian independence from foreign domination. Swaraj lays stress on **governance**, not by a hierarchical government, but by **self-governance through individuals and community building**.
128 **Oriflamme:** a principle or ideal that serves as a rallying point in a struggle.

Eventually she was given a bundle of letters and papers that had come from America five months previously.

Jim's fortnightly visit nourished her soul. She was delighted to greet him towards the end of September with a new yellow khaddar dress she had made. He was not having a happy time at Madanapalle, and she longed to be able to lighten his burden. When that would be was still uncertain. Hints from the office pointed towards 14 October, counting the remission due to her for 'hard labour.' Towards the end she was happy seeing that her 'other sisters' had caught the urge to plant seeds, thus giving a touch of natural beauty to their dreary surroundings in the prison.

"The roll of political prisoners was reduced by the release of baby Meenu and her mother, Kuthimalu Amma. So dehumanised was the psychology of incarceration that it could not allow mother and child to be freed with her husband, K. Madhava Menon. The remaining handful in the political wing celebrated the two famous birthdays on October 1 and 2. On the first we sang Mrs Besant's words beginning "God save our Motherland," which she had set to the tune of "God save the King," and repeated her prayer for brotherhood beginning "O hidden life vibrant in every atom." On the second we said some of Gandhiji's favourite prayers.

My release was fixed for 21 October 1933. The farewell tea-party on the 20th had *one* political prisoner besides myself. The day went by chiefly in bickering with the office over my possessions. Everything I had was searched. Biographical notes of my fellow prisoners were confiscated. I broke down at the sight of what I regarded as some of my sacred things being mauled by a stupid and vulgar young man. I let him have some straight talk on what I, a former magistrate, would do when I got outside. I scared him into giving the notes back."

At noon a car with Jim aboard was announced arriving at the gate of the jail. The last words uttered by the matron of the prison were: "Mrs Cousins, for God's sake try and get a stop put to the hanging of women."

In a few minutes she was beside Jim in the care of their spiritual brother, C R Parthasarathi Lyengar, front rank lawyer and Congress Member of Parliament. She was "Free! Free! Free!" They were both whipped away to a lunch-party in the home of Mr Gangadhara Sastri, prominent lawyer and also a Congressman.

Through the whole eighty miles from Vellore to Madanapalle Gretta appreciated the lush greenness of the countryside. Having approached

Madanapalle they stopped at the foot of the little temple-crowned Basamkonda where they were met by their spiritual brother, R. Seshagiri Rao, and took him in on the driver's seat.

"We reckoned to be home in twenty minutes, but it took us what seemed to be hours. From the entrance to the old town there was a crush of welcoming people through which the car could hardly make its way. Doors, windows and roofs were crowded. At street corners the car was held up while speeches were made, fruits and sweets presented, and garlands given. At the gate to the College compound we could hardly get out of the car. I was smothered in garlands and flowers. My head was splitting with the noise. A procession headed by a country band escorted us on foot from the gate to Krishna Cottage. The simple but distinctive two-storeyed building that was to be our future home was outlined in the darkness by small clay saucers holding oil in which wicks were burning. We were home, and home was heaven."

# CHAPTER THIRTY

## 'WE TWO TOGETHER AGAIN'
## College Financial Crisis
## Vacation in the Nilgiri Hills
## The Untouchable

Gretta thought about her time-out in prison and being away from her life-partner.

"It was wonderful to "we two together" again. Ten months and some days of jail fell away into the story-book of life. I could not think of the time as lost. I knew that influences and thoughts had been released that would have an enormous effect on the future of India. My own share in this would be forgotten, or perhaps thought of in a theatrical or self-important kind of way. It was sufficient to have earned the love and confidence of women and girls who were apparently of a new order, who had entered the world at one of its major crises, and would either carry it forward to an era of peace such as could arise out of the conserving and nourishing quality of free womanhood, or act as a brake on the descent to ruin that seemed to be the inescapable end of the purely masculine way of life."

Soon she fell into the routine of school and college life. In the 12-year interval between their first and second Madanapalle periods there had been some official expansion beyond text-books. To the official curriculum was added gardening, exploratory walks with the girls, picture-framing, drama and singing. Friends came and went. She went and came. In the middle of November 1933 Gretta attended the annual meeting of the Women's Indian Association in Madras. She was elected to preside by public demand, and took the opportunity to fulfil the desire of the prison matron by making a public protest against the hanging of women.

On the way to Calcutta (Kolkata) to a session of the All-India Women's Conference, she had a chance of showing up once more at a 'beach meeting'. The chief speaker was Mahatma Gandhi. He had an audience estimated at 200,000. Gretta met him at the train and had been given the honour of garlanding him.

Her travelling companion to Calcutta was Dr Muthulakshmi Reddi.

At the breakfast stop next morning they discovered, from crowds on the platform, that Gandhiji was on the same train. Luckily she was dressed in a new khaddar[129] frock, so they scrambled out to greet him. He was happy to see them and invited them to come to his carriage. They hurriedly changed into khaddar saris between stations, and had a whole hour's delightful talk with Bapu on all kinds of political and social topics.

The crowd of delegates at the All-India Women's Conference made seating somewhat of a squash, however they made up for the want of room with jovial banter. At the opening public meeting Sarojini Naidu and Sir Radha-Krishnan gave great distinction to the occasion with their accomplished oratory. Gretta gave her share of proposals and seconding's at the delegates meetings. Her resolution on capital punishment was enthusiastically passed. Rabindranath Tagore came to one of the meetings and sang "Jana gana mana"[130] in very quick time.

## College Financial Crisis

The year 1934 presented a crisis over Madanapalle College finance. As if that was not enough there were thefts on the compound. Collections were made by Jim and Gretta but it was nowhere near the sum required to wipe out losses. An ultimatum from Madras University had been received demanding an endowment fund of Rs.75000 should be banked soon. They were both anxious. A deputation with Gretta being one, went to Abdul-Hakim, a rich and philanthropic Muslim dealer in animal hides, at his big village beyond Chittoor. He sat on the platform of his house, a bearded patriarch. The deputation stood around and spoke about the various aspects of educational finance. He promised Rs.3000 at once, and a lakh (Rs.100000) during July. This was a significant sum enabling them to answer the University. It was added to by a cheque from the Tata Trust in Bombay (Mumbai) for Rs.8000.

The irony of this gift did not escape Jim and Gretta, that their financial deficits were resolved for these two '*ardent vegetarians*', by '*animal hides*', unless of course all the animals had died naturally!

---

129 **Khaddar:** Indian homespun usually cotton cloth. Due to imported costly cloth from England Gandhi started spinning himself and encouraging others to do so. He made it obligatory for all members of the Indian National Congress to spin cotton themselves and to pay their dues in yarn. He further made the chakri (spinning wheel) the symbol of the Nationalist movement. Initially the Indian flag was supposed to have a chakri, not the Ashoka Chakra at its centre.

130 "**Jana Gana Mana**" is the National Anthem of India, composed in Bengali by poet Rabindranath Tagore. It was adopted, in its Hindi version, by the *Constituent Assembly* as the National Anthem of India on 24 January 1950.

## Vacation in the Nilgiri Hills

Gretta preceded Jim by a day (16 April 1934) to a place she had found for vacation in the Nilgiri Hills which stride the borders of Kerala and Tamil Nadu. They were only a week settled when Gretta was noticed by workers who revered the Mahatma. She was promptly invited to visit a scavenger's village, where the inhabitants lived almost totally on searching refuse heaps for useful items and, sadly, food as well. They were poor beyond measure.

"I was lacerated by the awful conditions under which this downtrodden group of human beings had to exist. The only water available for them was polluted by other 'alleged' human beings. I got busy with those in authority, and before long had a tap of pure water installed. Then I went to a Kotah village three miles away. The Kotahs had acquired the art of blacksmithery, and supplied us with crude but usable household and garden tools.

When the British had discovered the plateau in Kotagiri, where the tribe had been living for ages, they thought it would be an admirable place for their wives and children for vacation as well as their nurses. They had ousted the Kotahs. The only available site was that which I trudged to, and I was exasperated at the inconsiderate nature of so-called civilised people, who could migrate another group to a place not fit for cattle. And so began an agitation for human amenities.

By request I visited the little temple in the scavengers' village to receive ceremonial thanks for the help I had given them: so much kindness for so little service."

During their vacation they did not have use of a car of their own. Friends kindly transported them on occasional jaunts to special beauty-spots. These made the days pass quickly. They were invited to musical parties that spread good fellowship through art and shattered any sectarian feelings. Dr Muthulakshmi and her young son, with baskets of Indian dainties for a picnic tea in Longwood Shola[131], were a great delight. While they rested on the bank of a mountain stream, Jim produced inspired lines that turned nature into a ritual in which Protestantism, Catholicism and Hinduism were beautifully entangled.

Water among pebbles tinkling
Needs no ceremonial sprinkling
Here to consecrate an altar,

---

131 **Sholas** are the local name for patches of stunted tropical forest found in valleys amid rolling grassland in the higher regions of South India.

Holy scripture, holy psalter.
Yea, past all dogmatic fission,
Here is ritual provision:
Multi-coloured cloths and bands,
Holy water for the hands
Flowing neither cold nor torrid,
Sacred ashes for the forehead
Gathered where the flame of day
Burns a glory into clay.

After vacation the official inauguration of the new College year at Madanapalle was a happy event. The Minister of Education, Mr Kumaraswami Reddy, and Janab Abdul Hakim attended. At the inaugural meeting the latter made a public promise of Rs.25000. This was not as high as their expectations and, indeed, their needs, but a good example to others. This put new life into the other item of the occasion, a new night school that had been built in the outcaste village, which was to be supplied with voluntary senior students from the College who would teach.

### The Untouchable

One incident indicated the subtle and rapid fall of morale that had emerged. Their only Harijan[132] College student asked permission to have his meals in the hostel. This was given. There were rumours of resentment, not among the students or teachers, but from amongst the servants. At the midday meal, which Jim as Principal shared with the residents in the hostel dining-room, they seated the Harijan between them. Food was served, but when the meal was finished, the 'petty servants' who saw to cleaning up and getting the place ready for the next meal, disappeared. They, who were themselves 'low caste,' had decided to go on strike against being polluted by a member of a still lower social grade!

When the Principal's lips went tight and his eyes lost their twinkle something was about to happen. What he did next proved very effective. He sent into town for a new set of servants to come immediately. They came, glad to earn a day's pay. All went well for afternoon 'tiffin'[133] and the evening meal, with the Harijan on friendly terms with everyone. Next morning the striking servants slunk back and resumed their duties.

132 **Harijan** is a term popularized by Mahatma Gandhi referring to **Dalits**, traditionally considered to be Untouchable. However the euphemism is now regarded as condescending by many, with some Dalit activists calling it insulting. As a result, the Government of India forbade its use for official purposes. The term harijan, literally meant children of god.
133 **Tiffin:** a snack or light meal. (Indian definition). Usually refers to 'afternoon tea'.

# CHAPTER THIRTY-ONE

## Art Advisor to the Maharaja of Travancore

Shortly after Jim had returned to Madanapalle as Headmaster he saw in the press that a palace was being prepared for the young Maharaja of Travancore, who had acceded to the throne in 1931 at the age of nineteen. Known as Maharaja Chithira Thirunal Balarama Varma II, he had succeeded Pooradam Thirunal Sethu Lakshmi Bayi (Regent Queen 1924-1931).

Something inside Jim moved him to write a letter to the Maharaja expressing the idea that the conjunction of the new reign and a new palace would provide an occasion for giving Indian art the place it deserved in the homes of Indian Rulers. He got no response. A year later he was invited to visit the State to preside over a Humanitarian Conference.

"Through the offices of those who sponsored my visit I was made a State guest, and put up in a spacious house with wide verandas opening on to the groupings of coconut palms, jack trees,[134] and other members of the arboreal kingdom whose beauty and usefulness had made Travancore and its neighbour State, Cochin, famous for centuries."

Although Jim's letter had been unanswered at the time his idea had not been without organic growth. In fact a conjunction of events brought him into direct contact with the young Maharaja and His mother:

a) The Superintendent of Archaeology, Mr. R. Vasudeva Poduval had suggested the establishment of a 'State Art Gallery'.
b) The Ruling family had entered their new home - Koudiar Palace - only a few days previously and needed help in the artistic arrangement of its contents.

Maharaja Chithira Thirunal
Balarama Varma II

When he got through the Humanitarian Conference, Jim was received by Their Highnesses the Maharaja and his mother. The young Ruler, though obviously alert and intelligent but not perhaps as knowledgeable in the arts,

---

134 **Jack Tree:** A short form of the name for the Jacaranda Tree

left for his afternoon exercise on the tennis court. Her Highness continued to talk with Jim, who began to sense the quality of her mind. She was sharp in every detail as well as general principles, and quick in picking up ideas and phrases that appealed to her.

"My disclosure of some degree of artistic intelligence apparently passed the test, for she rose with a "Come, Doctor," and took me up a flight of stairs, palatial but not ornate, to the second floor of the palace. In a room, which I perceived to belong to a lady, she waved a plump arm ending in a tiny hand around the contents, and asked me what I would do with them. I made a suggestion. "Do it," she said. "Well, if this were put there?" "Admirable." And so the game began.

For two hours we shifted objects of art from place to place in the room, and from the room to another. Servants appeared offering to carry ivories and bronzes, but she waved them away. In a small room a silver-framed photograph of Maharaja Krishnaraja Wodiyar of Mysore, famed for sanctity and chastity, stood against a pair of elephant tusks and looked with a slight photographic smile at a marble Venus de Milo without a stitch on from below the waist up. Her Highness, looked for some indication of my apparently amused reaction to the room. 'His Highness and Venus' seem somewhat incongruous, I suggested. Thereupon she moved the portrait elsewhere, and left the Goddess in the uncompromising company of a pair of elephant tusks."

Talk turned to the possibilities for a State Art Gallery. This brought up the question of accommodation. A new gallery was outside the current budget. A modest estimate for a first group of exhibits was possible, but a place to put them would have to be found among available buildings that could then be adapted. Two contiguous buildings in the Museum Gardens were suggested. The locale seemed perfect, but the bungalows had not been in use for quite some time. However the transformation from the domesticity to the treasuring of *objets d'art* would be possible. Jim astutely noted at first glance that the two buildings could fall into an order that would allow the exhibits to be grouped in chronological eras, and so add educational value to them in addition to the aesthetical quality within each group.

Further to his obvious knowledge and skills with regard to Indian, and indeed Asian art, Jim, by command, was appointed the **Art Advisor to the Maharaja** and the organiser of the Chitralayam, which developed into one of the most beautiful art-centres in India, and still is today.

In the latter part of September 1935 Gretta followed Jim to Trivandrum, and while he was absorbed in the opening of the Chitralayam,[135] she was busy with music. Once her musical commitments ended she took a long afternoon drive out to Padmanabhapuram Palace, and was amazed at her discovery of old-time beauty and skills in architecture, sculpture, wood-carving and wall-painting that Jim had helped in restoring. On their way back their car got mixed up in a procession of country people headed by three large decorated elephants accompanying a deific image from one temple to another.

As a finale to a busy ten days Gretta as 'Dr Cousins' wife,' when the entire Ruling Family visited the Chitralayam for a detailed inspection. Jim was naturally the guide, and fulfilled his duty with his usual enthusiasm. Gretta had not, up till now, fully realised his scholarship in the history and qualities of the arts of India from BC until the current time. His exposition was flawless and his knowledge vast. At intervals Her Highness the Maharana drew Gretta aside from art to chat on other topics. She was intensely interested in the problem of the 'backward classes'. It was not until a year later that Gretta saw the significance of some of her speculations, when His Highness proclaimed the opening of the temples of Travancore to the 'outcast' population of more than a million. Her Highness was also very concerned with the deterioration in the morale of students all over India, and was anxious to find some way of harnessing young energy and channelling it into constructive and unifying ways. When they were parting at the door of the gallery, Gretta found that Her Highness had noticed her love of flowers and had sent to the Museum Gardens for a large bouquet of orchids which she graciously placed in her hands.

It took several years, but finally, on 25 September 1935 the Sri Chitralayam (Art Museum) was opened to the public by His Highness. Five hundred invited guests attended. Jim was invited to read a ten minute statement on the educational and artistic ideals it was intended to fulfil. The Diwan[136] was good enough to offer the gratitude of the Government for creating such an inclusive gallery of art. He invited His Highness the Maharaja to declare the Sri Chitralayam open.

---

135 **The Sri Chitralayam (The Place of Art)** popularly known as Sri Chitra Art Gallery, was opened to the public by the then Maharaja of Travancore Sri Chitra Thirunal on the 25th of September 1935 for the 'enjoyment, education and development of the artistic taste of the people'.

136 **Diwan:** During the effective rule of the Mughal Empire, the Diwan served as the chief revenue officer of a province. Later, when most vassal states gained various degrees of self-determination, the finance and/or **chief minister** and leader of many princely states such as Baroda, Hyderabad, Mysore, Kochi, Travancore was referred to as **Dalawa** until 1811 then became known as a Diwan..

Jim and Gretta left Travancore after the grand opening and returned to Madanapalle. Towards the end of October Jim returned again for His Highness's birthday durbar.[137] The whole affair was grand and formal evening dress was worn. Jim had been placed to the left of His Highness the Maharaja. What happened next was a complete surprise to him. The Maharaja arose and addressed Jim as well as the audience:

Dr Cousins.
From ancient times it has been the custom of the Rulers of Travancore to confer the *vira srinkhala*, or bracelet of prowess, on persons who had rendered special service to the State. Formerly the decoration was given for prowess on the battlefield. That time has passed. But you have been a valiant warrior for art and culture, and I have great pleasure in giving you this *vira srinkhala* which is the highest decoration of the State. And in order to show that your prowess is for art and culture, I have great pleasure also in giving you this pandit's[138] shawl.

His Highness then presented Jim with the *vira srinkhala*. Sir Ramaswami Aiyar draped the shawl around his shoulders and then placed the *srinkala* on his right wrist. This 'bracelet of prowess' was a heavy bracelet in gold, encrusted with flat diamonds, rubies and emeralds.

The Sri Chitralayam (Art Museum). Opened by Maharajah Chithira
Thirunal Balarama Varma II on 25 September 1935 with Dr James Cousins,
Art Advisor, present.

---

137 **Durbar:** A public reception held by an Indian prince or Maharaja, a British governor or viceroy in India.
138 **Pandit:** a wise or learned man in India —often used as an honorary title

Once again a sudden and inspired action by Jim in writing to the young Maharaja had resulted in a major creation whose grace and beauty is still showered on many thousands of visitors today.

Later that year Gretta missed most of the Diamond Jubilee Convention of the Theosophical Society held at Adyar, as she had to go to Trivandrum for the annual session of the All-India Women's Conference from 25 December 1935 to 4 January 1936.

"Dr Poonen Lukhose, the first woman to become the head of the medical department of an Indian State, sent her car to meet me at Shencottah railway station, the first within the Travancore frontier, which was five hours by train from Trivandrum itself. I arrived in time and enjoyed a speech by Margaret Sanger.[139] With her and Muriel Lester, Gandhiji's hostess in London, I spent a day showing them over Padmanabhapuram Palace. A full day went in meetings and reports at the Conference. Her Highness the Maharani heard a magnificent speech on birth control by Margaret Sanger. Another day of discussions ended in a garden party at Koudiar Palace, laid out with exquisite thought and taste on the beautiful terraced lawns. After refreshments a first class Kathakali[140] performance was given. The closing day of the session was distinguished by an excellent speech by Her Highness."

After the AIWC meeting was over she and Jim enjoyed a refreshing interlude of six days at Thipagondana-halli ('village at the foot of the hill'). This enabled them both to overcome unpleasant health issues. They were guests of Humayun Mirza, son of Sir Mirza Ismail, at a rest-house beside the lake and reservoir from which water was electrically pumped for a number of miles to Bangalore. Humayun, a tall, stately young man, had driven them to the rest house, and subsequently called from time to time for chats on all sorts of subjects. Mornings were so refreshing that they sauntered early along the plateau overlooking the lake, until the beauty of the undulating country moved Jim to verse. Gretta left him to himself, until he had completed a fine poem that he dedicated to their host. The last double verse ran:

---

139 **Margaret Sanger**: (Sept 1879 – Sept 1966), was an American birth control activist, sex educator, writer, and nurse. Sanger popularized the term "birth control", opened the first birth control clinic in the United States, and established organizations that evolved into the Planned Parenthood Federation of America.

140 **Kathakali** is one of the major forms of classical Indian dance. It is a "story play" genre of art, but one distinguished by the elaborately colourful make-up, costumes and facemasks that the traditionally male actor-dancers wear. Kathakali primarily developed as a Hindu performance art in the Malayalam-speaking southwestern region of India (Kerala).

In the hour of the passing over from night to day
I heard one Voice through myriad voices say:
"Give ear to the silent, as unto that which speaks.
All life with life a rich communion seeks."

And as this was only saying that life was love,
A thing I had always known, like a mated dove
My heart to the heart of nature chanted this lay
In the hour of the passing over from night to day.

# CHAPTER THIRTY-TWO

The Maharaja of Travancore opens temples to all castes
Jim & Gretta spark a highly significant reform in Hinduism
Jim enrolled into the Hindu Faith
A small temple for 'untouchables' at Madanapalle

On 12 November 1936, His Highness the Maharaja of Travancore, after the Hindu manner of giving gifts instead of receiving them on the annual celebration of His birthday, was planning to proclaim the opening of the Government controlled temples of the State to all classes of Hindus irrespective of caste or indeed no caste. Gretta and Jim had been invited to Trivandrum as State guests and to develop some of the schemes for diffusion of art in the State.

At the State Banquet on 13 November Gretta was dinner partner to the Chief Secretary to Government, Dr Kunjan Pillai. In the course of table talk she put a question to him that she and Jim had discussed privately. They had wondered if the Temple Entry Proclamation did not, in **two** of its words, signify a much wider application than only to the one million outcaste Hindus to whom it would generally apply. The **two** crucial words were italicised by Jim in the following transcript of the Proclamation:

> "Profoundly convinced of the truth and validity of Our religion, believing that it is based on Divine guidance and on an all-comprehending toleration, knowing that in its practice it has, throughout the centuries, adapted itself to the needs of changing times, solicitous that none of Our Hindu subjects, by reason of birth or caste or community, be denied the consolations and solace of the Hindu faith, We have decided and hereby declare, ordain and command that, subject to such rules and conditions as may be laid down and imposed by Us for preserving their proper atmosphere and maintaining their rituals and observances, there should henceforth be no restriction placed on any Hindu by birth *or religion* on entering or worshipping at the temples controlled by Us and Our Government.
> (Sign manual)."

The distinction between a Hindu by birth or by religion seemed to Jim and Gretta to break down the tradition that to be a Hindu one had to be born into the Hindu community.

If accepted this would be the most significant reform in the long history of Hinduism. The Chief Secretary responded to Gretta that their interpretation, as far as he knew, was in accordance with the idea behind the Proclamation. This was confirmed by the Diwan, Sir C. P. Ramaswami. This boosted in them both a sense of responsibility to have new enlightenment of the Proclamation demonstrated clearly and not allow it to remain a theoretical possibility. This would be another step, if small, towards the realisation of the oneness of the human race.

Nothing, however, could be done until after the Rules for Temple Entry were published. On the way home on the train, the real significance of the Travancore Temple Entry Proclamation came to Jim, and with it a deep desire that its full importance should be made known and demonstrated widely. He drafted a proposed public statement for Indian as well as international publicity. He sent a copy to the Diwan for his information also informing him that he had seen a press announcement that Gandhiji would visit Travancore to celebrate the Proclamation in January, and that it would be important that he be present in order to see what could be done to make the celebration complete; if necessary taking the responsibility of doing so on himself.

On the morning after Jim's arrival back in Trivandrum (12 Jan 1937) the Diwan called him to discuss his 'Temple Entry proposal', and the preliminaries for the organisation of a State University. It so happened that two orthodox officials of Temples from the east coast were with the Diwan when he called. The Diwan brought them together for a discussion on Jim's determination to 'test the terms of the Proclamation as they appeared to relate to non-Indians'. Their orthodox officials had nothing to say with regard to the State. They gave their personal opinion that before many years had passed the restrictions that had prevailed for centuries in the temples of South India, would probably have disappeared. They proved good prophets. Jim wired Gretta, and she replied leaving the matter entirely to his judgement.

When Jim reported his final decision to go ahead to the Diwan, he was so impressed with the uniqueness and historical importance of the occasion that he would like it marked with a special ceremonial if he had no objection. Jim was ready for anything if it might help to demonstrate the history-making religious revolution of the Proclamation.

Next afternoon as the climax of a tour of the State, Gandhiji presided over a celebration of the 'Temple Entry Proclamation' by a vast quiet multitude in the military parade ground backed by twenty huge caparisoned[141] elephants. He squatted on a high platform under a canopy against the sun, and spoke in

---

141 **A caparison** is a cloth covering laid over a horse or elephant or other animal for protection and decoration. In modern times, they are used mainly in parades and for historical re-enactments. The word is derived from the Latin **caparo**, meaning a cape.

English, translated to the multitude in Malayalam by a leader of the formerly excluded one million. No hint came from him or anyone else of the wider-than-India importance of this occasion.

## Jim enrolled into the Hindu religion

At 8 o'clock next morning, 14 January 1937, a representative of the authorities of the great Sri Padmanabhaswami Temple of Trivandrum called officially to interview Jim as to his eligibility for temple entry. This ceremony would show that one did not any longer need to be born a Hindu to enter the temples. He, a born Methodist of the Christian Faith, was about to be invited ceremonially into the Hindu Faith. Assuming his willingness to take this step it had been decided that, as he had been known as a "white Brahmin" for many years, the fire ceremony for spiritual purification was unnecessary.

At an arranged time he presented himself at the quarters of the chief priest (Nambudhri) of the Temple in 'temple dress.' This was usually a white cotton skirt hanging from the waist with a similar cloth around the body, both having narrow embroidered borders. But as a mark of importance, on this occasion, he was asked to wear a special temple dress of white silk with deep borders of gold thread.

To his surprise, when conducted into the large ceremonial room, he faced a huge congregation, most of them squatting on the floor, some standing around the walls and looking in through doors and windows. Many were familiar to Jim as leaders of the Hindu community, Government officers, lawyers and teachers. All were, like himself, in temple dress. He took his seat, directed by the 'ceremonialists', on a small wooden plank. Frequent participation in Hindu ceremonies in connection with Madanapalle College and School and elsewhere, had made him familiar with their symbolical simplicity. He, more than anyone present, was keenly aware of the historical significance and worldwide importance of this event. Also that he had the honour of being part of this enlightened move forwards suggested by Her Highness in her concern for the 'outcaste' population of more than one million.

"Before the ceremony began I asked permission to make a statement in explanation of what I was doing.

I had been, I said, born into the Wesleyan Methodist sect of Christianity. My naturally reflective mind became dissatisfied with the religious exclusiveness of my upbringing. Modern science cut me away from all dogma; but an inborn religious sense and a truth-seeking mind would not allow me to rest in a negative state.

I studied psychical research as it related to the dogma of immortality and the states of heaven and hell. I studied Theosophy, and found in the Three Objects of the Society what appeared to me to be the fullest and most consistent method of approach to realisation of the truth of life. I studied books on the Vedanta, got to know certain of the Upanishads, memorised much of the Bhagavad Gita, and practised some phases of yoga. When I came to India I came to know of the cosmic and human symbolism of deific figures, especially as embodied in sculpture and painting; also of the psychic influences that were gathered round and expressed in consecrated places and images. From these extensions of knowledge and experience I derived a deeper understanding of the universals of Christianity….

I said these things in order to make it clear that my public declaration of belief in Hinduism as a way to union with the Divine Life, a way most in affinity with the devotee, the artist and the philosopher in me, did not imply any denial of the spiritual truth that was to be found in all religions, or any repudiation of their ceremonial and discipline. To me the commonly used term conversion did not mean a turning away from one religion to another: it had for me the meaning of turning from the externals of any religion towards its internal and eternal verities.

If my reception into the religious community of Hinduism was contingent on my denying the validity of other faiths as ways to the spiritual life and light, the proposed ceremony should be dropped; if otherwise, it might proceed."

Diwan Bahadur V. S. Subramania Aiyar, ex-Diwan of Travancore, speaking for the temple authorities and those assembled, said that denial of truth in other religions than Hinduism would be against its spirit and teachings. No one had any doubt as to Jim's fitness for the religious communion of Hinduism. The simple ceremony then proceeded, and at the end the venerable old Nambudhri whispered in his ear the name 'Jayaram'.[142] This was to be the name by which he would be known in Hindu circles in Travancore, and by whoever chose to recognise it elsewhere in India. At the end of the ceremony he was escorted by the temple authorities into the Temple, and taken from shrine to shrine, where he offered his palm-to-palm salutation to the images of various aspects of the one Universal Being.

"In the afternoon I was telephoned to call at the Diwan's home at 7.30pm to accompany him to Koudiar Palace for dinner with the Maharaja and the ruling family. His Highness welcomed me warmly

---

142 **Jayaram** incorporates qualities of spontaneity, creativity, and exuberance.

into the family, meaning the Hindu community, of which he was not only the Ruler but the spiritual head in succession from Maharaja Martanda Varma, who had brought a number of disunited and fighting princelings under one banner, and then laid his sword before the image of Deity and vowed his kingdom and its administration to God, and gave himself the title Sri Padmanabhadasa (follower of Vishnu). All that was 200 years ago."

From the reception room they went to an open space within the palace precinct. He found himself with Her Highness the Maharana's mother at the head of the informal procession. This gave her an opportunity to inform Jim that it was she who had selected his Hindu name. She had noticed that his chief desire was for **light**, not just for knowledge. The name Rama came from an original meaning 'spiritual light'. To this she prefixed Jaya, which both wished for and prophesied victory. So Jayaram meant "victory to the light;" and, she added with a mischievous little laugh, "It will save you having to change your initial!"

"During the procession from the shrine to the dining hall His Highness the Maharaja asked: "What do you think of the artistic aspect of the temple, Doctor?" I replied: "I was so engrossed, Your Highness, with the proceedings and the part I had to play in them, that art was temporarily in abeyance. But there was one item that somehow got into my consciousness. I was shown the stone on which, I was told, Maharaja Martanda Varma laid his sword when dedicating the State to God; and the *corrugated sheeting* above it did not seem worthy. "Quite right, Doctor." I knew a mental note had been made. Sometime later I was asked to inspect a piece of wood-carving; a well-designed and admirably executed triangle that might have been a survivor from the heyday of local craftsmanship, but was plainly new. It was, I learned, a new cover for the dedication stone instead of corrugated iron. Her Highness had herself made the lovely indigenous design."

Repercussions to Jim's Temple entrance and ceremony enrolling him as a Hindu were varied. Travancore accepted the matter without the least problem. His visits to temples on artistic quests were welcomed and facilitated by those in charge. There were few criticisms. An Indian Christian wrote condemning his "base denial" of Christ, and pleaded with him to confess his error, and acknowledge Him as the only hope of salvation, before he stood before the Judgement seat.

Others congratulated him on his courage and nobility. A sadhu (holy man) unofficially conferred the highest Sanskrit titles on him. The daily press gave over many columns to the event. The news had apparently escaped abroad. He received a cable from Ireland four days later asking him to confirm press reports.

A relative wrote in complete understanding. Another deplored what he had done making it clear that it was likely to prejudice their family reputation and position. The farthest repercussion came from the United States of America, from a lady bearing the name – Cousins - of Belfast parentage. From publications she had thought of Jim as a "very intelligent gentleman" but he had "turned his back on God." He was asked to think of his soul, and where he would spend eternity. Jim did not reply to any of them.

### A Consequential Act – Opening a small temple for untouchables in Madanapalle

That Jim was incorrigible was shown by declaring open a temple for Harijans (Dalits) near Madanapalle College shortly after returning from Trivandrum. For a village that was sodden with illicit spirits he had been instrumental in having a small temple built. He received from Mr & Mrs D. Appa Rao, a gift of the images of Sri Rama, Ska, Lakshman and Hanuman. In declaring the simple and basic temple open, Jim said to the crowd of villagers, squatted under the early stars in the clear sky of the southern Deccan, words which were translated into the regional language, Telugu. They had, he reminded them, chosen Sri Rama as the object of their worship; and if they wanted their temple to be a centre of spiritual power and purification they should strive to live day by day in the spirit of Sri Rama, who became the perfect Ruler by first learning to rule himself, to put away all tendencies of self-indulgence, violence and impurity.

# CHAPTER THIRTY-THREE

## BACK TO WOMEN'S ISSUES
### Jim's retirement and the ghost of insecurity

Gretta had returned to Madanapalle on 4 Jan 1937, while Jim was involved in the historic Temple Entry Proclamation in Trivandrum. Routine kept her busy, though politics called on her energies for an election campaign with a woman candidate in a south Indian constituency. She assisted with organisation and talks, translated into Tamil, at huge meetings in various villages. On polling day, 20 Feb 1937 she was on the move in a car from 11.30am to 10pm. They visited 11 polling stations notching up a total of 200 miles. They were mobbed by crowds of enthusiastic supporters. Villagers were intoxicated with the assurance of success. A week later the country was overjoyed with the triumph of the Congress candidates in the General Election. Gretta was as buoyed up as anyone with the success, but not naïve enough to think that this one election would bring about a nationwide summer of peace and prosperity. She had all too often observed that human beings have a habit of being contrary, and can change as often as the wind. Put another way, crowd mentality, or should we say emotionality, can swing like a pendulum.

Next afternoon she was off to Delhi to attend a session of the All-India Women's Conference and hopefully collect donations for the College. She was put up in aristocratic comfort in the home of Mrs Sultan Singh, and from this traditionally hospitable centre sallied forth in an ever ready car to various meetings, one in the large official home of the Viceroy.

Music helped to fill the days between the women's meetings and a session of the Indian National Congress. She had, in fact, been invited to give a piano broadcast.

"A delightful renewal of friendship was seeing John Foulds[143] again, who was Director of the Western section of the All-India Radio. He remained an optimist on the orchestrating of Indian melodies. He

---

143 **John Herbert Foulds** (1880 – 1939) was an English composer of classical music. He was largely self-taught as a composer, and belongs to the figures of the English Musical Renaissance. A successful composer of light music and theatre scores, his principal creative energies went into more ambitious and exploratory works that were particularly influenced by Indian music. Travelled to India in 1935 where, among other things, he collected folk music, composed pieces for traditional Indian instrument ensembles, and worked for All-India Radio. Foulds was an adventurous figure of great innate musicality and superb technical skill. Among his best works are *Three Mantras* for orchestra.

played his fascinating Gandharva music. He also played the opening chorus of his Requiem which had been performed in the Albert Hall, London. This was a masterly piece of music that had in it the prophecy of a classic. It was real aesthetical nourishment."

On 19 March 1937 Gretta spent six hours at the National Congress. One pleasant job was transcribing Sarojini Naidu's speech for a reception. Her handwriting had the 'illegibility of genius', and took some concentration as well as a sizeable chunk of intuition to decipher. A huge crowd gave a tremendous send off to Gandhiji and Rajaji.[144]

After some weeks Jim and Gretta set off again, 11 April, via Mysore to the hills of Ootacamund. Gretta continues:

"We settled in rooms in a comfortable house, and revelled in the beauties of nature. Jim told me of an unexpected break in our plans by an invitation to go with the Maharaja and Elayaraja of Trivandrum and their mother to Java and Bali. I shrank from the threatened separation at a time when we much needed each other. But I felt that the trip to Java and Bali would be a significant event in his life and also have repercussions in my own."

So, while Jim headed off, Gretta was left alone at 7,500 feet not feeling even slightly elevated. The only consolation was: 'every day he snatched time to write to me, and that he was the best corresponding lover any girl at sixty could desire'.

### Jim's retirement and the ghost of insecurity
### What about the future?
They both returned again to Madanapalle on 15 January 1938:

"In a few days Jim went to Mysore, feeling ill with the future uncertainty as to income, home and status, though he had taken steps to retire from the College to join Travancore and try to overcome inartistic prejudices by the positive display of real beauty.

No sooner was I alone than I had to try and stop the marriage of a 12yr-old girl to an adult. Such outrages against womanhood, so far

144 **Rajaji: Chakravarti Rajagopalachari** (Dec 1878 – Dec1972) informally and affectionately called **Rajaji** , was an Indian politician, independence activist, lawyer, writer, historian and statesman. Rajagopalachari was the last Governor-General of India, as India soon became a Republic in 1950

down in the scale of humanity compared with the equivalence in age and education in marriages in the early Hindu era, made me wild. But I could do nothing in face of the monster custom. Happily opinion and legal change, that could not be set aside as foreign prejudice, raised the age of marriage and brought equality between the sexes a shade nearer. At this time a feminist expedition to a number of small towns took me into peculiar places, one being over-night in a small dingy room off a police court, with a drunken woman in custody near me."

While in Trivandrum Jim's formal notice of retirement as Principal of Madanapalle College came by post in the middle of March. At the same time Gretta got news that his insomnia had started again, so she went to Trivandrum on 21 March to see what could be done.

"I found him very much down in tone through worrying over frustrations to schemes for the new University. I could do nothing about this; but living over an office at the corner of a main road, with every kind of noise and interruption, could be got over to some extent by finding another home. So we prowled about house hunting, and eventually found a small bungalow in a cul-de-sac. The nearest noises were softened by distance, and were more natural than the hootings and grindings of mechanical civilisation. They were the cries of rare birds, barkings of animals, roaring of lions, growling of tigers, from the neighbouring zoo. We settled on this, and after five days I left to see to packing up at Madanapalle. After that, a month of wrangles among the College staff, and sadness over the discovery of leprosy contracted by the wife of our valued house-boy, were not making me too happy. Feelings were running so high that I was outvoted at a packed meeting of the High School Management; and a teacher for whom we had much affection accused me of all people, of 'foreign prejudice' because I stood up for a European member of the staff on plain principle. It was an immense relief to get away for the summer vacation on April 30."

Jim oscillated again between Madanapalle and Trivandrum, with anxieties at each end. They enjoyed the fifty mile bus drive to Kodaikanal, at 7,000 feet. A flat was found in a large house on a small but superbly wooded estate for a month's relaxation. The lovely view, the spaciousness, the peace and quiet, and the flowers, lifted life at least an octave and gave the imagination a chance to soar and their spirits to fly free.

They returned to Trivandrum on 2 June to begin life again in a home of their own. For how long they could not prophesy, as forces were at work that threatened their future. Days went by with picture-hanging, sewing, gardening and paying calls.

One of Jim's lectures, as Head of the Department of Fine Arts in the University, was a mixture of art and political agitation. On their way to the lecture room in the Science College they had to pass through rows of police and cavalry who, they were told, were protecting the legislators against threatened assault as they came out of the hall.

At the entrance to the College they stood to see what would happen. Street boys and school boys had got into the College compound. Some were throwing stones across the railings at the horses and setting them rearing and bucking. Others began to stone the police at the entrance to the legislative hall. Suddenly the gate at the end of the College compound facing the Jubilee Town Hall was thrown open, and the police began to clear the compound of the stone-throwing boys. This they did with lathis.[145] Of the mob of boys only two received slight head-wounds. Protests were stimulated by Congress and students' organisations in many parts of India. Gandhiji, even he, was deceived into treating the incident as something terrible, but changed his attitude when he heard both sides.

At Christmas 1938 Gretta was again in Delhi, for the annual session of the All-India Women's Conference. The move from the perspiration of Trivandrum to a hot-water bottle in Delhi brought on the early symptoms of a 'cold' in her, but they receded. The session was full of good resolutions as usual.

She began 1939 with a piano broadcast from Delhi under the auspices of her acquaintance John Foulds. Gretta played piano which was recorded to be incorporated into a film. After that she set off on the seventy hours train journey to Trivandrum, reading and darning stockings!

She found 'the Art Adviser' up to his eyes in preparations for a visit from the Viceroy, Lord Linlithgow,[146] the Vicereine and her two daughters. For three days he showed them over the art galleries; and in their company saw a superb performance of Kathakali. Gretta was one of the hostesses when Her Excellency and daughters visited the Baby Welcome, and also when the Ladies Club was formally opened with a tennis match between two Indian and two British ladies. Later a banquet was laid on and a Palace garden party in which Maharani Setu Parvati Bayi was the directing genius. A dinner party

---

145 **Lathis**: long, heavy iron-bound bamboo sticks used as a weapon, especially by police in India.

146 **Victor Alexander John Hope, 2nd Marquess of Linlithgow**, KG, KT, FRSE, GCSI, GCIE, OBE (Sept 1887 – 5 Jan 1952) was a British Unionist politician, agriculturalist and colonial administrator. He served as Governor-General and Viceroy of India from 1936 to 1943. He was usually referred to simply as **Linlithgow**.

was given by His Highness in honour of the retiring British Resident[147], Mr C. F. Skrine.[148]

"Formality was left outside. We were all friends, the Ruling Family, being the friendliest of the lot. An unforgettable event was a treasure hunt. The game is usually played indoors, the clues guiding or deluding the hunters from room to room. But this was different. The company were given fancy names and paired by lot. Some literary imp enjoyed itself by giving me the Scottish name of Flora Macdonald, and giving Mr Skrine, a Scotsman, the name of Bonnie Prince Charlie, and completed the whimsy by bracketing our names for the hunt. The trail soon took us beyond Kanakakunnu, and we were scampering along the avenue to Koudiar Palace, half a mile away, and after zig-zags through the illuminated gardens scampered back again—'Flor' and 'Charlie' were first in; Jim and his partner were lower down the list; but none too low not to carry away a prize as a memento of a jolly occasion."

Gretta spent hours in the Legislative Hall of Travancore one day, listening to a debate on a Child Marriage Bill.

"Speaker after speaker kept up long-winded obstructionist speeches, and ultimately talked it out—a sad demonstration of the tenacity of the male of the species to the position of sexual domination, and a sharp challenge to the free-minded women of the State."

---

147 **A Resident** or Political Agent was an official of the East India Company (after 1813 the British Government). The Resident, who was based in a princely state, served as part diplomat, part adviser to the native ruler, and part monitor of activities in the princely state.
148 **Sir Clarmont Percival Skrine** (1888–1974) was a British civil servant and administrator who served as Under-Secretary of State for India. On 20 November 1936, Skrine was appointed agent for the Madras States where he served till 1 April 1937, when the agency was abolished and replaced with a residency. He also served as the British Resident for the Madras States from 1 April 1937 to 15 January 1939.

# CHAPTER THIRTY-FOUR

## VERBAL ATTACK IN SEMI-PARADISE
### Meeting Dr Montessori
### Recording their memoires – 'We Two Together'

Their journey homewards (3-8 July 1939), from an unforgettable month with what Jim called 'Himalayan humanity,' was a descent from a semi-Paradise to an almost complete inferno of temperature. At Madras there was a division of the ways. Jim went to Trivandrum on duty as Art Advisor, and Gretta to Kotagiri to search for a place where they could settle in coolness and dryness for most of the year. A cheerful Tamilian greeted her as a friend, though she had never seen him before, and placed himself and his car at her disposal during her search. He was an angel incognito.

"Twists and turns from one impossibility to another ended at a single-storeyed cottage on a hill side with a wonderful view over hills and valleys to the blessedly far-off sweltering plains, just what we needed in size, with a leafy bower for the poet, and a shaded lily-pool fifty feet downhill with a terraced garden between. "Ghat View"[149] had no electric light or running water. So our new home at 6,200 feet was

Kotagiri, in the Nilgiri Hills (6000ft), lying close to borders between Tamil Naidu and Kerala. (Modern day picture)

---

149 **Ghat View:** The Western Ghats is a mountain range within the Nilgiri Hills. It is likely that Gretta and Jim could see the Ghats from their front door.

settled on, as we hoped, for the remainder of this incarnation, with periodical shuttling by my partner to Travancore, 500 miles away. His continued earnings would keep the larder full and pay the rent and hire of a piano that I had heard a rumour of.

The garden fell steeply from the path in front of the cottage to the road. At each end of the path a hibiscus tree had been planted. One of them had grown to twenty feet or more; the other had stopped at five. Their long-tongued bright-red flowers were plentiful but not as vital as I felt they should be. So I put them on a full diet of fresh earth and rotting leaves, with plenty of water carried up from the well at the bottom of the garden."

Then Jim arrived from Trivandrum.

"August 8 was a gala day. My 'comrade' got off the bus from Mettupalayam at the corner of our avenue. I semaphored with my arms to him from the door, and then leaped down like a deer to greet him. I had plucked flowers from a neighbouring garden, with consent, and the rooms were pictures in natural colours. Jim was delighted. We were 'two together' again. In front of a cheery wood-fire after dark we read Æ and Vedanta and Theosophy, and talked high and broad, and I suppled my fingers and strengthened my memory on the piano with Bach's fugues and Beethoven's sonatas and many other classics. Jim worked up old songs in anticipation of sing-songs as of old."

They both looked through old diaries and letters for indications of social life in the area. This was bound to be multi-coloured, since Kotagiri was the vacation centre of all the Christian missionary sects who, in addition to their shades of difference in organisation and observances, came from England, Holland, Denmark, Germany and America. The social rounds began some days after Jim's arrival, when they were invited by the Kotagiri Missionary Union to give a piano-and-poetry recital.

The peace and quiet was not to last. Following a lovely tea with Jim in the Longwood Shola[150] Gretta felt it her duty to visit a neighbour who had previously rented to them. The road from the shola passed the foot of the garden of that bungalow. She had heard that the owner had returned after a long absence. Gretta wanted to express their appreciation, though they had paid a fairly stiff rent at the time.

---

150 **Shola:** a high-altitude evergreen forest in southern India.

"When I announced my name she came to the door and berated me as a dangerous woman, a wicked Theosophist! If she had known then who I was she would never have allowed her house to fall into the hands of such a person. There was nothing for me to say, and I withdrew as politely as I could. The dear lady was to cross my path again."

Their Theosophical way of life and Jim's affiliation with Hinduism in Travancore were well-known. Friendliness and cultural pleasures made a neutral meeting-place.

"What others thought and did in their own circles did not concern us. Some of them, we heard, in the kindness of their hearts, and in view of 'post mortem' possibilities, prayed for us. We were glad of this, for we knew that prayer was good for the person who prayed, apart from its effect on the subject of the prayer.

My piano-playing and Jim's light baritone singing and his original verse, brought us invitations to tea and dinner parties. Then a big concert was arranged and promised well. The evening arrived, and we were dressed for the event and awaiting a friend's car when another car turned up bringing the Archdeacon. This was quite an honour, we felt. But it turned out otherwise.

He had come to ask me not to attend the concert. Why? Mrs So-and-so had returned to Kotagiri after an absence. She had read in the press that Mrs Cousins had been in a Hindu temple just outside Kotagiri. She had also found that she was a Theosophist. She had got up a petition, headed by a Bishop, against Mrs Cousins being associated with the Missionary Union and she threatened to lead a demonstration if Mrs. Cousins was allowed to attend the concert that had been announced. [J=Jim A=Archdeacon]. The conversation went thus:

(J) Is she a member of the Union?  (A) No.

(J) Have you ever been in a Hindu temple? (A) Many a time.

(J) Then of course *you* will face such hypocritical zealotry.

(Gretta) I am quite ready to fulfil my engagement.

(A) Well, we do not want to disturb the peace of our community by any strong action.

I saw, notwithstanding my indignation, that it was impossible to override the obviously fixed intention of the local head of one of the groups in the Union. Like the objector, I was not a member and could not assert any rights. So I took off my evening wrap and submitted. The Archdeacon said, with probably more truth than he intended, that I was the best Christian of the lot. The concert, I was told next morning, went off so-so. Letters of sympathy came in. I sent round word that the invitation I had already given for an evening party still stood. Members of the chorus could bring friends. The result was a crush in our little drawing-room plus Jim's study and the glassed veranda, with refreshments and songs and piano and poetry and jolly good fellowship that would have remained unexpressed but for this occasion.

The collision with the zealous lady did not reduce my visiting list. Our missionary friends graciously left us either to our doom or to the Will of God."

Occasional visitors from beyond India expanded their social contacts. Their friend Emilie Van Kerckhoff from Capri stayed with them for a while, reminding them of the 'Mediterranean Sea', vineyards and olive groves and the midday bell on the tower of Axel Munthe's home. She arrived on the day when Britain and France declared war on Germany after its invasion of Poland (23 August 1939). All prayers for peace had yet to be answered. Their guest left again ASAP to get back home to her aged husband before sea-travel to Italy was likely to be cut off.

"Work for women kept calling me. When Jim was on duty periodically at Trivandrum I scurried around a number of towns fanning up interest in women for their own welfare and the realisation of the duties of citizenship when it came to them. I made a detour through several towns to Trivandrum to be present at the Birthday celebrations of the Maharaja."

Eventually she got back to Kotagiri and their new home and beautiful garden a full day before Jim. He came back from Travancore looking thin and pale, but in a dozen days of creative mental and emotional unity, with music, poetry, and the enjoyment of nature, he was back to his cheery self again.

Soon after they both headed back to Adyar, for the annual International Convention of The Theosophical Society, where they were sure to find old sustained friendships, free spiritual aspiration, artistic fellowship, the dynamism and encouragement of the President, Dr Arundale, and the genius, idealism and loveliness of his partner, Rukmini.

A pre-Convention experience for them both was a talk by Dr Maria

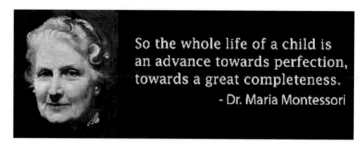

So the whole life of a child is an advance towards perfection, towards a great completeness.
- Dr. Maria Montessori

Montessori[151] to three hundred teachers in training, who had come from all parts of India to attend a course in a specially built cadjan[152]hall. Gretta heard Rukmini Devi give a public performance of Bharatanatyam solus[153], a perfect collaboration of rhythm, gesture, posture and hand-signs, sometimes as a pure fantasia and cadenza, sometimes in telling a story from the ancient Indian scriptures.

## The conception of WE TWO TOGETHER

It was about this time in late 1939-40 that both Gretta and Jim began the task of planning to record their experiences and adventures over the years. It is an insight to see how they considered this mammoth task: Gretta speaks for both.

"But the work that was to absorb our joint interest and time was what, for short, we called our 'duography.' Our travels in many countries, our contacts with eminent persons and important organisations, and our pioneering in activities that had taken their place in history, had naturally come out in the reminiscent moments when chatting to friends. Indeed they often made suggestions that we should put our experiences in a book. Settling up our accumulation of old papers in our new home, we came across notes of persons and places and a number of diaries. I took on the job of arranging these chronologically. We discussed the matter from every point of view. Why should we think

---

151 **Montessori** is a method of education named after its founder and based on self-directed activity, hands-on learning and collaborative play. In Montessori classrooms children make creative choices in their learning, while the classroom and the teacher offer age-appropriate activities to guide the process. The main purpose of a Montessori school is to provide a carefully planned, stimulating environment which will help the child develop an excellent foundation for creative learning.

152 **Cadjan:** The matted cocoa-palm leaves used in southern India for thatch.

153 **Bharatanatyam** is a major genre of Indian classical dance that originated in Tamil Nadu. Traditionally, Bharatanatyam has been a solo dance that was performed exclusively by women, and it expressed South Indian religious themes and spiritual ideas, particularly of Shaivism, but also of Vaishnavism and Shaktism.

our lives worth recording? Jim recalled Benvenuto Cellini's[154] saying, in justification of *his* autobiography that: "Anyone who had reached forty and had done anything worthwhile should write it down."

What had we done that was worthwhile? We had pioneered for the liberation and elevation of womanhood and for culture and beauty in education and life. But to what effect? Much had been accomplished; or it seemed much when you had your eyes on it. But when you raised them and looked at the vast area of necessity, what had been done seemed as nothing. Anyhow, we had been so close to movements that had made history that we could record them with an intimacy that few possessed."

The way of telling the story had its problems. Their eminent friends the Pethick-Lawrences told their story in separate books. Gretta and Jim could not get away from the fact that their story was **one story**, even though its bits and pieces, it stories and adventures, its historic encounters as far apart as Madras or Los Angeles, or as separate in conditions as Vellore Women's Gaol and the island of Capri were scattered.

Once plans were laid the work became steady, almost too absorbing on the part of Jim, with his Celtic poem-drama still unfinished. It amused and indeed illuminated them to get a more or less objective view of themselves. They discovered that both separately and together they rarely had gone anywhere or did anything that had not been worthwhile, promoting a just civilisation in an atmosphere and context of working for the unification of the human race.

Gretta stated:

"I do not think there was any smugness or superiority, nor did our seriousness reduce our sense of humour. I began writing my share of the 'duography' on St. Patrick's Day, 1940".

---

154 **Benvenuto Cellini** (1500-1571) was an Italian goldsmith, sculptor, draftsman, soldier, musician, and artist who also wrote a famous autobiography.

# CHAPTER THIRTY-FIVE

## Developing child welfare in Kotagiri
## A cable to HG Wells – 'The Rights of Man'

The general unsanitary state of most homes of the people in Kotagiri moved Gretta to do something to rectify this. A group of good-spirited women both Hindu and Christian were eager to join her. Together they were not able to assist financially, as giving one square meal to each hungry person in the whole neighbourhood would have taken a considerable sum of money, and would, in the end, have made little or no difference. There were not enough helpers to provide significant care to all the crowded and dingy homes that needed it. Gretta's experience in the Baby Welcomes in Madras came to her aid. She recollected how mothers brought their new-borns for a morning bath, medication and a sweet.

Those attending this new and improving service fluctuated for a number of indigenous reasons. When they fell towards zero she made sorties into side streets with an interpreter and usually returned like a clucking hen with a brood of 'chickens' around her.

With warm-hearted help they organised a 'Child Welfare and Maternity Centre' convenient to the most densely populated area of the town, in a roomy and comfortable building equipped with all the paraphernalia for helping babies into an already overcrowded world. They welcomed toddlers, and some older ones, to a warm bath, simple medicines, and a sweet, as an inducement to come back again. Maintaining the Centre was difficult. A record of each child had to be kept, supplies and staff maintained as well as a rotation of voluntary visitors. There was a general feeling of fulfilment in trying to liberate these children, and through them their parents, from sectarian restrictions of caste.

"When I appeared a furlong from the Baby Welcome at my visiting hour, I was usually hailed by a group of village children with joint smiles and salutations that sometimes cancelled and sometimes heart-breakingly accentuated their poverty, and made me resolve revolutionary vows concerning the dreadful treatment during childhood not only by a foreign Government but by their own kindred."

While Gretta was keeping the 'home fires burning' as a refuge for her hard-worked and harassed husband, between his duty periods in Trivandrum with its humid heat and ever increasing frustration with mostly ignorant staff, she was occasionally challenged to come down from her lofty hill-top retreat and mix in the ground-level affairs of people.

### The Rights of Man

One such outside-world diversion was the journalistic hubbub raised by H. G. Wells in his campaign for the Rights of Man. He, both his helpers and critics were all male. Reading the daily column in the newspaper made Gretta think that no man ever had a mother or a sister, not to mention a wife. Not an inch of progress, apparently, had been made in thirty years towards expressing the dual nature of humanity. She came to feel this so strongly that she cabled Wells asking him to alter the title of his campaign for Human Rights. He merely acknowledged, grudgingly and evasively, this demand on behalf of an 'awakened womanhood' in the booklet reprint of his articles. Gretta felt that:

H.G. Wells, Science Fiction Writer and Reformer

> "No progress would be made until women took their place as the numerical and voting equals of men, and hammered sense into their nouns and pronouns."

Gretta was only concerned with the absence of women's mention and not the content, with which she was totally in agreement. H.G. Wells published his Rights of Man in 1940.

This predated the Universal Declaration of Human Rights (UDHR) adopted by the United Nations General Assembly at its third session on 10 December 1948. Of the fifty-eight members of the UN, forty-eight voted in favour, none against, eight abstained, and two failed to vote.

Wells began his statement on The Rights of Man as follows:

> "Since a man comes into this world through no fault of his own, since he is manifestly a joint inheritor of the accumulations of the past, and since those accumulations are more than sufficient to justify the claims that are here made for him, it follows:

"(1) That every man without distinction of race, of colour or of professed belief or opinions, is entitled to the nourishment, covering, medical care and attention needed to realise his full possibilities of physical and mental development and to keep him in a state of health from his birth to death.

The Human Rights Declaration of the United Nations did remedy the lack of female mention. Within its preamble it stated:

"Whereas recognition of the inherent dignity and of the equal and inalienable rights of all members of the human family is the foundation of freedom, justice and peace in the world,
   Whereas the peoples of the United Nations have in the Charter reaffirmed their faith in fundamental human rights, in the dignity and worth of the human person and in the equal rights of men and women and have determined to promote social progress and better standards of life in larger freedom."

It then stated in two of its 30 Articles:

### Article 1
All human beings are born free and equal in dignity and rights. They are endowed with reason and conscience and should act towards one another in a spirit of brotherhood.

### Article 2
Everyone is entitled to all the rights and freedoms set forth in this Declaration, without distinction of any kind, such as race, colour, sex, language, religion, political or other opinion, national or social origin, property, birth or other status. Furthermore, no distinction shall be made on the basis of the political, jurisdictional or international status of the country or territory to which a person belongs, whether it be independent, non-self-governing or under any other limitation of sovereignty."

# CHAPTER THIRTY-SIX

Frightening health issues & accidents for Jim and Gretta
The Failure of the Cripps Mission
The All India Educational Conference in Srinagar, Kashmir
Gretta crashes to the ground
Gretta's inability to serve becomes a reality

Anno domini, as well as wear and tear, were beginning to restrict efforts to serve and caused anxiety for both of them. In 1940 Gretta was now sixty-two years old and Jim a few years older. Living in India's fierce climate, especially for westerners, is particularly difficult for prolonged periods. Hence the need every year to 'go to the hills' for temporary ease from the searing heat. This luxury was not open to the vast majority of Indians.

Gretta comments:

"A short collapse of Jim, blamed by the doctor on overwork, gave me a fright. He lost his memory, and had to lie in his day clothes for a while. A blood clot in the brain was suggested, but he slowly recovered, and became as alert and cheery as ever. I was much helped by kind neighbours. A slacking off of work was prescribed, but that was one of the bright scientific ideas that made the patient impatient."

Then Gretta had a fall.

"I had my own upset on a visit to Bangalore to assist Jim's full recuperation, when I fell in the bathroom of the State Guest House and badly injured an arm. Jim carried me bodily, naked, covered with soap lather, and in agony, onto my bed, and called for a doctor. Happily expert aid was immediately at hand, and X-rays showed no fracture. Time was helped to pass by chats with that great mind, The Hon. V. S. Srinivasa Sastri,[155] who was making a short stay in the Guest House. He was an orator of the same eminence as Mrs Besant had

---

155 **Valangaiman Sankaranarayana Srinivasa Sastri** (1869 – 1946) was an Indian politician administrator, educator, orator and Indian independence activist. He was acclaimed for his oratory and command of the English language. Sastri served on the Indian National Congress from 1908 to 1922, but later resigned in protest against the Non-Cooperation movement. Sastri was one of the founding members of the Indian Liberal Party. In his latter days, he was strongly opposed to the partition of India.

been. He had made a deep impression as official representative of India in South Africa, the land in which Indians were on about the same level of discrimination as negroes in the United States of America. He was now aged and delicate, but his mind was as clear and his speech as golden as ever."

Sir Mirza Ismail,[156] the Diwan in Bangalore and Mysore, and their official host, now had two invalids on his hands. So he drove Gretta and Jim some eighty miles from Bangalore to Mysore and put them up in his official home while dispensing a rosy glow of hospitality and intellectual friendship. Another visitor was Miss (Dr) Albuquerque, one of the heads of the State Medical Department. She saw that instead of helping one another back to health they were pulling each other down. On an hour's notice she drove Gretta back to Bangalore, and secured her a special room in the Women's Hospital, which had five-hundred beds. Gretta was the only one who was not pregnant. In three days she was quite well. She did not like the stark bareness of the wards, and the overwhelming sense of sickness without any growing plants or flowers around. She put in a plea for flowers, put into decorative vases, and plucked from their well-stocked gardens. This was authorised. Gretta never heard, however, how long this welcome innovation was maintained after she was discharged.

Once back at Ghat View they had visitors all the time, except when Jim was doing something else. This 'something else' was the completion of one of his major epics. Gretta spent some hours by the side of a stream reading the first complete chapters of "The Hound of Uladh."[157] They gripped her completely. She realised how full it was of imaginative genius.

Sad news arrived on 8 August 1941 of the death of Rabindranath Tagore. Arrangements for a memorial meeting created a sense of unity, not in loss, but in what life had gained through him. The commemoration gathering on 12 August, organised by Jim, was unique. Every phase of his eighty years was marked by intellectual and artistic genius. In the end he had achieved world-fame and literary immortality.

---

156 **Sir Mirza Muhammad Ismail** (Oct 1883 – Jan 1959) was the Diwan (Prime Minister) of the Kingdoms of Mysore/Bangalore Sir C P Ramaswami Iyer, Diwan in Travancore considered him 'one of the cleverest men in India'. Long-time friend Sir Chandrasekhara Venkata Raman said that 'Sir Mirza's accessibility and personal charm coupled with his depth of knowledge and his keen sense of human and cultural values made him a great and highly successful administrator'.
157 **The Hound of Uladh – A Play of Brahma:** and essay on the drama of national revival.

## The All India Educational Conference in Kashmir

News of the 'Churchill-Roosevelt Atlantic Charter' [158] (14 Aug 1941) was coming in when they started out for Srinagar in Kashmir, as delegates to the annual session of the 'All-India Educational Conference'. In addition, Jim was commissioned by the Government of Travancore to give an exhibition of copies of murals of temples in Travancore. These did good work for the history of Indian art by bringing the achievement of the south to the other end of India, 2850 miles away. He was in a true position to explain their significance to delegates from all over the north.

The Conference opened on 26 September 1941 with the Maharaja of Kashmir & Jammu delivering a short but impressive speech. The President, Dr Amarnath Jha, Vice-Chancellor of the University of Lucknow, a man of large body and large mind, gave an uplifting presidential address. Jim spoke on his favourite theme of 'Art in Education'.

## Gretta crashes to the ground

The second day of the Conference brought a traumatic crisis for Gretta. Whether it was the result of bad manners by a youth, who pushed himself forward to express his anti-female complex, or the excessive heat and light of the thin roof of the big marquee, no one could say. Whatever the reason, Gretta crashed to the ground. When she recovered she was told she had been unconscious for three hours. She insisted, despite protestation, on fulfilling her duty as President of a sub-conference on women's education. She then suddenly had another period of unconsciousness, but, this time, was taken from the home of Mr and Mrs Brijlal Nehru to a nursing home. A European doctor diagnosed sun-stroke. An Indian doctor diagnosed malaria. She appeared to have symptoms of both. Her own private opinion was that she was suffering from a break-down, and that her treatment was to leave Srinagar. But two more days were required before she was well enough and strong enough to attempt the long journey homewards.

At Nagpur she left Jim on the train on his way to duty in Travancore as she felt strong enough for a small detour before arriving back in Kotagiri.

158 The **Atlantic Charter** was a pivotal policy statement issued during World War II on 14 August 1941, which defined the Allied goals for the post war world. The leaders of the United Kingdom and the United States drafted the work and all the latter confirmed it. The Charter stated the ideal goals of the war—no territorial aggrandizement; no territorial changes made against the wishes of the people; self-determination; restoration of self-government to those deprived of it; reduction of trade restrictions; global cooperation to secure better economic and social conditions for all; freedom from fear and want; freedom of the seas; and abandonment of the use of force, as well as disarmament of aggressor nations. Adherents of the Atlantic Charter signed the Declaration by United Nations on 1 January 1942, which became the basis for the modern United Nations.

"Our family doctor gave me a thorough look over. He found no malaria, and diagnosed that I was somewhat exhausted after heat-stroke. I was up and down in energy for some time, but was ultimately able to take large draughts of my favourite tonic - natural beauty and exercise on foot."

The end days of 1941 were divided between the Theosophical Convention at Adyar and the Standing Committee of the All-India Women's Conference. Jim organised an exhibition of twelve large paintings by Nicholas Roerich, a very choice and impressive demonstration of art at its highest in an equally artistic setting in the Pavlova Theatre, Adyar, beside the great banyan tree, in the wide-spread shade of which the public meetings of the Convention were held.

Nicholas Roerich
(1874 –1947)

The first Convention lecture was to be given by Dr Radhakumud Mookerjee, but he arrived from Calcutta too late to recover from the fatigue of the long train journey. Out of the blue came a request from the President, Dr Arundale, for Jim to take his place at very short notice. Gretta always felt that he did best as a speaker when he was given little or no time to get complicated and nervous. He gave the sixty minute lecture to the big crowd with little or no preparation. His subject - "Art and Reconstruction."

**Failure of the Cripps Mission**
In the spring of 1942 political tension was tightening. There seemed no hope of finding a solution to the Indo-British problem. The Indian leaders were determined to carry their agitation to the extreme, short of violence. But the second world war was raging, and the preoccupations, implications and the dangers of this made the prospect of any legislation on anything Indian look extremely academic and peripheral.

A Coalition Government in London had been formed in May 1940 by the circumstances of war. Winston Churchill was its leader. In November 1941 the leader of the Opposition died, and Frederick Pethick-Lawrence, was chosen as Chairman of the Parliamentary Labour Party, a position that made him leader of the Opposition in place of Clement Attlee, who had taken a seat on the Coalition War Cabinet. This Coalition made a change in the relationship of the Labour Party to the Government. Now, as a 'supporter' of the Government, the Labour Party could influence and modify Governmental intentions.

So, on March 14, 1942, Jim and Gretta put their heads together and cabled Pethick-Lawrence urging the necessity for Britain to hand over power to India, all of it, once and for all. Hopes were raised as a result of the visit of Sir Stafford Cripps to enquire into the position within India. Gretta spent a sleepless night drafting a letter to Cripps. The urgency she felt was eased by an announcement from Delhi that he would like to see representatives of Indian women. After it was all over, came the devastating announcement of the failure of the Cripps mission.[159] The appalling prospect for the future made both of them feel quite ill. Later, as mass emotion heightened, together they issued a press statement putting the situation in as balanced a way as possible, though yielding 'not an inch' of their claim for India's freedom.

They took refuge from these national complexities by individually pursuing their own special interests, Gretta in the growing work for children, with excursions to Madanapalle and Trivandrum, Jim in literary work and his duties as Art Adviser. Any hours of relaxation in the gardens of Government House at Ootacamund and in Simms Park at Coonoor were gladly taken. At the height of nearly 7000 feet, it gave climatic conditions for a rich and varied culture of trees, shrubs and flowers. Bus travel to and fro was always full of delighted astonishment at the contours of the Nilgiri Hills.

They ended 1942 in Adyar, taking part in a support Convention of The Theosophical Society, where their contribution was an artistic evening, when Jim recited a number of his own poems and Gretta performed piano solos interspersed between the recitations. Gretta records:

> "From Adyar 'we two together' went to Trivandrum and had the usual double varied enjoyment. While I went around the various feminine institutions, Jim was in great form getting the beautiful Government Museum rid of a moth-eaten set of stuffed and anatomical animals so as to transform it into a Museum of craftsmanship worthy of the noble building.
>
> By the time Jim got back from Trivandrum, thin and tired and worried, I had quite a lot of what we called the 'duography' ready to read to him. By our wood-fire in the evenings we discussed it, and made

159 **The Cripps Mission** was a failed attempt in late March 1942 by the British government to secure full Indian cooperation and support for their efforts in World War II. The mission was headed by Sir Stafford Cripps, Lord Privy Seal and leader of the House of Commons. Cripps was sent to negotiate an agreement with the nationalist leaders, speaking for the majority Hindu population, and Muhammad Ali Jinnah, speaking for the minority Muslim population. Cripps worked to keep India loyal to the British war effort in exchange for a promise of full self-government after the war. He also promised to give India dominion status and to hold elections once the war was over. Both the major parties, the Congress and the Muslim League rejected his proposals and the mission failed.

plans for more. We went on with the work systematically and rapidly. The literary partnership was mentally energising. I hugely enjoyed the objectivising of my former self. We got spasms of modesty now and again. The mere stating of simple facts seemed to be saying what wonderful persons we had been. Yet we couldn't help being intensely interested in all sorts of worthwhile adventures of the mind and heart."

The Indian situation steadily got worse. Gandhiji had again been forced to announce another fast. Gretta, as she usually did, went on a sympathetic fast. She longed to be in the struggle but had the feeling that direct participation by herself was no longer required, or even desired by the leaders of Indian womanhood, who were now strong enough and confident enough not to require support from a non-Indian woman.

**Gretta's inability to serve becomes a reality**

"My health was becoming something of a nuisance, perhaps a menace. I was tied by the leg to home sweet home and its problems with servants whose daily round was beyond me—bringing up buckets of water from the well, keeping the hillside from reverting to jungle, cleaning dry closets, cooking and washing up. I could, as a result, only take a long-distance share in politics, such as cabling Winston Churchill and wiring the Viceroy urging them to release Gandhi. Of course, being who and what they were, they didn't. The anxiety and strain, including my own, increased. A breakage of nerves was prevented or postponed by callers and their special interests.

News of Gandhiji's breaking of his fast in the middle of March brought some relief to tension. It was interesting to learn that a copy of Francis Thompson's 'Hound of Heaven' was on his bed at the time. I had been revising the notes on that wonderful poem that I had made on the steamer going to New York to join my 'collaborator' for our sky-scraper year."

The fortieth anniversary of their wedding - 9 April 1943 - passed quietly. They had planned a walk and picnic tea. But nature had some other anniversary to attend. Rain plumped. Holidays for airmen having a rest from war resulted in six of them coming to Ghat View for an extempore party. They crammed in, with a tennis champion, the head of a tuberculosis sanatorium, a Lutheran clergyman, an Archdeacon, a Reverend of the Anglican Church and a Major 6ft 4in tall. They had an informal and thoroughly enjoyable afternoon.

"Jim was not on form on this occasion. Part of the day he was in bed, coughing and fidgeting, trying to get away from the body by reading Emerson's poetry, and a big American biography of Trelawny lent to us. The latter became the chief aid to Jim's recovery. His illness made me contemplate the obvious deterioration in my own health, and my growing inability to do field service for the freedom of India, which I felt to be a basic necessity for the world. The pull between necessity and inability took toll on my emotions, nerves and heart, much to the concern of Jim. Between downs and ups of mood I pushed on with my chapters for the book."

# CHAPTER THIRTY-SEVEN

### The autumn leaves of Gretta's life start to fall
### Gretta attends her last All India Women's Conference

Gretta's contribution to the book of their memories, 'We Two Together', finished early in July of 1943. Deterioration in her health continued. Almost indecipherable entries in her diary suggested an increasing lack of brain-hand coordination. Jim was at Trivandrum on duty as Art Advisor and unaware of this. Letters to him had their customary cheerfulness, but her handwriting was obviously becoming shaky. On one of her journeys her nerves were not helped by finding out that the ladies' second class compartment, where she was sound asleep, had been plundered and all movable items stolen including a favourite cloak of hers.

A fall on the steep and rough path down from Ghat View gave her a bad jolt on 14 August. Two days later she slipped again on the very same path. On 17 August she walked the two miles for the anniversary of the Child Welfare and Maternity Centre. Her sight became clouded, so that she was unable to read properly after Jim returned. On 21 August she tried, as usual after dinner, to look over the newspaper. She could only decipher the large-type headings, but unable to make any meaning out of them. Next morning, when even a good night's sleep had not shown any improvement, Jim sent for an eye specialist, Dr Jeffreys, an American female doctor who had opened a clinic on the other side of the town. Examination indicated high blood pressure and symptoms of a brain haemorrhage.

Hospital was ordered. Next afternoon Dr Herlofsen, the assistant lady doctor at the clinic, and Jim took her by taxi to the Civil Hospital at Ootacamund, a 90 minute slow drive. She had become restless and delirious, and was sick from the movement of the car. The District Medical Officer, Lieutenant Colonel Cox, was very pessimistic, and quite critical when Jim told him she was a vegetarian and should be suitably catered for. She had become paralysed down the right side. Jim went home to tidy things for a prolonged absence and to attend to the varied correspondence which awaited him. He then returned to Ootacamund to be in daily attendance on Gretta.

Professor Speight gave him a room in his bungalow. Jim was then able to visit the hospital on foot twice a day, a mile and a half each way. The six miles a day tramp in a heavy overcoat with an umbrella, against wind and rain and cold, at first a drag, soon became a healthy exercise. The ups and downs in the patient's condition dissolved any thoughts of imminent death.

Little touches of recognition on one occasion, a lifted mouth for a kiss, sent him home happy.

Speight's versatility as poet, musician, connoisseur and scholar helped Jim along in their separation. There could be no real progress until the patient was taken to a much lower level, say 2500ft instead of 7500ft. The doctor advised that this should not be done suddenly. So on 17 September she was taken by ambulance to Ghat View, and after a couple of anxious days with help from a friend Helen Veale, she was allotted the one empty bed attached to Dr Jeffrey's clinic in Kotagiri. Jim's visiting had to be reduced to once a day, from just before midday lunch to after teatime, with a siesta on an extra 'cot'[160] in the little ward. As the dreary month of September slowly passed, Gretta became less helpless, and could be moved onto a chair or to the tea-table at a window from which, through one eye, she could see the outline of the hills and smile at their beauty though she could speak no words to express the joy of the view. When the time drew near for taking her even farther downhill Jim found that restrictions on petrol made transport for the twenty miles to the station impossible. By some fluke he discovered a military ambulance going that way that gave them a lift to Mettupalayam station, along with another friend Barbara Bannerman. And so began their descent for the last time from their beautiful Indian retreat on 17 October 1943, four years after their arrival.

Signs of improvement in the patient's condition gave heart that getting her to a lower level would increase her chances of recovery. She had given a slight response in her paralysed right hand. When both the doctors and Jim were having a pow-wow in a whispered conversation, she startled them by clearly saying, "Jim, I accept everything."

They were allotted a four-berth second class compartment on the train, Gretta and Barbara Bannerman on the lower two, Jim on one of the upper berths, luggage on the other. From Bangalore City station next morning Gretta and Barbara were taken in an ambulance to the Vani Vilas Hospital. Jim went to Race View, where he would stay in the State Guest House for as long as was necessary, with the use of a car for daily visits to the hospital. On 7 November, Gretta's birthday, she had so far improved that she wanted to give a lunch party for the Matron of the hospital, the nurse and two ayahs[161].

In spite of restrictions in her movement and loss of some memory, she obviously enjoyed herself in the role of Irish hostess, once again trying to make her guests eat more than they had capacity for. A helpful visitor was Major Somerville-Large, ophthalmologist to the British Army, a resident practitioner in Dublin in peace-time and nephew of the famous novelist,

160 **Cot:** In Indian culture refers to a narrow bed, especially one made of canvas on a collapsible frame.

161 **Ayah:** A maid or nurse usually employed by Europeans in India.

Miss E. Somerville-Large. He gave Gretta a thorough ocular examination, and found nothing wrong except from the effects of the stroke, which should wear off in due course.

It was a day of rejoicing when she walked four steps from her bed and back, leaning on Jim's arm. Shortly afterwards she moved slowly, with a limp, from her bed to the opposite side of the room and gazed out of the window. Across the wide garden was a main road. Jim asked her to tell him who was passing the gate. "A man on a cycle wearing a Gandhi cap," she said in broken speech. She was right.

On 26 November she was discharged, needing home surroundings more than the hospital environment. Still in Bangalore, Jim took her and her belongings to a cottage a short distance from the home of Sir Mirza and Lady Ismail. Sir Albion Banerjea, a former Diwan of Mysore, the permanent occupant, rented it to Jim while he went on a month's visit to relatives in northern India.

Dorai Raj, came with his wife and family of small children from Kotagiri, and looked after the cooking and home arrangements. Two ayahs looked after Gretta in rotation, and fed her sitting at the small dining-room table.

Her power in walking soon increased to the extent that her ayah could be entrusted to go with her on an hour's slow walk beyond the home and compound of Captain Bettala Durgiah Naidu close to the cottage. So much had the patient improved that Jim was able to leave her in the care of friends for a short visit to Madras at the end of the annual Convention of the Theosophical Society. Once Jim returned to Bangalore he found Gretta considerably better in expression but still restricted in movement. They had happy times on chairs in the garden, joking, reading, reciting poems some of which she repeated line by line from memory after Jim prompted her with the first two words.

The post brought a letter from Dr Arundale suggesting Jim 'resumed residence, with Mrs. Cousins, at Adyar'. Another letter arrived from Sir Mirza Ismail inviting Jim to take up a post in Jaipur, where he was Prime Minister. Jim saw opportunities for service with both these offers, but felt that Gretta's condition would ultimately decide their future location. Jim again:

"One day on our longest walk yet she said: "I feel much better today, almost my old self, only for memory." She was full of interest in everything. Her love of nature was undiminished. My long intimacy with her thought and her likes and dislikes enabled us to communicate freely. It was different with others. They knew nothing of the surges of deep soul-affection that passed between us. Our unity in the things of daily life was obvious; but only we and a few others were aware of our affiliation with loftier aspects of life. "What would I do without you?" was one of her questions. The answer was that she would not have to do without me for any length of time so long as I was alive. But I had to fulfil my duties as Art Adviser to Travancore State so long as my annual contract was renewed. This necessitated a three week visit from mid-February (1944). Through the kind offices of Dr Muthulakshmi Reddy, our old Madanapalle friend, Srimati Padmasani, came from her home outside the Theosophical Society's estate at Adyar to take care of Gretta in Bangalore during my absence.

Her experience as mother of a family and her geniality and intelligence gave us assurance of the patient's care, and sent me off with a kiss and a hand-wave and good wishes for a month."

Jim got back to Bangalore on 14 March and found progress maintained. However, as fate would have it, on 22 April Gretta's life was changed by a flower-loving cow.

Jim had left Gretta on a chair in the garden, with the ayah (nursemaid) nearby in case of any needs. He had walked to the Mirza home, and had just arrived when Dorai Raj came racing up on a bicycle blurting that Madam had been hurt by a cow. Jim rushed back and found that the ayah had taken advantage of Jim's absence and gone on business of her own. A neighbouring cow had come into the garden and begun to devour the few flowers left. As there was no one to drive it away, Gretta had risen from her chair to chase it. The cow, however, had other plans. It put its head down and glared at her, so she had turned to avoid the threatened attack. The sudden movement over-balanced her and she fell.

A local lady doctor found no breakage. But spasms of pain, especially when Jim helped her onto the bed-pan, in the absence of the night ayah who had deserted us. This persistent pain made Jim suspect that the local doctor had been mistaken in her diagnosis. After three days she was taken to the X-ray department of the 'Bowring and Lady Curzon Hospital'. This confirmed a vertical fracture of the right hip-bone. Admission to the hospital was urgent, her fourth hospital in two years.

She was eight weeks in plaster, but took it calmly and wisely. "It will give me the opportunity to reach my higher self," she said. Ups and downs in the patient's health, and what appeared to Jim to be 'drug-poisoning' from the analgesics prescribed for pain, so increased his anxiety that he insisted on a special nurse. He was very happy one morning to find Gretta enjoying herself with a tall, pleasant, articulate young woman who appeared to know just what to do to make her happy and comfortable in her immovable splints.

Jim noticed her almond-shaped eyes and queried "Burma?" "No!" she replied, "Singapore." "And what may we call you?" "Mrs Ho." "But that is not from Singapore. That's Chinese." "I am Chinese."

Jim then recalled a Chinese friend from Singapore who had come to the Ashrama at Adyar twenty-five years previously. "Perhaps you could tell me something about a Chinese dentist in Singapore whom I knew long ago, but haven't heard about for ages, Mr Mensen Fones."

"He was my father!" she said with veneration. "I remember you calling at our home in Singapore when I was a little girl. He was always full of praise for the Ashrama, of which you were the head. He died some time ago."

Before long Mrs Ho was called off to north India on an official mission, and they had to revert to the services of hospital attendants. A bed-sore at the base of Gretta's spine soon developed and necessitated the removal of the plaster. This was intended to be temporary, but the fact that she could move the fractured leg vigorously made a difference. An x-ray showed no sign of fracture. It had apparently healed quicker than anticipated. The doctors decided that, as far as the fracture was concerned, she could leave the hospital in a few days.

Privately they told Jim of their concern for Mrs Cousins' mental state and urged an examination by the foremost mental specialist in Bangalore, Dr Govindaswamy. He was very expensive but very experienced. Jim waved aside the expense, as her welfare was now the central issue. The doctor turned up on the afternoon of 2 June 1944. He was amazed to find that his patient was none other than Mrs Margaret Cousins. He saluted Jim as if he was an old friend, then saw the patient alone. His conclusion was: "There is nothing wrong with her mental state. Her condition is purely physical". He diagnosed it as 'expressional aphasia due to paralysis.' This would recede without medicines, though perhaps not entirely. She was to rest in the hospital for some days and then go home. Her treatment was to be word-making, games, use of a ball to squeeze, turning a spinning-wheel and very light massage.

Jim then asked him if his fee would be paid through the hospital or directly to him. "Neither through the hospital nor direct. How are you going home, and where?"

"Shanks pony,[162] to 3 Miller Road." "My car goes that way." "How fortunate".

On the way he began to recite poetry. Jim suddenly recognised familiar lines. Surprise, surprise, they were from his own drama, 'The King's Wife.' Jim naturally asked him where he had learnt them. The gist of the reply was something like:

---

162 **Shanks pony**: A phrase used to refer to one's own legs and the action of walking as a means of conveyance.

"When I was taking my higher studies in the United States some years ago, I was occasionally asked to give talks on Indian philosophy. I used to tell my audiences not to bother with Max Muller and his 'Six Darshans' but to absorb the lines in 'The King's Wife' by James H. Cousins that were straight from the Bhagavad Gita and put into the mouth of the singing and dancing saint, Rani Mirabai. That is why there is no fee."

On 14 June Jim brought Gretta home in an ambulance. As to the future she was calm and content. One angel, in the form of a warm invitation from Ammu Swaminathan, to stay in her big house on the outskirts of Madras, arrived promptly. She was always very happy in the company of Ammu who had become an important political personage and destined to become a member of the Central Legislature of India. A week after Ammu's arrival Jim was so reassured that Gretta would receive all the loving attention necessary that he accepted an invitation from Sir Mirza Ismail to go to Jaipur to look over the art treasures of the State of Rajasthan and make suggestions with regard to their future. Gretta was quite happy with this arrangement.

Returning to Madras, after a miserable, crowded, sleepless, hot and dusty forty-eight hour train journey from Delhi, he arrived on 1 October 1944. While he had had encouraging reports about Gretta's health, he was not prepared to see her in a car at 6.30am at the railway station to welcome him. She had clearly improved in expression though not in movement and was obviously very happy in the Swaminathan home with cheery friends, and very interested in sketching trees in the big compound.

At coffee with Dr Arundale, President of the Theosophical Society, and his wife Rukmini Devi, they were invited to become once again residents at Adyar. Jim records:

"Dr Arundale wanted to put me on his 'Civil List'[163] on account of my long record of work for the ideals of the Theosophical Society, for my founding of Lodges as far apart as Ireland and Japan, for my six years of work as Director of Studies of the Brahmavidya Ashrama, and for my numerous writings and lectures in which I expounded the principles and implications of the law of Brotherhood, which is the only dogma of the Society. I maintained that while I was able to earn sufficient to cover living expenses I had no justification for being a drain on the Society."

163 **A civil list** is a **list** of individuals to whom money is paid by a government. It is a term especially associated with the British Empire and its former colonies. It was originally defined as expenses supporting the monarch. In this case it refers to a list held by the Theosophical Society and administered by the President.

Jim was persuaded to accept, however, and they were escorted by Mr Sri Ram, Vice-President, to 'Sevashrama,' a handsome Saracenic[164] building at the confluence of the Adyar River and the Bay of Bengal. It had been arranged for them to occupy its ground floor after some preliminaries of tidying and furnishing. They finally moved in on 19 October 1944.

So far as Gretta was concerned, her active participation in service, in all her multiple capacities in helping humanity to progress, had come to an end. Jim knew now that he was to become her permanent helpmeet, doctor and nurse. Jim describes Gretta at this time in the autumn of her life.

"A noble, unselfish, wise, affectionate, happy spirit in adapting itself to an injured 'instrument of expression' (body). With occasional help during absences on duty, it was my sacred privilege to be what we called her 'lady's maid' by night and day. This did not give the stretches of quietude necessary for concentration on large-scale literary activity. But afternoon hours in an easy chair under a crimson bougainvillea, while she hobbled about the compound, "M. visiting the sick" as she called it, allowed my creative imagination to find its way into verse, and to add two small books to the twenty-seven already in my name."

---

164 **Saracenic** was an **architectural style** mostly used by British **architects** in India in the later 19th century, especially in public and government buildings in the British Raj, and the palaces of rulers of the princely states.

# CHAPTER THIRTY-EIGHT

## Jim's swan-song
## Termination of the Art Advisor's job

Jim's indoor work at Adyar, at what was now their final home, consisted of plans for the completion of a book on 'The Arts and Crafts of Travancore,' and continuing the drafting of their memoirs. Gretta was escorted on shopping trips by her gentle, spiritual hostess.

"When we got back to Adyar in Oct 1944 we had finished our many thousands of miles of an incredible journey for this life. As I had always been a pucca[165] fool over emoluments,[166] finding more joy in working than in being paid for it, being more engaged in feathering other people's nests than my own, I had, willy-nilly, to anticipate necessity as closely as possible lest necessity might take too close an interest in me. My appointment at Travancore seemed as certain as sentiment could make it, in spite of opposition. But sentiment is not always a sure prophet. Meantime I shuttled from my office at Adyar to my workshop in Travancore, 500 miles away. The main features of the visits were much the same with feelings of inspiration, encouragement, intelligent criticism, considerateness and kindness from those in authority. The reverse from those below authority who darkened the atmosphere and frustrated efforts. These obstructive influences came from a side that indicated both political and religious animosity. Behind this was a growing agitation against Sir C.P. Ramaswami, the Diwan. I was counted among these objectionable people.

These forces, wrongfully against me, may be grouped as coming from the Congress party with its as yet vague notions of electoral democracy, and Communism with its quite clear plan of reducing persons and institutions to the level of a pyramid. I had seen some of the moves in the intensifying attempt to get rid of the doubly detested 'Brahmin'[167] and 'Tamilian 'foreigner.'[168] I was aware of men goading small boys to throw stones after his car and shout "C.P. go back."

---

165 **pucca**: 'solid' and 'permanent'.
166 **Emolument** is a salary or fee obtained for holding office or for employment.
167 **'Brahmin'** refers to CP Ramaswami, the Diwan – or Prime Minister of the state.
168 **'Tamilian foreigner'** refers to Jim being a Hindu and from Madras. He was seen as an unwanted foreigner.

The chief and final event of Jim's association with Sir C. P. Ramaswami in Travancore took place on the evening of 25 July 1947, the inauguration of the death-centenary of Maharaja Swati Thirunal, a composer of the highest rank. This drew an audience of some 2000 men and women to an immense and beautiful venue on the compound of the new School of Music. After the formal opening by the Maharaja at 4.45pm precisely and the retirement of the Ruling Family, the platform was cleared and a recital of Sri Swati Thirunal's music began.

The Diwan took a seat in front of the platform, on the floor level, with an empty chair left and right. As the programme proceeded he called a Madras visitor, Sri Jayaram, a lawyer, to occupy the chair to his left. Shortly afterwards Jim was signalled to occupy the other chair. At 7pm precisely the Diwan looked at his watch, arose and passed along the aisle between saluting friends. He had to keep an appointment. Jim remained sitting. The lights went out for a moment or two. There was some fuss around the exit, but no one inside knew what was happening.

Srimati Rukmini Devi from Adyar, wife of Dr Arundale, the President of the Theosophical Society, had come on a short visit, and was staying as a guest at the Diwan's official residence. Jim had taken her there in the car assigned to him as Art Adviser, so that she would be ready for dinner on his return from his appointment. Next morning Jim called to take Rukmini Devi to see the Palace, and was shocked by news that an attempt had been made to assassinate the Diwan as he left the shamiana.[169] He had been stabbed in the jaw and the neck. His jugular vein, thank God, had been narrowly missed. He had been rushed hospital and expertly treated, eventually making a full recovery.

These dramatic events occurred three weeks before what must, from almost any point of view, be counted as one of the greatest political events in human history. As Jim put it: "The complete non-violent liberation of 400 million people from foreign rule."

Involved in this were problems that went to the root of Travancore's relationship with India, and Sir C.P. Ramaswami's relationship with the State. He had made a valiant attempt to rally the people under the proud banner of a sovereign independent State.

Advisory duties, for Jim, continued. An extension to the Chitralayam (The Art Gallery) added a number of small rooms, each given to a particular aspect of oriental painting. His belief that the grouping and hanging of paintings was itself an art found full expression and approval. Large numbers of visitors

169 **Shamiana** is a popular Indian ceremonial tent shelter or awning, commonly used for outdoor parties, marriages, feasts etc. Its side walls are removable. The external fabric can be multi-coloured or can hold exquisite designs.

came, and Jim gave peripatetic talks on various features of the gallery. Eminent visitors to the State had the art institutions in their programmes with the Art Adviser, Jim, in charge.

He was detailed to act as host at Padmanabhapuram Palace to Viscount Wavell,[170] the Viceroy, on his way to Trivandrum by road together with the Vicereine and staff. They had been officially received by the Diwan and given lunch in a tented camp. The Diwan left them in Jim's charge for a look over the previous seat of Government, while he went on to Trivandrum to be present at the State reception arranged by the Maharaja. His Excellency the Viceroy was remarkably interested in the old Palace and its architectural and sculptural relics and insisted on seeing the mural room which threatened to overlap tea-time and their required departure. Tea was laid for the party of twelve, with a chair unobtrusively in the background for Jim in case he was needed. Jim, however, was commanded to take his seat on the Viceroy's right-hand side. During tea, at which His Excellency took neither tea nor coffee or a cold drink, cake or even a cigarette, plied him with questions about the old palace and its history.

* * *

Sometime later, around March 1948, came a visit of Lord Mountbatten, the last Viceroy, whose job was to find a way of making the Viceroy a figure of the past. This visit was rather different.

Jim describes:

"Lady Mountbatten was the questioner. In the introduction interval after the banquet I was, much to my surprise, called first by the Aide-de-camp to have a five minute chat with Her Excellency. She had called me, she said, to see what could be done about her visits to the art institutions. She broke off and said: "Where were you born?" I had to think for an instant, and an answer to a similar question by someone else floated up from memory. "I was born, Your Excellency, in the greatest city in the world, as any Belfast-man will tell you, especially if he has never been out of it." "I thought as much. I quite understand. What I want to know is, why I am given ten minutes to see the School of Arts. I am intensely interested in arts and crafts. I shall take an hour off my afternoon rest for a visit."

---

170 **Field Marshal Archibald Percival Wavell**, GCB, GCSI, (1883 – 1950) was a senior officer of the British Army, who served in the Great War, and was wounded in the Second Battle of Ypres. He served in the Second World War, initially as Commander-in-Chief Middle East. He served as Commander-in-Chief, India, from July 1941 until June 1943 and then served as **Viceroy of India** until his retirement in February 1947.

I did not explain that the programme had not been made by me, but I arranged it accordingly. Her Excellency saw all the departments of the School, and dispensed expert appreciation and criticism. She had the foreman of each section introduced, and shook hands with him. Everyone was up in the air. On the same day I showed Their Excellences over the other art-centres, and at night assisted at a reception at Koudiar Palace, when 500 guests included sixty Congress Members of Parliament from the first election under the new regime of a free India, a wonderfully significant sight in their white khaddar dresses and the world's most commonplace head-gear, the Gandhi cap."

The new political era had its highest personal expression, for Jim, on 22 August 1947, when the first Indian Governor General visited Travancore. His Excellency C. Rajagopalachariar, affectionately known as Rajaji. Jim had been called from Adyar to show him over the Chitralayam. His Highness the Maharaja of Travancore accompanied him and they both shared descriptions of various items in the Gallery with Rajaji.

This was Jim's last official act as Art Adviser to the Government of Travancore.

# CHAPTER THIRTY-NINE

Jim packs up in Travancore and goes home to Adyar
Plans to write a magnum opus on Mrs Besant and her legacy
Gretta attends her last Session of the AIWC

Next morning Jim started for Adyar and the final stage of his life.

This particular visit to Trivandrum should have been the first month of a new year of service. Jim had written months previously asking for formal extension. In the new excitements and insecurities within the Secretariat his letter was not dealt with.

He had spoken to the new Prime Minister and the Minister of Education. However their preoccupations with getting half a dozen new Ministers into unfamiliar work resulted in postponing the decision yet again. And so it went on for half that year. Finally he received notification that his services were no longer required.

> "The clearance of my mind of Travancore affairs and duty periods with long taxing though interesting train journeys, allowed me to come nearer and more continuously to the phase of activity that more than any other satisfied my temperamental desire for service in the raising of the quality and circumstances of the life of the people."

The way to this, he felt, was through making the appreciation of art and its practice obligatory throughout education at all its levels. From his realisation in 1935 of the artistic magnitude of Srimati Rukmini Devi, and the work she could perform in imbuing the arts with pure and joyous idealism, Jim had taken a keen interest in her activities. She had embodied her enormous talent in the Kalakshetra (place dedicated to art.) She had founded this at Adyar in 1936 on part of the compound of the Theosophical Society within a rented building. In this project she had been warmly and understandingly supported and inspired by her husband, Dr George Arundale, President of the Society in succession to Dr Annie Besant.

Another project that Jim was delighted to look forward to was his proposed book about Annie Besant, their mentor and long-term friend, now sadly passed on in 1933.

> "The magnum opus that it became my luck to create was 'The Annie Besant Centenary Book.' It became 264 pages containing tributes

from men and women of eminence East and West from George Bernard Shaw and George Lansbury downwards, and a succession of photo-illustrations from her beautiful young womanhood to her noble age. The death of Dr Arundale on 12 August 1945 was followed by a constitutional six month interval before his elected successor as President of the Theosophical Society could be installed. This was Mr Jinarajadasa, the only candidate, who gave his Presidential address on February 17, 1946.

The British General Election had occurred during July 1945. The Labour Party had come into power with a 200 majority. Eight days after the victory the hope of help for India seemed almost assured with the announcement that F. W. Pethick-Lawrence had been made Secretary of State for India and elevated to the Peerage.

By now both Jim and Gretta had known the Pethick-Lawrence's for more than thirty years. He and his wife were uncompromising liberationists, and beyond the subtle corruptibility of power and place. They knew also that the cause of India was no political expedient. India's freedom was a cardinal item of his programme indeed a fundamental principle.

Mr C Jinarajadasa,
President of the
Theosophical Society
(1946-1953)

Two years went into the complicated arrangements for transfer of political power from Britain to India. Sadly a huge concession had been agreed. A large part of the sub-continent was partitioned off - Muslim Pakistan. This developed rapidly into a colossal and extremely violent transfer of populations. For Jim and Gretta, this had echoes of the partitioning of Ireland in 1921.[171] This division of India, however, was on a much larger scale where many thousands of Hindus and Muslims were killed during the process. The House of Commons passed the India Bill, and on July 17, 1947, and soon after the House of Lords passed it without dissent.

The Partition of India officially came into being at midnight on **14th August 1947** resulting in the division of British India into three independent dominions. The Dominion of India is today the Republic of India, and the

---

171 The **partition of Ireland** (Irish: *críochdheighilt na hÉireann*) was the division of the island of Ireland into two distinct jurisdictions, Northern Ireland and Southern Ireland. It took place on 3 May 1921 under the Government of Ireland Act 1920. Today the former is still known as Northern Ireland and forms part of the United Kingdom, while the latter is now a sovereign state also named Ireland. All efforts by Nationalists, violent and non-violent, have been towards reunification of Ireland without involvement of the British.

Dominion of Pakistan is today the Islamic Republic of Pakistan and the People's Republic of Bangladesh, previously East and West Pakistan.

On that hugely historic evening of 14 August 1947, Jim lectured in Gokhale Hall at Adyar that Mrs Besant had built for free speech, and in which she had used her unrivalled oratory and mental power to arouse the people of India from their lethargy. Jim spoke that night on 'Dr Besant and World Problems.'

### The Last Annual Session of AIWC for Gretta

In December 1947, the 20th Annual Session of the All-India Women's Conference was held at Madras (Chennai). This was where it all started. This was where Jim had suggested, "What about votes for women?" This was where Gretta had launched her Irish afternoon teas and where the Women's Indian Association had been born. The All-Indian Women's Conference, Gretta's brainchild, came into being in 1927. Finally the All-Asian Women's Conference was created in the 1930s.

Was this where it would all end?

Jim took her to the opening meeting.

"She was delighted to see many old friends from various parts of India. She could remember their faces and facts concerning them, but could not recall their names. Her halting walk along the path from the entrance of the large temporary hall to the platform became a procession of new-comers anxious to pay their respects to the Mother of the Conference. Camera-men and reporters of the day were all anxious to put the occasion into newsreels and newspaper blocks.

She realised that the organisation she had begun had become a national institution of unique achievement and profound influence, and *she was satisfied*."

# CHAPTER FORTY

Jim finishes his half of "We Two Together"
Gloomy about the immediate future for mankind
Jim ponders their future

With the horrific nightmare of the mass killings of Hindus by Muslims and Muslims by Hindus. India was yet to suffer another catastrophe.

Jim records his feelings at the time.

"Unregenerate human nature asserted itself; and the dreams of a free country turned into a succession of nightmares of murder and destruction and unspeakable misery, with the world-staggering assassination, on January 30, 1948, of Mahatma Gandhi, the apostle of non-violence, by a follower of the faith in which ahimsa (harmlessness) is an integral tenet. That fanatical event was not a climax of evil but a symptom. The morale of a section of the people of the new Dominion of India fell to a low level. Happily the sordid stories in the press of corruption, hoarding and black marketing, and the dreadful list of wrecking of loaded trains with the cold-blooded killing and maiming of inoffensive women and children, has awakened the public mind to the need for a drastic reorganisation of life in such a manner as to allow the constructive and ideal elements in humanity to obtain ascendency and to become a transforming influence over the destructive and material elements. Our interests and activities brought us a number of such friends, to whom, though unnamed, we offer the salutation of good fellowship."

It appears that Jims last publication was a book of Twenty four Sonnets published in 1949.

His last contribution to his part of their memoirs was finished on 27 October 1950.

His gloomy thoughts on that day are left for posterity.

"Unhappily the newspaper of today October 27, 1950, when I put these end words to this record of personal reactions to life, does not inspire optimism as to the near future of humanity the world over.

The chasms between religion and religion, between religion and anti-religion, between country and country, between classes and castes, between sex and sex, show no sign of soon closing up; and without such closing-up there does not appear to be any chance of a worldwide plateau on which the future could establish itself in peace.

The leaders of the various groups are carried from crisis to crisis by an incalculable power for an inscrutable purpose. If they could but see this, see that they are not the originators of events but their agents, collaborators in a design that, for all its apparent complexity, is ultimately simple; not a forensic dissertation, but a work of creative art, a fugue or a sonnet, as Sir James Jeans put it in 'The Mysterious Universe,' the one with its criss-crosses and over-laps and repetitions, the other with its settled pattern of expression providing for incalculable communication of ideas and feelings; if they could see this, it would be "the darkest hour before the dawn" in the ongoing struggle of humanity towards the light.

But a civilisation is not enclosed in a constitution, and is only incompletely enunciated in an ideology. It is made living and meaningful in its citizens, and perfectly so only to the extent that each is himself and herself an aesthetical phenomenon; that is, an embodiment of the principles that are inherent in the arts, and a practitioner and exponent of them in the inclusive art of living.

We may not be able to cause or influence major decisions in the organisation of human relationships; but there is always the possibility that a constant example and a well-timed precept from an individual effort to live life as ever in the great Art-Master's eye, may touch some ready spirit to achievement of world-shaping influence."

Finally, after this heart-felt hope that leaders would see the light through the darkness of the current world situation at that time, and that they, he and Gretta, had in some small way contributed to the spiritual raising of their fellow women and men, he turns back to his deeply held bonds with his beloved, since their marriage in Sandymount Methodist Church in Dublin in 1903.

"And so it happens that, as the signal goes down some distance from terminus at the end of the rails, short or long as the distance may be, we realise - one of us at 77yrs, the other at 72yrs —that the values of life have a way of arranging themselves in an order that alters, sometimes reverses, and one comes face to face with ultimate realities.

For ourselves, we have long anticipated the realities by looking for light in darkness and for ends in beginnings. We know for certain in the sense of experience observed and tested, that the human consciousness can function beyond its instruments of expression and beyond the phase of life called death.

We face the future with a realisation of the discrepancies and shortcomings of our own relationship with reality. We cannot be content to remain in this less than perfect state. That reality stretches its hands, which enfold us, impelling us forwards 'life after life' for its completion."

# CHAPTER FORTY-ONE

## ACORN TO OAK

Margaret & James Cousins – Ireland 1913

In 1927, with the inauguration of the first session of the All-India Women's Conference, there was created, for the first time in the history of India, a democratically elected body composed of Indian women delegates from throughout the subcontinent. They were meeting in a single gathering, resolving to seek equality in all things for men and women. After women's franchise was achieved, this new and powerful body worked tirelessly for the education of all girls, and boys for that matter. Gretta had unwittingly initiated this process when a young girl as a result of an encounter with her donkey, in a field, in Boyle, in the west of Ireland.

> "I was born a natural equalitarian, and rebelled exceedingly from that early age against any differential treatment of the sexes.

Her mission began with a focus on suffrage in Ireland expressed through the foundation of The Irish Women's Franchise League. Once settled into life

241

in India, it was Jim, thinking of what they had done in Ireland, who kick-started the process:

> One day, Jim, with his customary intuition of my mental states, asked me. 'What about Votes for women?

Out of this question came the birth of the: Abala Abhivardini Samaj - 'The Weaker Sex Improvement Society.' Dorothy Janarájadása took this model to form the Women's Indian Association in Madras. Gretta was its Honorary Secretary.

Then Gretta was charged with organising the first All India Women's Conference in Poona. Today there are more than 200,000 members of the AIWC in 500 centres.

The work over decades has covered a vast array. All political, legal and social efforts to raise the status of women have been aimed at women's education of both mind and spirit. Many Laws have been introduced to the Indian Parliament in connection with justice and equality for women.

Not yet finished, Gretta conceived the idea for the All-Asian Women's Conference.

With her inner deep passion, ignited by suggestions from Jim, it seems that Gretta acted as a powerful catalyst with a golden gift for bringing people together and generating inspiration. Her deep and sincere love for humanity, with a passion for justice, was the driving spiritual force which enabled her to become this huge dynamo-for-change.

These, perhaps, are their lasting legacies.

The marriage of this unique couple brought enormous creativity to many fields, but especially to their walk together on the long road towards full equality at all levels for men and for women, the two wings of humanity.

Margaret 'Gretta' Elizabeth Cousins
Died Adyar, Chennai, India
11 March 1954

James 'Jim' Henry Cousins
Died Madanapalle, India
20 February 1956

Margaret & James Cousins – India 1947

# BIBLIOGRAPHY

## BOOKS OF POEMS AND PLAYS BY JAMES H. COUSINS

**POETRY**

Ben Madighan and other poems. Belfast, Marcus Ward & Co., 1894.

Sung by Six (Collaborated). Belfast, Aiken & Co., 1896.

The Legend of the Blemished King. Dublin, Bernard Doyle, 1897.

The Voice of One. London, T. Fisher Unwin, 1900.

The Quest, 1906.

The Awakening, 1907.

The Bell-Branch, 1910.

Etain the Beloved, 1912. Dublin, Maunsel & Co., Ltd.

Straight and Crooked. London, Grant Richards, 1915.

The Garland of Life, 1917.

Ode to Truth' 1919.

Moulted Feathers, 1919

The King's Wife (drama), 1919;

Sea-Change, 1920;

Surya Gita, 1922. Madras, Ganesh & Co.

Forest Meditation. Madras, Theosophical Publishing House, 1925.

Above the Rainbow, 1926;

A Tibetan Banner, 1926;

The Shrine, 1928.

The Girdle, 1929. Madras, Ganesh & Co.

A Wandering Harp (first selection), 1932; A Bardio Pilgrimage (second selection), 1934. New York, Roerich Museum Press.

The Oracle. Madras, Ganesh & Co., 1938.

Collected Poems (1894-1940). Adyar, Madras, Kalakshetra, 1940.

The Hound of Uladh (dramas). Adyar, Madras, Kalakshetra, 1942.

Reflections before Sunset. Adyar, Madras, Kalakshetra, 1946.

Twenty-four Sonnets. Adyar, Madras, Kalakshetra, 1949.

## PROSE

The Wisdom of the West. London, The Theosophical Publishing Society, 1912.

New Ways in English Literature. Madras, Ganesh & Co., 1917.

The Kingdom of Youth. Madras, Ganesh & Co., 1917.

Footsteps of Freedom. Madras, Ganesh & Co., 1919.

Modern English Poetry. Madras, Ganesh & Co., 1921.

'The Play of Brahma'. Bangalore, Amateur Dramatic Association, 1921.

'The Cultural Unity of Asia'. Adyar, Madras, 1922.

**'We Two Together' by** James & Margaret Cousins – their 'duography' Published 1950

'Work and Worship. Madras, Ganesh & Co., 1922.

The New Japan Madras, Ganesh & Co., 1923. The Philosophy of Beauty.

Adyar, Madras, The Theosophical Publishing House, 1925.

Heathen Essays. Madras, Ganesh & Co., 1925.

Saxnadarsana (Indian Psychology). Madras, Ganesh & Co., 1925.

The Work Promethean. Madras, Ganesh & Co., 1933. A Study in Synthesis. Madras, Ganesh & Co., 1934.

The Faith of the Artist Adyar, Madras, Kalakshetra, 1941.

The Aesthetical Necessity in Life. Allahabad, Kitabistan, 1944.

## BOOKS BY MARGARET E. COUSINS

The Awakening of Asian Womanhood. Madras, Ganesh & Co., 1922.

The Music of Orient and Occident. Madras, B. G. Paul, 1935.

Indian Womanhood Today. Allahabad, Kitabistan, 1941.